W9-BOB-625

K 000008
NEW BOOK
NO REFUND IF REMOVED

A 15.95

The Democratic Invention

A *Journal of Democracy* Book

•

Published under the auspices of

the International Forum for Democratic Studies

The Democratic Invention

*Edited by Marc F. Plattner
and João Carlos Espada*

The Johns Hopkins University Press

Baltimore and London

© 2000 The Johns Hopkins University Press and the National Endowment for Democracy
All rights reserved. Published 2000
Printed in the United States of America on acid-free paper
9 8 7 6 5 4 3 2 1

Chapter 8 of this volume originally appeared in the *Journal of Democracy,* October 1999; chapter 6 appeared in the July 1999 issue of the *Journal;* chapters 3 and 5 appeared in the April 1999 issue; chapter 11 appeared in the January 1999 issue; chapters 4 and 10 appeared in the October 1998 issue; chapter 13 in January 1998; and chapter 1 in October 1997. Chapter 12 appeared in the Spring 1998 issue of *The Public Interest.*

The Johns Hopkins University Press
2715 North Charles Street
Baltimore, Maryland 21218-4363
http://www.press.jhu.edu

Library of Congress Cataloging-in-Publication Data

The Democratic Invention / edited by Marc F. Plattner and João Carlos Espada.
    p.   cm. — (A Journal of democracy book)
    Essays originally presented as part of a year-long lecture series sponsored by the International Forum for Democratic Studies of the National Endowment for Democracy and the Soares Foundation of Portugal. They also appeared in the Journal of democracy.
    Includes bibliographical references and index.
    ISBN 0-8018-6419-4 (pbk. : acid-free paper)
    1. Democracy. 2. Revolutions 3. Utopias. I. Plattner, Marc F., 1945– II. Espada, João Carlos. III. Series.
    JC423.D44176 1999
    321.8—dc21   99–048599

A catalog record for this book is available from the British Library.

CONTENTS

ACKNOWLEDGMENTS

The past quarter-century has witnessed an unprecedented flowering of democracy around the globe. This period has been famously labeled the "third wave" of democratization by the author of this volume's opening essay, Samuel P. Huntington, who traced its beginning point to the overthrow of the authoritarian regime in Portugal on 25 April 1974. The ultimately democratic outcome of the Portuguese revolution, however, was by no means assured, as that country's powerful communist movement almost succeeded in gaining power. It was only due to the persistence and effectiveness of Portuguese democratic forces, led by the country's future prime minister and president Mário Soares, that Portugal became one of the third wave's pathbreaking new democracies.

Mário Soares is also the initiator of this volume. The essays that follow are based on a lecture series initially held in Lisbon and subsequently reprised in Washington, D.C. This series, entitled "The Democratic Invention," constituted the first public initiative of the Mário Soares Foundation, which was established in Lisbon as a nongovernmental organization when Mário Soares stepped down after two terms as Portugal's president in 1996. The subject of democracy—a cause on behalf of which Mário Soares fought all his life, and with which his name is indissolubly linked—was chosen as the most appropriate subject for the new foundation's inaugural program, which was coordinated by João Carlos Espada.

The Soares Foundation's lecture series came to the attention of Marc F. Plattner, codirector of the National Endowment for Democracy's International Forum for Democratic Studies, through an invitation to lecture in Lisbon extended to his codirector Larry Diamond. Plattner conceived the idea of reproducing the lecture series in Washington, and he traveled to Lisbon in October 1996 together with John Brademas and Carl Gershman, chairman of the Board and president, respectively, of the National Endowment for Democracy (NED), to attend the opening lecture in the Lisbon series. There they met with Mário Soares, João Carlos Espada, and Carlos Barroso of the Mário Soares Foundation, and with Rui Machete and Charles Buchanan of the Luso-American Development

Foundation (FLAD), to work out the arrangements for a Washington version of the series under the joint sponsorship of the International Forum and these two Portuguese institutions.

A decision was made to broaden the geographical range of the Washington lecturers by inviting speakers from outside Western Europe and the United States. Thus three lecturers spoke in Washington who had not previously spoken in Lisbon—the Dalai Lama, Bronisław Geremek of Poland, and Fatima Mernissi of Morocco. (Invitations were also extended to a distinguished Latin American and African, but neither was ultimately able to participate.) To accommodate these additions, three Americans—Larry Diamond, Terry Karl, and Robert A. Pastor—who had delivered lectures in Lisbon, were invited instead to join in a panel discussion at the inaugural event of the Washington program on 3 June 1997. This event, held at the Cannon House Office Building of the U.S. House of Representatives, featured a lecture by Samuel Huntington, followed by a panel discussion including Diamond and Pastor (Terry Karl was ill and could not attend) and three distinguished Portuguese commentators—former foreign minister José Manuel Durão Barroso, former deputy prime minister Rui Machete, and João Carlos Espada. The evening concluded with a reception honoring Mário Soares for his many contributions to democracy, with Senators Edward Kennedy and Jack Reed, Representatives Richard Pombo and Patrick Kennedy, and former U.S. ambassador to Portugal Frank Carlucci among the speakers.

The remaining Washington lectures, scheduled from September 1997 through December 1998 (a postponed lecture by Bronisław Geremek was not delivered until April 1999), were hosted by The George Washington University. All the lectures delivered in Washington are included in this volume except for that of Fatima Mernissi, who was unable to provide us with a written text in time for our deadline. Two of those who lectured in Lisbon, Ralf Dahrendorf and Federico Mayor, were unable to accept our invitation to speak in Washington and are not included here. The only lectures not presented in Washington included in this volume are those presented in Lisbon by Larry Diamond and Robert Pastor, who participated in the opening panel discussion in Washington. François Furet had accepted an invitation to speak in Washington in November 1997 but died in a tragic accident in July of that year. A translated version of his Lisbon lecture was presented in Washington by Marc F. Plattner, along with comments by Francis Fukuyama and Jeane J. Kirkpatrick and a tribute to Furet by France's ambassador to the United States, François Bujon de l'Estang. Two of the speakers in the series, Seymour Martin Lipset and Alfred Stepan, spoke on different topics in Washington than in Lisbon, and several of the other Washington lecturers modified their remarks to take into account the shift in venue. In all these cases, it is the Washington version that appears in this volume. (A volume in Portuguese containing the lectures delivered in Lisbon is being published jointly by the Instituto de Ciências Sociais of the University of Lisbon and the Mário Soares Foundation.) The majority of the essays published here—those by Huntington, Soares, Lipset, Diogo Freitas do Amaral, Geremek, Stepan, Andrea Riccardi, the Dalai Lama, and Furet—first appeared in the International Forum's quarterly *Journal of Democracy*.

As this project involved the cooperation of a large number of institutions, there are many people who contributed to its success and who are deserving of our thanks. One of the cosponsors of the Washington series, FLAD, was also the largest funder of the project, and we are especially grateful to its president, Rui Machete. A second substantial funder was the Lynde and Harry Bradley Foundation, which has also given continuing support to the *Journal of Democracy,* and we are pleased to have an opportunity here to thank its president Michael Joyce and its former vice-president Hillel Fradkin. Other funders included the Ford Motor Company and Lehman Brothers; the latter supported printed materials connected with the project and thus merits special thanks with regard to this volume.

We are enormously grateful to The George Washington University and especially its president Steven Joel Trachtenberg, not only for hosting the lectures at the University's Cloyd Heck Marvin Center, but also for their active involvement in the series. Steve Trachtenberg introduced a number of the lectures himself and regularly hosted the splendid dinners that the University graciously provided for 20 to 30 guests following the lectures. Lynn D. Shipway, a special assistant at the university, was unfailingly helpful in planning these events and was always a pleasure to work with. Other prominent administrators who frequently represented the university at the lectures were Vice-President Donald R. Lehman; Harry Harding, dean of the Elliott School of International Affairs; and University Marshal Jill F. Kasle.

The Washington series represented a high order of cooperation between Portugal and the United States. On the Portuguese side, in addition to Rui Machete, we wish especially to thank Ambassador Fernando Andresen Guimaraes and José Sasportes at the Portuguese Embassy in Washington and Carlos Barroso, the secretary-general of the Mário Soares Foundation in Lisbon, for all their help and generosity.

The president of the National Endowment for Democracy, Carl Gershman, was intimately involved with every aspect of the lecture series. His efforts secured the participation of the Dalai Lama and Bronisław Geremek, and he introduced many of the speakers and attended all the dinners. Sydnee Lipset and Jane Riley Jacobson at NED and Debra Liang-Fenton and Art Kaufman at the International Forum made indispensable contributions to arranging the lectures. Philip J. Costopoulos, Mark Eckert, Zerxes Spencer, Miriam Kramer, Stephanie Lewis, and Mahindan Kanakaratnam all were involved with the editing of these essays, and Stephanie prepared the text for publication. Jordan Branch did a fine job with the index. Larry Diamond gave us the benefit of his advice at every stage of this project, and his influence is no doubt visible throughout the volume. Henry Tom of the Johns Hopkins University Press also helped to shape and improve the final form of this book.

Finally, we wish to conclude with a word of tribute to Mário Soares. Though many people labored on the project that gave birth to this book, he was its inspiration, and only someone of his stature could have attracted the extraordinary group of speakers who lectured on "The Democratic Invention" both in Lisbon and in Washington. We hope that this volume will stand as one testament to the accomplishments and the influence of this outstanding democratic leader and remarkable man.

INTRODUCTION

Marc F. Plattner and João Carlos Espada

The title of this volume, "The Democratic Invention," was borrowed from a book of the same name by French political scientist Claude Lefort published in 1981. As Mário Soares notes in his own contribution to these pages, this phrase is intended to emphasize "democracy's need for continuous and progressive improvement," as well as the fact that "any democratic construction will constantly generate problems and remains incomplete by definition." Thus "democracy cannot be taken for granted as something established once and for all, nor can it be viewed as a single static model applicable to any country, as if it were a finished and unchangeable work." But there is a further reason why this phrase is particularly appropriate for new democracies like Portugal. If such a lecture series had been inaugurated in Britain or the United States, it might instead have been called "The Democratic Tradition." Of course, no social reality is entirely inherited, just as none is entirely invented. But a new democracy in a country with a significant authoritarian past must necessarily rely heavily on invention.

The essays included in this book, although they share both a high standard of intellectual excellence and a commitment to democracy, are in most other respects quite diverse. In a lecture series dedicated to celebrating the democratic invention, it seemed only fitting to include differing points of view and to cover many aspects of democratic theory and practice. At the same time, the essays do focus on certain common themes, and we have grouped them accordingly under four headings: 1) "The Democratic Prospect"; 2) "Transitions to Democracy"; 3) "Beyond and Below the Nation"; and 4) "Religion, Morality, and Belief."

The opening section, featuring essays by Samuel P. Huntington, Larry Diamond, and Mário Soares, offers broad-ranging global assessments of the recent history and the future prospects of democracy. The second section comprises three essays that focus on specific cases of democratic transition: Seymour Martin Lipset on the founding of democracy in the United States, Diogo Freitas do Amaral on Portugal's democratic transition, and Bronisław Geremek on the postcommunist transitions in

Central Europe. The third section features three essays that deal with democracy at different levels in terms of scale: Jean Daniel, focusing on the issues raised by the deepening of the European Union, examines the critical but precarious status of the nation as the seat of democracy; Alfred Stepan considers the challenges that confront populous (and especially multinational) democracies in allocating power to their smaller subunits; and Robert Pastor addresses the role that the "international community" can play in promoting democratic progress. Finally, the concluding section, containing essays by Andrea Riccardi, His Holiness the Dalai Lama, Gertrude Himmelfarb, and the late François Furet, examines the perennial issues of religion, morality, and belief that confront all democratic societies, whether they are newly emerging or long established.

The Democratic Prospect

Our volume opens with Samuel Huntington, who inaugurated the lecture series in Lisbon in October 1996 (and in Washington the following June), reflecting on the future of what he was the first to dub the third wave of democratization—the set of regime transitions since 1974 that by now has more than doubled (to 60 percent) the percentage of the world's countries whose governments are based on reasonably fair and open elections. He argues that the future fortunes of democracy in the world "will depend largely on two factors: economic development and the receptivity to democracy of non-Western cultures." When economic growth brings countries to intermediate levels of development, they enter a "zone of transition" where pressures arise for them to democratize their political system. The economic factor, however, may be offset by that of culture, with Western countries (or those most exposed to Western influence) much more likely to democratize than non-Western countries. Thus Huntington defines as "the central issue" for the future of the third wave the following: "To what extent can modern democracy, a product of the West, take root in non-Western societies?"

In discussing this question, Huntington draws upon the distinction made by Larry Diamond between liberal democracy and electoral democracy. Huntington's conclusion seems to be that while electoral democracy may readily spread to non-Western societies, it is not likely to give rise there to liberal democracy, which is rooted in Western concepts of individual rights and the rule of law. Electoral democracy, as he puts it, "is a parochializing, not a cosmopolitanizing influence." Therefore extending democratic elections to non-Western societies may only strengthen their nativist and anti-Western elements. While acknowledging that "at least one liberal democracy exists in almost every other civilization," he seems pessimistic about the willingness of most Muslim and Confucian societies to adopt Western-style liberal democracy. Thus his practical advice to promoters of democracy is to concentrate their efforts not on tough cases in Asia, Africa, or the Middle East, but on transforming electoral democracies into liberal democracies in areas like Latin America and Eastern Europe that are more akin to the West.

In his own contribution to this volume, Larry Diamond presents a somewhat more optimistic assessment of the future prospects for the expansion of democracy. Agreeing with Huntington that sustainable democratic transitions are unlikely any time soon in the many countries in East Asia, Central Asia, the Middle East, and Africa where cultural or economic conditions are unpropitious, he acknowledges that the third wave has probably come to an end. Looking toward the future, however, he argues that "no country should be written off" in the quest to build a more democratic world. While noting the deterioration in the quality of democracy in many key third-wave countries and reemphasizing the gap that separates electoral from liberal democracy, he urges that we view democracy "in *developmental* terms, as emerging in fragments or parts." Thus even mere electoral democracy, no matter how illiberal or imperfect, can become a building block for the eventual construction of liberal democracy.

For the immediate future, Diamond stresses the importance of preventing a new "reverse wave" of the kind that followed the two earlier waves of democratization identified by Huntington. To avoid such an outcome, he argues, like Huntington, that democratizers should give priority to consolidating the third-wave democracies. But at the same time he urges policy makers "to encourage the many disparate currents of change that could at some point in the future gather into a fourth wave of democratization." Diamond cautions that neither the consolidation of democracy where it exists nor its eventual spread to other countries is inevitable. For it to happen will require skilled leadership and commitment, not only within countries aspiring to democracy, but also on the part of the established democracies. Through reinforcing international rules and structures favorable to democracy and through providing diverse forms of assistance to democrats abroad, the established democracies can pave the way for a fourth wave that, in the next generation, could spread democracy through much of Asia and Africa.

In the following essay, Mário Soares explores the question of democracy's future, but from the perspective of a statesman rather than a political scientist. His own painful experience under dictatorship in Portugal leads him to view democracy "as a frail and precious flower that needs care and permanent vigilance." Reacting to those who believe that the end of the Cold War has brought about the worldwide triumph of liberal democracy and the market economy, he points to the misguided optimism that reigned in the early 1900s before the twentieth century was engulfed by tragedy and terror. Recounting the many grave social and economic problems that continue to plague contemporary societies,

Soares insists that we cannot be complacent about the future of democracy.

Much more than either Huntington or Diamond, he emphasizes the extent to which the successful functioning of "formal democracy" and its political rules and institutions depends upon the ability of democratic societies to ameliorate the social, economic, and cultural conditions of their citizens. Democracy, he argues, can become "deeply rooted in the hearts of the people" only if it responds to their social, economic, and cultural concerns. Thus Soares sees "the new forms of international speculative capitalism" and growing inequality both within and among nations as posing serious obstacles to the future flourishing of democracy. While calling attention to the dangers of globalization, however, he also finds signs of hope in the progress of the European Union (EU), the emergence of a global public opinion, and the growing role of civil societies, which can "gradually help to build a global civic awareness."

Transitions to Democracy

With the next set of essays, this volume moves from an examination of the global democratic wave to an exploration of regime transitions in individual countries. Two essays focusing on key third-wave cases are preceded by Seymour Martin Lipset's essay on what might be considered the first modern democratic transition—that of the United States. While focusing on the crucial role played by George Washington in America's struggle for independence and the founding of its new democracy, Lipset draws lessons that have broad application to other new democracies. As he points out, the history of postrevolutionary regimes has generally been marked by democratic failure. "It is rare for all the major players, including the military, economic, and political elites, to accept the need to conform to the rules of the new system. New political regimes inherently have weak or low legitimacy."

As Lipset reminds us, the postrevolutionary United States experienced many crises—including attempts at secession—during its early years, but it was able to maintain and institutionalize its democracy. He gives much of the credit for this to the contribution of George Washington. To preserve national unity, new regimes, lacking a traditional basis for authority, usually have need of a charismatic leader. The danger of charismatic leadership, however, is that because it is so personalized it is inherently unstable. Though he was venerated, even idolized, as much as any revolutionary hero, Washington possessed the moderation, commitment to civilian constitutional rule, and understanding of the requirements of republican self-government that were needed to institutionalize democracy. Perhaps his greatest contribution, Lipset suggests, was to step down after two terms as president, thus setting an example that helped spare the United States from the affliction that has plagued democracy in Latin America and elsewhere—the desire of presidents to remain in power indefinitely. As Lipset notes, the third-wave figure who has the greatest claim to be the George Washington of his country is South Africa's Nelson Mandela, who has just set a similar example by retiring from office at the height of his popularity.

The next essay is the first of two by prominent participants in the democratic transitions about which they write. Diogo Freitas do Amaral was a founder and leader of Portugal's Social Democratic Center, one of the three leading democratic parties that contested the April 1975 Constituent Assembly elections. He has been a leading political figure under Portuguese democracy, narrowly losing the presidential election to Mário Soares in 1986. Yet he writes not to praise the Portuguese revolution but to underline its costs. For while approving its democratic outcome, he contends that "Portugal's democratic transition occurred far later and far less peacefully than it could have," and therefore that it does not provide "a model worthy of emulation by other countries."

Freitas contrasts Portugal's revolutionary transition unfavorably with the peaceful transition in neighboring Spain. He suggests that if Marcello Caetano, the successor to longtime dictator Antonio de Salazar, had been as adroit as Spain's post-Franco prime minister Adolfo Suarez, he could have overcome the opposition of the extreme right to bring about a transition prior to the revolution. Moreover, after Caetano was over-thrown in the April 1974 military coup, a peaceful transition could have been achieved were it not for the communist attempt to imitate the Bol-sheviks by initiating a second, socialist revolution. Although Portugal's democratic forces were miraculously able both to defeat the communists and to avoid civil war or military dictatorship, Freitas argues that Portugal paid a heavy price. Not only was its economic progress severely retarded by economic measures imposed by the communists, but the country did not succeed in eliminating Marxist economic provisions from its consti-tution until 1989. Freitas acknowledges that the story eventually ended happily in a strong and flourishing Portuguese democracy, but he remains insistent on the superiority of peaceful transition to violent revolution.

The final essay in this section is by Polish foreign minister Bronisław Geremek, who was a key advisor to Lech Wałęsa from the earliest days of Solidarity and played a key role in the 1989 "roundtable talks" that led to Poland's first partially free elections. Just as Portugal took the lead in initiating the third wave of democratization, which spread from Southern Europe in the mid-1970s to Latin America in the 1980s, Poland launched the remarkable series of postcommunist transitions that vastly extended the range of the third wave in the 1990s. As Geremek points out, Hungarians, Czechs, and Poles had paid a high price for their resis-tance to communist rule in 1956, 1968, and 1981, but in 1989 they chose the path of dialogue rather than confrontation. The "roundtable talks" between Solidarity and Poland's communist regime led to a "negotiated revolution" rather than a bloody one, and produced a model that was emulated by many other Soviet Bloc countries. Like Freitas, then, Geremek points to the advantages of peaceful transition over violent revolution.

The postcommunist transitions were complicated by the fact that they entailed an effort to build free-market economies as well as democratic political institutions. Geremek emphasizes the complementarity between democracy and the free market and hails Poland's success as a sign that an efficient economy can be constructed under democratic auspices. He also notes, however, that while a number of other Central European countries have been similarly successful, the transition has faltered in much of Eastern and Southeastern Europe. He cautions against the threat of "a new wall dividing the democratic and affluent countries of Europe from those sunk in political chaos and economic stagnation." To help prevent such an outcome, he calls upon NATO and the EU to support the postcommunist transformations and to show an openness to accepting new members. Just as democratic consolidation was assisted in Portugal, Spain, and Greece by integration into European structures, Geremek suggests that the same processes can help secure democracy in the postcommunist countries.

Beyond and Below the Nation

Jean Daniel begins the next section by focusing not on the enlargement of the EU but on the deepening of the ties between its existing members, as symbolized by their May 1998 decision to adopt a single currency. Daniel sees this event as being comparable in historic significance to the 1648 Treaties of Westphalia and as representing an unprecedented willingness of sovereign nations to relinquish part of their power in peacetime. For him, the progress of the EU raises a fundamental question: "Is democracy possible outside the framework of the nation-state?" His complex meditation on this theme explores the "dialectic between wandering and rootedness, between universality and identity, between the individual and the community." While acknowledging that the democratic concept of the sovereignty of the people has historically been associated with the territorial nation, he concludes that "democracy is conceivable in a framework other than the nation-state, but the organization of such a democracy must take national sovereignty into account." What he seems to envision is a Europe that will eventually comprise a federation similar to that of the United States.

Daniel also devotes a portion of his essay to the internal American debate about exporting democracy. In this debate he seems to side with more skeptical authors like Henry Kissinger and Samuel Huntington rather than with those like Strobe Talbott who champion a universalist concept of democracy and call for an active U.S. role in promoting it.

Although Daniel himself argues that there is a "universal minimum" of moral principles on which all the main human civilizations can agree, he is strongly opposed to a single power taking it upon itself to enforce even this common standard. Instead, he argues that any such intervention or assistance should be undertaken by a "community of nations." Thus he concludes his essay by reaffirming his support for "the federation of democratic nations because the nation is halfway between the individual and the universal, and as such only it can enable *the universal to take root*."

In the next essay, Alfred Stepan comes at the question of federalism from a different angle. The question of scale has long been critical in thinking about democracy. The authors of the *Federalist* sought to counter the long-held view that democracy was appropriate only for very small polities by making a case for the "enlargement of the orbit" of popular government through the principle of federalism. American-style federalism has indeed proven to be a great success, but in Stepan's view that success has tended to obscure other variations of federalism that might be better suited for many newer democracies. Stepan accepts that federalism is all but essential for democracy to work in very large and diverse societies, but he contends that, especially in multinational and multilingual polities, the best choice may be a federalism with very different characteristics than those most familiar to Americans.

Stepan categorizes the variety of federalisms along three different dimensions. First, he distinguishes between "coming-together" and "holding-together" federalism: In the former model, which describes both the United States and the EU, previously sovereign polities agree to give up part of their sovereignty in order to obtain the benefits of union; but other federations, including India, Belgium, and Spain, result from previously unitary polities agreeing to devolve some power to subunits. Second, Stepan constructs a continuum ranging from "*demos*-constraining" to "*demos*-enabling" federalism: At the *demos*-constraining end of the continuum, the power of popular countrywide majorities is limited both by a relatively powerful upper chamber of the legislature where less populous subunits have disproportionally greater representation and by the constitutional allocation of significant powers to the subunits, as in the United States. Other federations, however, have weaker and less disproportional upper chambers and reserve fewer significant powers to their subunits. Finally, Stepan distinguishes between "symmetrical" federations (like the United States), where all the subunits enjoy the same powers, and "asymmetrical" federations (like Canada), where different subunits (for example, Quebec) may enjoy different rights and privileges. Stepan concludes that asymmetrical federations, including those that grant group-specific rights, may offer the best option for large multinational polities, and that they need not be incompatible with the effective protection of individual rights.

The final essay in this section, by Robert A. Pastor, explores the relationship between politics at the international level and the effort to establish democracy in individual countries. He begins by invoking the American Declaration of Independence, emphasizing not only the universal character of the rights that it proclaims but also its profession of "a decent respect to the opinions of mankind." Just as the American revolutionaries received support from external powers, Pastor notes that the Portuguese struggle for democracy was powerfully assisted from abroad, especially by social democratic forces in Western Europe. Yet the legitimate role of the international community in supporting democracy in a particular country has never been clearly defined, with conflicting guidance being provided by two international norms: "the right of a people to have a democratic government and the right of a state to be free of outside intervention."

Over the past decade, however, the balance has increasingly tipped in favor of an active role by the international community on behalf of democracy, a trend that Pastor defends on both moral and practical grounds. He traces these recent developments on two parallel fronts: efforts to promote democratic transition and consolidation within individual states and attempts to forge structures that can provide a collective defense of democracy at the international level. On the intrastate level, he recounts the rise of election monitoring by nongovernmental and intergovernmental organizations, beginning with the 1989 "breakthrough" when the Sandinista government invited the UN, the Organization of American States (OAS), and the Carter Center to observe Nicaragua's elections. Regarding the collective defense of democracy, he cites the precedent set by the UN Resolution authorizing member states to use "necessary means" to restore to power Haiti's freely elected president Jean-Bertrand Aristide, who had been overthrown by a military coup. Pastor also recounts the approval of the "Santiago Commitment" by the OAS and its successes in forestalling military coups in the Western Hemisphere, as well as the prodemocratic policies of other regional organizations. He concludes with a plea to democratic world leaders to "dedicate themselves to a global strategy of democratization."

Religion, Morality, and Belief

While the previous essays in this collection focus primarily on the political or institutional aspects of democracy, the concluding section takes up key questions of religion, morality, and belief. Its first two essays, by prominent religious leaders, point to a growing reconciliation between major religious traditions and the principles of democracy. Andrea Riccardi, president of the Community of Saint Egidio, a Rome-based lay Catholic nongovernmental organization, recounts the story of this Community in the context of the wider evolution of the Roman

Catholic Church. As Samuel Huntington first pointed out, the third wave until 1989 had primarily involved Catholic countries (in southern Europe, Latin America, the Philippines, and Central Europe), a development made possible by the shift in Catholic doctrine associated with the Second Vatican Council in 1962–65. Riccardi confirms that for his own generation (the children of 1968), "the Second Vatican Council signified a profound detaching of Christian experience from political authoritarianism. . . . The Council ushered in the full acceptance of religious freedom and pluralism . . . [and] the conviction that Christian life matures more profoundly in democracy and freedom."

Riccardi describes the Community of Saint Egidio's dedication not only to democracy but also to the related goals of solidarity and peace. He defines solidarity as "the recognition that the poor and the nonpoor share a common destiny," an understanding that informs the commitment of Saint Egidio's 15,000 members worldwide to living with and assisting the poor. And he explains how Saint Egidio's struggle against poverty led it into a struggle against war as well, culminating in the key role that it played in the diplomacy that brought to an end the brutal civil war in Mozambique. Finally, noting that religion sometimes "can add fuel to the flames of war," he describes Saint Egidio's efforts to bring together people from different religious traditions to pursue "a path of religious recognition of 'the other,' of faith-inspired work for peace, of dialogue (undergirded by religious values) that enhances democratic respect for others."

The next essay, by Tibet's exiled spiritual and political leader, His Holiness the Dalai Lama, considers the relationship between the Buddhist tradition and democracy and concludes that they are indeed compatible. In the first place, both Buddhism and modern democracy are "based on the principle that all human beings are essentially equal, and that each of us has an equal right to life, liberty, and happiness." While emphasizing that each individual is the master of his or her own destiny, Buddhists "also believe that the purpose of a meaningful life is to serve others." Here, too, the Dalai Lama sees a compatibility between Buddhism and democracy, contending that, although all forms of government are imperfect, democracy "allows us the greatest opportunity to cultivate a sense of universal responsibility."

The Dalai Lama explicitly confronts the claim made by some Asian leaders that democracy and individual freedom are essentially Western concepts that tend to undermine the "Asian values" of order, duty, and stability. He rejects this viewpoint, on the grounds that "all human beings share the same basic aspirations." He cites not only the example of India, which shows that democratic government can take root in Asia, but also the calls for equality, freedom, and democracy emanating from opposition groups in Burma, Indonesia, and China. Finally, he recounts his own efforts to develop democratic structures for Tibetans living in exile, and voices his hopes that in the not-too-distant future such institutions may be introduced within an autonomous Tibet. The Dalai Lama concludes by reemphasizing the importance of "acknowledging the universality of the key ethical and political values that underlie democracy," and of recognizing that the basic institutions derived from those values are "necessary conditions of a civilized society."

The final two essays in this section are by secular historians who focus on the moral and intellectual condition of the established democracies and present a somewhat darker view than the other authors in this volume. Gertrude Himmelfarb sees democracy threatened not by weaknesses in its political institutions but by "diseases" in the moral and cultural realm: "the collapse of ethical principles and habits, the loss of respect for authorities and institutions, the breakdown of the family, the decline of civility, the vulgarization of high culture, and the degradation of popular culture." Although these afflictions are besetting most Western democracies, she concentrates her analysis wholly on the United States, reviewing both the symptoms of moral decay and the possible responses to it. She is skeptical about efforts to apply political remedies to social and moral disorders, but also dubious about the highly touted restorative potential of civil society, for much of civil society has been infected by the same ethical and cultural relativism that is the source of the problem.

Himmelfarb then turns to an analysis of religion, noting the importance that Tocqueville had attributed to religion in providing the underpinning of American liberty. She sees signs of a religious revival that is also a moral revival, and it is here that she finds the best hope for arresting moral decline. Yet Himmelfarb is by no means sanguine that this revival will quickly sweep through American society as a whole. In fact, borrowing the term from Disraeli's description of nineteenth-century England, she characterizes America as divided into "two nations," separated not into rich and poor but into cultural conservatives and progressives, with the latter now forming the dominant cultural elite. The traditionalists, whom Himmelfarb terms the "other nation," not only lack influence in such key institutions as academia and the media but also form a minority in the population as a whole. She believes that this "other nation," which is capable of mitigating (though not curing) the "diseases incident to a democratic society," is likely to grow in reaction to the excesses of the dominant culture. But far from calling for an intensification of the "culture wars," she hopes that, as the religious groups grow more self-confident, they will also "shed some of their sectarianism and intransigence." Drawing once again upon the analogy of Victorian England, Himmelfarb concludes with the suggestion that the two nations not only can live together without civil strife but may even be able to achieve an eventual reconciliation.

In this volume's final essay, eminent historian François Furet explores the utopian impulse in modern politics, beginning with "the French

Revolution, that laboratory of modern democracy." For Furet, the seeds of utopianism are to be found in the democratic idea itself, with its promise of both unlimited liberty and unlimited equality. Since "it is impossible to make liberty and equality reign together or even to reconcile the two in a lasting way," actual democratic regimes always appear unfaithful to their own principles and thus are constantly exposed to demands for revolutionary change. Moreover, the anticlerical and even antireligious character of the French Revolution led to an abandonment of all otherworldly hopes and turned the passions of the revolutionaries toward achieving a utopian outcome purely at the level of the political. A wholly good society was to be achieved solely through the unfolding of human history.

This, of course, is the outlook of Marxism, and Furet devotes the second half of his essay to analyzing the extraordinary worldwide influence and appeal of the idea of communism from the birth of the Soviet Union in 1917 until its demise in 1991. He notes that Marx himself "never ceased oscillating" between two contradictory conceptions of the revolutionary idea, and the same has been true of his followers. On the one hand, the revolution is seen as the product of the deterministic evolution of human history; on the other, its achievement requires a Promethean effort of the human will—"political invention" in its most extreme sense. The collapse of the Soviet Union, in Furet's view, has brought about the death of the communist idea (and perhaps of the revolutionary idea as such). Given the tragedies this idea has generated and the threat it posed to liberal democracy, we can be grateful for its demise. Furet adds, however, that the disappearance of the communist idea "has deepened the political deficit that has always characterized modern liberalism." The idea of democracy has long been linked to a progressive view of history. But today, "The democratic individual finds himself poised before a closed future, incapable of defining even vaguely the horizon of a *different society* from the one in which we live, since this horizon has become almost impossible to conceive." Does modern democracy require a utopian vision to energize its citizens and to give them a sense of where their societies are heading? Can and will a new "revolutionary horizon" emerge? These are the profound questions with which Furet concludes his essay, questions that may provide the greatest challenge of all to "the democratic invention" in the century ahead.

A Complex Picture

The diversity of perspectives represented by the statesmen, scholars, and religious leaders who have contributed to this volume provides a more balanced and rounded understanding of the challenges facing democracy than could be found in the view of any single observer. But what is one to conclude from the complex picture that emerges from this collection of essays? We would highlight the following conclusions.

First, the last quarter of the twentieth century has been the greatest period of global democratic advancement in human history. Democracy has spread to many more countries and civilizations than ever before, and it currently enjoys unrivaled worldwide intellectual and political hegemony. Major religious traditions that once evinced skepticism or even hostility toward the claims of democracy are increasingly coming to accept its basic principles. Leading international and regional organizations explicitly endorse democracy and are devoting greater efforts than ever before to assisting its establishment and maintenance in many parts of the globe. The economic and technological developments often grouped under the label of "globalization" are eroding opposition to democracy and facilitating its expansion.

Yet these undeniably powerful trends by no means guarantee a democratic future. Some non-Western cultures remain resistant to liberal democracy. Ethnic conflict threatens democracy in multinational states. Globalization, despite breaking down barriers and promoting international integration, is also exacerbating inequality and threatening to marginalize significant segments of the world's population. The nation-state, which has been the only real home of modern democracy, appears to be losing its centrality and facing an uncertain future. Most worrisome of all, even long-established democracies seem vulnerable to moral decline and spiritual exhaustion. Democracy has vanquished all its most potent external opponents, but it seems surprisingly shaky at what should be the moment of its greatest triumph. The story is by no means completed, nor is it fated to come to a happy end; the need for "democratic invention" is perhaps as great as it has ever been.

I

The Democratic Prospect

1

THE FUTURE
OF THE THIRD WAVE

Samuel P. Huntington

*Samuel P. Huntington is Albert J. Weatherhead III University Professor
and director of the John M. Olin Institute for Strategic Studies at Harvard
University. His many books include* The Third Wave: Democratization
in the Late Twentieth Century *(1991) and* The Clash of Civilizations
and the Remaking of World Order *(1996).*

Some five hundred years ago a small group of Portuguese leaders and
thinkers—including King John II, Prince Henry the Navigator, Bartholo-
mew Dias, and Vasco da Gama—acting with courage, determination,
and imagination, inaugurated a new phase in human history, the age of
discovery. They set an example that Spain, France, Britain, and the
Netherlands were to follow. Slightly more than two decades ago, Mário
Soares and his colleagues, acting with comparable courage, determination, and imagination, inaugurated a new phase in human history, the
age of democracy. They too set an example that Spain, Greece, Brazil,
and many other countries have followed.

This result, however, was not foreordained. Chaos and conflict existed
in Portugal in the months following the military's overthrow of the
dictatorship in April 1974. At that time the prospects for democracy did
not seem bright, and many thought that Portugal's Stalinist communist
party would come to power. This pessimism was shared by U.S. secretary
of state Henry Kissinger. When Mário Soares, then foreign minister in
the provisional government, visited Kissinger, the latter berated him
and his government for not taking a stronger line against the communists.

"You are a Kerensky," Kissinger said, "I believe your sincerity, but
you are naive."

To which Soares replied: "I certainly don't want to be a Kerensky."

And Kissinger shot back: "Neither did Kerensky."[1]

Mário Soares and his colleagues, however, proved Kissinger wrong.
In Portugal, the Kerenskys won, democracy was consolidated, and Mário
Soares went on to be prime minister and later president. The third wave
of democratization that Portugal initiated literally created the age of

democracy, in which for the first time in history more than half the countries in the world have some form of democratic government.

Let us briefly look at the record. The first, long wave of democratization that began in the early nineteenth century led to the triumph of democracy in some 30 countries by 1920. Renewed authoritarianism and the rise of fascism in the 1920s and 1930s reduced the number of democracies in the world to about a dozen by 1942. The second, short wave of democratization after the Second World War again increased the number of democracies in the world to somewhat over 30, but this too was followed by the collapse of democracy in many of these countries. The third wave of democratization that began in Portugal has seen democratization occur much faster and on a scale far surpassing that of the previous two waves. Two decades ago, less than 30 percent of the countries in the world were democratic; now more than 60 percent have governments produced by some form of open, fair, and competitive elections. A quarter-century ago, authoritarian governments—communist politburos, military juntas, personal dictatorships—were the rule. Today, hundreds of millions of people who previously suffered under tyrants live in freedom. In addition, since democracies historically have not warred with other democracies, there has been a major expansion of the zone of peace in the world and a reduction in the likelihood of interstate conflict. This dramatic growth of democracy in such a short time is, without doubt, one of the most spectacular and important political changes in human history.

But what about the future? Will democracy become consolidated in the countries where it has recently emerged? Will more countries become democratic? Are we about to see a world in which democracy is not only the predominant system of government but the universal system of government?

Economics and Culture

The answers to these questions, I believe, depend largely on two factors: economic development and the receptivity to democracy of non-Western cultures.

First, as we all know, an extremely high correlation exists between levels of democracy and levels of economic development. Setting aside the oil-rich states as a special case, all the wealthiest countries in the world, except Singapore, are democratic, and almost all the poorest countries in the world, with the notable exception of India and perhaps one or two others, are not democratic. The countries at intermediate levels of economic development are in some cases democratic and in other cases not. Yet correlation, as we know, does not prove causation. Hence we are left with a set of questions: Does economic growth produce democracy? Does democracy produce economic growth? Or are economic growth and democratization both products of some other cause or independent variable?

As Seymour Martin Lipset pointed out decades ago, the evidence is overwhelming that economic development has a strong positive effect on democratization.[2] In short, if you wish to produce democracy, promote economic growth. There are several reasons for this relationship. Economic development involves higher levels of urbanization, literacy, and education. It also involves a shift in occupational structure, with a decline in the size and importance of the peasantry and the development of a middle class and an urban working class. The latter groups increasingly want a voice in and influence over policies that affect them. With higher levels of education, they are able to organize trade unions, political parties, and civic associations to promote their interests. Second, economic development produces more resources, public and private, for distribution among groups in society. Politics becomes less of a zero-sum game, and hence compromise and toleration are encouraged. Third, economic growth produces a more complex economy that becomes increasingly difficult for the state to control; as we have seen in the case of the command economies, state control can only be maintained at the price of economic stagnation. Fourth, the easing of state control of the economy leads to the creation and growth of independent centers of power, based on private control of capital, technology, and communications. The bourgeoisie who hold these assets want a political system in which they can exercise influence, one that is not dominated by a military junta, a politburo, or a dictator and his cronies. Finally, while in the short term rapid economic growth often exacerbates income inequalities, in the longer term it produces greater equality in income distribution. Democracy is incompatible with total economic equality, which can be achieved only by a coercive dictatorship, but it also is incompatible with gross inequalities in wealth and income. Economic growth eventually reduces these inequalities and hence facilitates the emergence of democracy.

As a result of this positive effect of economic growth on democratization, it is possible to identify what in *The Third Wave* I called a "transition zone."[3] As countries grow economically and enter into this zone of intermediate levels of economic development, pressures develop within them to open up and democratize their political system. Most of the 40 or more transitions to democracy that have occurred in recent decades have been in countries that were in this transition zone. One would expect that future transitions to democracy will occur in those areas of the world, such as East and Southeast Asia, that are experiencing rapid economic development.

At this point, however, it is necessary to introduce the cultural element. Modern democracy is a product of Western civilization. Its roots lie in the social pluralism, the class system, the civil society, the belief in the rule of law, the experience with representative bodies, the separation of spiritual and temporal authority, and the commitment to individualism that began to develop in Western Europe a millennium ago. In the seventeenth and eighteenth centuries, these legacies generated the struggles for political participation by the aristocrats and rising middle classes that produced nineteenth-century democratic development. These characteristics may individually be found in other civilizations, but together they have existed only in the West, and they explain why modern democracy is a child of Western civilization.

Europe, as Arthur Schlesinger, Jr., has said, is "the source—the *unique* source" of the "ideas of individual liberty, political democracy, the rule of law, human rights, and cultural freedom. . . . These are *European* ideas, not Asian, nor African, nor Middle Eastern ideas, except by adoption."[4] The great achievement of the third wave has been to ensure the universality of democracy in Western civilization and to promote its manifestations in other civilizations. If the third wave has a future, that future lies in the expansion of democracy in non-Western societies. The central issue is: To what extent can modern democracy, a product of the West, take root in non-Western societies?

Elections and Democracy

This question raises the issue of the meaning of democracy to people of different cultures. Since the Second World War the dominant trend has been to define democracy almost entirely in terms of elections. Democracy is viewed as a means of constituting authority and making it responsible. In other political systems people become rulers through birth, appointment, examination, wealth, or coercion. In a democracy, in contrast, either the rulers and ruled are identical, as in direct democracy, or rulers are selected by vote of the ruled. A modern nation-state has a democratic political system to the extent that its most powerful decision makers are selected through fair, honest, periodic elections in which candidates freely compete for votes and in which virtually the entire adult population is eligible to vote. This procedural definition of democracy received its most significant modern exposition over 50 years ago in Schumpeter's *Capitalism, Socialism and Democracy,* and has been generally accepted by scholars working on this subject.[5] According to this definition, elections are the essence of democracy. From this follow other characteristics of democratic systems. Free, fair, and competitive elections are only possible if there is some measure of freedom of speech, assembly, and press, and if opposition candidates and parties are able to criticize incumbents without fear of retaliation.

Are elections, however, all there is to democracy? In a brilliant article in the *Journal of Democracy,* Larry Diamond elaborated a key distinction between liberal democracy and electoral democracy.[6] Liberal democracies not only have elections. They also have restrictions on the power of the executive; independent judiciaries to uphold the rule of law; protection for individual rights and liberties of expression, association, belief, and participation; consideration for the rights of minorities; limits on the ability of the party in power to bias the electoral process; effective guarantees against arbitrary arrest and police brutality; no censorship; and minimal government control of the media. Electoral democracies have governments resulting from reasonably free and fair elections, but they lack many of these other safeguards for rights and liberties that exist in liberal democracies. As Diamond points out, the number of electoral democracies has grown greatly in recent years, but the number of liberal democracies has been relatively static. According to the 1996 survey by Freedom House, 118 countries qualify as electoral democracies. Only 79 of these countries, however, are rated by Freedom House as "Free"—that is, as liberal democracies. Some 39 countries with elected governments are judged only "Partly Free," including such important countries as Russia, India, Ukraine, Turkey, Brazil, Pakistan, and Colombia.[7]

As a result of this distinction, some people have begun to question the identification of democracy with elections. They have talked of "the fallacy of electoralism" and "the free-elections trap." One distinguished American scholar has even suggested that elections may be superfluous in a democracy: If people have the freedom to protest, criticize, organize, demonstrate, and lobby their rulers, elections will not be necessary.[8] Another critic has argued that it is "more important for democratizing societies to have a free press than free elections." He, of course, was a journalist.[9] This disillusionment with elections stems from various sources, but in large part from the extent to which the results of elections in non-Western countries have differed from those in Western societies.

First, elections in non-Western societies may lead to the victory of political leaders or groups that seriously threaten the maintenance of democracy. Elected chief executives in Latin American countries and in former Soviet republics have often acted in arbitrary and undemocratic ways, suppressing their opponents and ruling by decree. Zviad Gamsakhurdia in Georgia was an early case in point, and Alberto Fujimori in Peru is a later one. Other elected chief executives in Latin America have subordinated their legislatures and forced through constitutional amendments allowing them to extend their term in office. In non-Western societies lacking the liberal tradition of the West, governments formed by elections may often pay little attention to individual rights, discriminate against minorities, curtail press freedom, and tolerate or even encourage police brutality.

Second, elections in non-Western countries provide incentives to politicians to make appeals that will win them the most votes, and these are often appeals of an ethnic, religious, or nationalist nature. Such appeals may exacerbate divisions within the country and may also result in the victory of anti-Western political leaders and policies. Paradoxically, the adoption by non-Western societies of Western democratic institutions often encourages and gives access to power to nativist and anti-Western political movements. Democracy is a parochializing, not a cosmopolitanizing, process. Politicians in non-Western societies do not win elections by demonstrating how Western they are. Religiously-oriented parties challenging Western secularism have scored electoral successes in Turkey, India, Israel, and the former Yugoslav republics. The Algerian military canceled an election that the fundamentalist Islamic Salvation Front was certain to win. The Turkish military forced out of office a government led by the Islamist Welfare Party. In some Muslim countries the choice appears to be between antidemocratic secularism and anti-Western democracy.

In the West, electoral democracy rests on and developed out of a liberal political heritage that included individual rights and the rule of law. Electoral democracy may also play a role, however, in nonliberal, non-Western political systems. Consider the case of Iran. It is a fundamentalist state. Ultimate power is in the Supreme Ayatollah and a Council of Guardians composed of religious leaders. Criticism of the revolution, the regime, or its religious leaders is rigorously suppressed. The media are either controlled by the government or subject to ruthless censorship. Religious minorities are harassed and some, such as the Bahai, are persecuted. Arbitrary arrests are frequent, and torture of prisoners is reportedly widespread. Dismemberment is a form of criminal punishment. There have often been large numbers of political prisoners. Iran is clearly a country far removed from the Western liberal model.

Yet Iran is, in some respects, an electoral democracy. In the 1997 presidential contest, Mohammed Khatemi scored a stunning upset victory over the establishment candidate, winning 69 percent of the vote in an election in which 88 percent of the adult population voted. In 1993, Hashemi Rafsanjani won with 63 percent of the vote in a hotly contested election against three other candidates. In the 1992 elections for the Majlis (parliament), the Council of Guardians disapproved more than a thousand aspiring candidates, but the remaining two thousand vigorously competed against one another for the 270 seats. In 1996 the Council disapproved two thousand Majlis aspirants, but that left three thousand competing for the 270 seats. While political parties are banned, candidates in both elections were affiliated with two semi-party political groupings representing more moderate and more fundamentalist views, respectively. Women both voted and ran for office, and in 1997 they made up 5 percent of the Majlis. The Majlis, moreover, has significant power. It has refused to approve the president's nominations for cabinet positions, and it has on occasion forced the resignation of cabinet ministers. It has hotly debated economic policies and other issues, and in 1994 and 1995 it effectively blocked many of the reforms that then-President Rafsanjani was attempting to put through. The Majlis is arguably the liveliest parliament in the Middle East after the Israeli Knesset. Electoral contestation has been more intense in Iran than in any Arab state and in all but one or two other Muslim states. Iran thus combines contested elections and some checks and balances with fundamentalist repression and gross violations of individual rights. In the Persian Gulf, Saudia Arabia, America's closest ally, is the least democratic country, while Iran, America's greatest antagonist, is the most democratic country.

The Influence of the West

Liberal democracy, rooted in the concept of individual dignity, is a Western product, and some have argued that liberal democracy is impossible outside the West. In fact, however, at least one liberal democracy exists in almost every other civilization. Liberal democracy, in short, is not inherently incompatible with major non-Western cultures. Yet the extent to which non-Western societies are receptive to either liberal democracy or electoral democracy varies with the extent to which they have been influenced by the West. The 39 countries that have governments produced by reasonably open and fair elections, yet also lack the full range of political liberties and civil rights, include ten Latin American, eight African, five Orthodox Christian, and five Muslim countries. Electoral democracy in these countries is not necessarily a step on the road to liberal democracy. India, Turkey, and Sri Lanka, to take but three examples, have been electoral democracies for almost half a century, yet they still remain deficient in the extent to which they protect the rights and liberties of their citizens.

The great civilizations of the world differ significantly in the degree to which their cultures are similar to that of the West or have been influenced by the West. Latin America is clearly a close kin of the West and, according to some, should even be considered a member of the Western family. Orthodoxy is a much more distant and more difficult relative. In Africa, Western rule was brief and its impact, outside South Africa, much more limited. The degree of Western influence among Muslim countries has varied, but in the Arab heartland of Islam it also has been limited. The same is true for China. Overall the extent to which non-Western societies have proven receptive to either electoral democracy or liberal democracy tends to vary directly with the extent to which those societies have been subject to Western influences.

Democratic development occurs when political leaders believe they have an interest in promoting it or a duty to achieve it. Such elites are missing from many parts of the world. In most Muslim countries, authoritarian rulers are in control and show no sign of opening toward democracy. In those few democracies that do exist in the Muslim world, the rulers often rule in undemocratic fashion and show little interest in moving from electoral democracy to liberal democracy. Perhaps even more importantly, in virtually all Muslim countries not governed by fundamentalist regimes, fundamentalist movements dominate and often monopolize opposition to the regime. Liberal democratic opposition groups are notable for their absence. "In one Muslim society after another," Fouad Ajami has observed, "to write of liberalism and a national bourgeois tradition is to write obituaries of men who took on impossible odds and then failed."[10] In addition, it is widely recognized that democracy depends on a vigorous civil society. A vigorous civil society is emerging in Muslim countries, but it is a fundamentalist civil society, not a secular and liberal civil society.

The elites of China and many other Asian societies have no use for liberal democracy. Indeed, it has been argued by some Western scholars that Asia is the home of "illiberal democracy," the product of a cultural heritage that stresses the tutelary and disciplining role of the state and the law as guides for citizen behavior rather than as protectors of individual rights.[11] In China political leaders vigorously oppose democracy, the emerging bourgeoisie is likely to be too intertwined with the state to challenge state power, and students and other dissidents lack any secure social base. The concept of human rights that limit the state is weak in East Asia; to the extent that individual rights are recognized, they are usually viewed as rights created by the state. Harmony and cooperation are preferred over disagreement and competition. The maintenance of order and respect for hierarchy are viewed as central values. Conflict between ideas, groups, and parties tends to be viewed as dangerous. Hence electoral democracy, to the extent that it develops in Asian societies, is likely to be designed to produce consensus rather than choice, to have different characteristics from electoral democracy in the West, and to lack the penumbra of the liberal practices and institutions that go with Western democracy.

A Strategy for Democratizers

The practical issue comes down to this: In the current phase of the third wave, should those concerned with the promotion of democracy give priority to extending electoral democracy to the more than 50 unfree countries of the world that lack any form of democracy? Or should priority be given to promoting liberal democracy in countries that are already electoral democracies? Obviously, in some measure it is desirable and necessary to do both. At this time, however, I believe that greater emphasis should be put on the transformation of electoral democracies into liberal democracies. The place to start is Latin America, where liberal democracy has taken root in several countries, and where there are ten electoral (but not liberal) democracies. Latin America's electoral democracies have been variously labeled as "delegative," "protected," "restrictive," "corporatist," and "quasi" democracies.[12] Yet Latin American culture closely resembles Western culture. Latin Americans speak Western languages and are overwhelmingly Catholic (and increasingly Protestant) in their religious beliefs. Migration and the expansion of trade are creating close ties between Latin America and North America. Economically, most Latin American countries are at middle levels of economic development. Latin American elites are far more committed to the liberal democratic values of the West than are the elites of other non-Western civilizations. All these factors dictate that a top priority should be countering the tendencies toward executive arrogation of power and transforming Latin American electoral democracies into liberal democracies. By similar reasoning, the next priority should go to Orthodox countries.

A second major need is to develop the sense of community and enhance the forms of cooperation among liberal democracies. One way of doing this is by the creation in more countries of publicly funded foundations or other institutions committed to the expansion of democracy. The third wave has already seen the formation of the National Endowment for Democracy in the United States and the Westminster Foundation for Democracy in the United Kingdom. Other Western democracies are moving toward the establishment of comparable institutions. It is also highly desirable that these institutions join together in an international association to coordinate their efforts and to become an effective lobbying group with national governments and international organizations on behalf of democratic development. Many years ago, when I was working at the White House in the Carter administration, we discussed the possibility of convening a meeting of the leaders of democratic governments and democratic movements from throughout the world in order to discuss how to promote democracy on a global scale. But somehow the time then did not seem ripe, and we did not pursue this project. It is difficult for governments, which have many other interests at stake, to take the lead in such an endeavor. Now, after 20 years of the third wave, conditions are much more favorable, and private groups should move to create an international association of organizations and movements dedicated to expanding democracy on a global basis and to enhancing the performance of democracy within countries. The Comintern is dead. The time for a Demintern has arrived. The creation of such an association will be a major step toward ensuring the consolidation and the continuation of the momentous expansion of human freedom that began under the leadership of Mário Soares a quarter-century ago.

NOTES

1. Quoted in Tad Szulc, "Lisbon and Washington: Behind the Portuguese Revolution," *Foreign Policy* 21 (Winter 1975–76): 3.

2. Seymour Martin Lipset, *Political Man: The Social Bases of Politics* (Garden City, N.Y.: Doubleday, 1960), ch. 2, "Economic Development and Democracy."

3. Samuel P. Huntington, *The Third Wave: Democratization in the Late Twentieth Century* (Norman: University of Oklahoma Press, 1991), 59–69.

4. Arthur M. Schlesinger, Jr., *The Disuniting of America: Reflections on a Multicultural Society* (New York: W.W. Norton, 1992), 127.

5. Joseph Schumpeter, *Capitalism, Socialism and Democracy* (New York: Harper and Row, 1976; orig. publ. 1942), esp. chs. 22–23.

6. Larry Diamond, "Is the Third Wave Over?" *Journal of Democracy* 7 (July 1996): 20–37.

7. Adrian Karatnycky, "Freedom on the March," *Freedom Review* 28 (January–February 1997): 4 ff. See also the list of "Electoral Democracies as of 31 December 1996," supplied by Freedom House.

8. John Mueller, "Democracy and Ralph's Pretty Good Grocery: Elections, Equality, and the Minimal Human Being," *American Journal of Political Science* 36 (November 1992): 984–90.

9. Leslie H. Gelb, "The Free Elections Trap," *New York Times,* 29 May 1991, A23.

10. Fouad Ajami, "The Impossible Life of Muslim Liberalism," *New Republic,* 2 June 1986, 27.

11. See Daniel Bell, David Brown, Kashka Jayasuriya, and David Martin Jones, *Towards Illiberal Democracy in Pacific Asia* (New York: St. Martin's, 1995).

12. Guillermo O'Donnell, "Delegative Democracy," *Journal of Democracy* 5 (January 1994): 55–69; Brian Loveman, "Protected Democracies and Military Guardianship: Political Transitions in Latin America, 1978–1993," *Journal of Interamerican Studies and World Affairs* 36 (Summer 1994): 108–11; Larry Diamond, Juan J. Linz, and Seymour Martin Lipset, eds., *Democracy in Developing Countries: Latin America* (Boulder, Colo.: Lynne Rienner, 1989), xvi–xviii; Terry Lynn Karl, "Dilemmas of Democratization in Latin America," *Comparative Politics* 23 (October 1990): 1–21. For a sophisticated analysis of the conceptual complexity and confusion with respect to types of democracies and semidemocracies, see David Collier and Steven Levitsky, "Democracy with Adjectives: Conceptual Innovation in Comparative Research," *World Politics* 49 (April 1997): 430–51.

2

THE END OF THE THIRD WAVE AND THE START OF THE FOURTH

Larry Diamond

Larry Diamond *is coeditor of the* Journal of Democracy, *codirector of the International Forum for Democratic Studies, and senior research fellow at the Hoover Institution. Earlier versions of this essay were presented in the July 1996 issue of the* Journal of Democracy *and in a lecture delivered in Lisbon in June 1997. This essay also draws on and updates work more fully presented in his most recent book,* Developing Democracy: Toward Consolidation *(1999).*

It is entirely fitting that the lecture series which gave birth to this book was launched in Lisbon. For it was there that what Samuel P. Huntington has dubbed the third wave of democratization began in 1974, though no one at the time anticipated anything like the transformation of the political character of Europe and the world that would eventually follow. I spent a month in Portugal in October 1974, and having come out of the intense political theater of student movements in the United States during the early 1970s, I found in Lisbon a milieu not entirely unfamiliar to me. The city was alive with revolutionary slogans and zeal and with the struggle between closed and open minds, between those who sought justice and social progress through a ruthless ideological certainty and those who sought it through a flexible, tolerant politics of dialogue, persuasion, and coalition-building. Quite in contrast to the United States or France, however, in Portugal a country's whole political future was at stake. Democracy hung in the balance.

I could not know what the outcome would be. But as I watched and conducted interviews, two things struck me most. One was not just the differences in program and ideology but the contrast in *spirit* between the drab, dogmatic, unquestioning atmosphere of the Communist Party, with its grim visages of Lenin and Stalin bearing down, and the life and color, the spontaneity and openness, the idealism and pragmatism, and the turbulent creativity that infused the offices, meetings, and rallies of the Socialist Party, the Popular Democratic Party, and the Social Democratic Center. The second was the talent and commitment of the people I met in the democratic parties and their obvious hunger for freedom.

If nothing else, this experience taught me what much subsequent research, reading, travel, and reflection have reinforced—that the fate of democracy is not simply driven by grand historical and structural forces. It is a consequence of struggle, strategy, vision, courage, conviction, and compromise—of politics in the best sense of the word. No political career in our times has more vividly embodied this lesson than that of President Mário Soares, who conceived and launched the lecture series on which this book is based. Whether history and structure are favorable or not, democracy is always more or less "an invention." Each society must invent its own democracy—and seek it, shape it, structure it, revere it, guard it, and improve it by that society's own sense of its values and needs. This lesson is crucial to thinking about the future of democracy, both to avoiding a "reverse wave" of democratic regression and to paving the way for a fourth wave of democratic expansion.

The Spread of Electoral Democracy

Over the course of the third wave of democratization that began in Portugal in 1974, democracy has spread to an extent unprecedented in world history. Today, according to the count of Freedom House (which I endorse), 117 countries—more than 60 percent of all the independent states in the world—choose their governments through more or less free and fair elections in which multiple political parties compete and the ruling party faces the risk of defeat. This is the minimal standard of what I term "electoral democracy," and while it may coexist with many undemocratic features, it marks a crucial threshold in a country's political development. The global expansion of democracy during the third wave has been breathtaking. In 1974, there were only 39 democracies, about 27 percent of all the world's independent states. Since then, the number of democracies has tripled and the proportion of democracies in the world has more than doubled in just a generation (Table 1).

More striking still is how much of this growth (both proportionally and in sheer number of democracies) has occurred in the 1990s, with the collapse of Soviet and East European communism and the diffusion of the third wave to sub-Saharan Africa. From 1990 through 1996, the number and percentage of democracies in the world increased *every year*. As recently as 1990, when he was writing *The Third Wave,* Huntington found only 45 percent of the world's states (with populations over one million) to be democratic, a proportion virtually identical to that in 1922 at the peak of the first wave.[1] Today, even if we similarly restrict our view to countries with populations over one million, the proportion of democracies in the world stands at 57 percent.

TABLE 1—NUMBER OF ELECTORAL DEMOCRACIES, 1974, 1990–98

Year	Number of Democracies	Number of Countries	Democracies as a % of all Countries	Annual Rate of Increase in Democracies
1974	39	142	27.5%	n/a
1990	76	165	46.1%	n/a
1991	91	183	49.7%	19.7%
1992	99	186	53.2%	8.1%
1993	108	190	56.8%	8.3%
1994	114	191	59.7%	5.3%
1995	117	191	61.3%	2.6%
1996	118	191	61.8%	0.9%
1997	117	191	61.3%	-0.9%
1998	117	191	61.3%	0.0%

Note: Figures for 1990–95 are for the end of the calendar year. Figures for 1974 reflect my estimate of the number of democracies in the world in April 1974, at the inception of the third wave.

Sources: Data from Freedom House, Freedom in the World: The Annual Survey of Political Rights and Civil Liberties, 1990–91, 1991–92, 1992–93, 1993–94, 1994–95, 1995–96, 1996–97, 1997–98 (New York: Freedom House, 1991 and years following); and Adrian Karatnycky, "The 1998 Freedom House Survey: The Decline of Illiberal Democracy," Journal of Democracy 10 (January 1999): 115.

This is the good news, and it has been heartening for democrats everywhere. But it is also somewhat superficial news and masks a much more variegated picture. First, the rate of increase in electoral democracies steadily declined after the huge surge in 1991 (when the number jumped by almost 20 percent), and since 1995 the overall expansion of democracy in the world has effectively halted. The year 1995 saw a net increase of only three democracies; 1996 saw only one—and that one was wiped out by a military coup in Sierra Leone. With four consecutive years of stasis in the number of democracies in the world (though not exactly in the identity of regimes, as a few have switched categories with one another), it appears that the third wave of democracy has come to an end. Even if the year 1999 brings a modest increase in the number of democracies, with a transition completed in Nigeria and one underway in Indonesia, and even though those two countries are among the largest and most influential in Africa and Asia, respectively, there is no immediate prospect of a new surge of democratic transitions in either of these regions, not to mention the Middle East. The world of the near-to-medium term may settle into a certain political equilibrium, in which transitions to electoral democracy are roughly offset by authoritarian regressions, even if they are more often in civilian guise.

The prospect of overall equilibrium is indicated by the conditions of the 70-plus countries in the world that now fall below the minimal threshold of electoral democracy. These countries fall into two categories. "Pseudodemocracies" have legal opposition parties, multiparty elections, and sometimes other significant features of electoral democracy, but they lack one defining feature: a sufficiently fair arena of contestation to allow the ruling party to be turned out of power. Like pseudodemocracies, "authoritarian regimes" may vary considerably in their levels of civil and political freedom, but they are generally even more repressive, and in any case they are less pluralistic in that they make no pretense of allowing competitive, multiparty elections.

Of the countries that fall into one or the other of these two non-democratic categories, most are in East Asia, Central Asia, the Middle East, and Africa, where culture, history, the level of economic develop-ment, and/or the character of the current regime make a *sustainable* transition to democracy unlikely any time soon. Neither does the regional context favor democratization in the way that regional economic, political, military, and cultural ties have pushed democracy forward in Southern and Central Europe and in Latin America. I emphasize here two words: "unlikely" and "soon." In the quest to build a more democratic world, in the spirit of "democratic invention," no country should be written off.

Following the political scientist Richard Sklar, I have urged that we view democracy in *developmental* terms, as emerging in fragments or parts, through distinctive paths in each country that follow no fixed sequence or timetable.[2] From this perspective, the presence of legal opposition parties that may compete for power and win some seats in parliament, and of the greater space for civil society that tends to prevail even in pseudo- or semidemocracies, constitutes an important foundation for future democratic development.[3] Not only in Mexico and Ghana, but also in Jordan, Morocco, and several other African states where former one-party dictators or military rulers engineered their reelection under pseudodemocratic conditions, these democratic fragments tend to press out the boundaries of what is politically possible. And this increases the prospects for an eventual breakthrough to electoral democracy, as occurred in Ghana in 1996 and may now be taking place in Mexico. Even if the achievement of electoral democracy seems a distinct prospect, every increment of democratic progress can become a foundation or impetus for further democratization and give a boost to political pluralism and human rights. International efforts to promote democracy should therefore engage these nondemocracies and support democratic forces within them, or in exile from them. But it should do so with a sense of strategic realism and a long-term perspective.

Tracking Liberal Democracy

A second current of sobering news has to do with the quality of democracy. Democracy encompasses more than just elections, even if they are regular, free, and fair. It requires the absence of "reserved domains" of power for the military or other social and political forces that are not accountable to the electorate. It also requires "horizontal"

TABLE 2—FREEDOM STATUS OF INDEPENDENT STATES, 1972–98

Year	Free	Partly Free	Not Free	Total
1972	42 (29.0%)	36 (24.8%)	67 (46.2%)	145
1980	52 (31.9%)	52 (31.9%)	59 (36.2%)	163
1985	56 (33.5%)	56 (33.5%)	55 (32.9%)	167
1990	65 (39.4%)	50 (30.3%)	50 (30.3%)	165
1991	76 (41.5%)	65 (35.5%)	42 (22.9%)	183
1992	75 (40.3%)	73 (39.2%)	38 (20.4%)	186
1993	72 (37.9%)	63 (33.2%)	55 (28.9%)	190
1994	76 (39.8%)	61 (31.9%)	54 (28.3%)	191
1995	76 (39.8%)	62 (32.5%)	53 (27.7%)	191
1996	79 (41.4%)	59 (31.1%)	53 (27.7%)	191
1997	81 (42.4%)	57 (29.8%)	53 (27.2%)	191
1998	88 (46.1%)	53 (27.2%)	50 (26.2%)	191

Note: Ratings refer to the status of the countries at the end of the calendar year. See text for an explanation of the basis of the ratings.

Sources: For 1972, 1980, and 1985, see Raymond D. Gastil, ed., Freedom in the World: Political Rights and Civil Liberties, 1988–89 (New York: Freedom House, 1989). For 1991–98, see Table 1.

accountability of office-holders to one another, so as to constrain executive power and protect constitutionalism, the rule of the law, and the deliberative process.[4] Third, it encompasses extensive provisions for political and civic pluralism, as well as for individual and group freedoms, so that contending interests and values may be expressed and compete through a variety of means beyond periodic elections.[5] All of these amount to a higher standard and a deeper phenomenon, what may be termed "liberal democracy"—not with reference to the relationship between the state and the economy but rather by way of emphasizing the greater presence of political and civic liberty.

In a liberal democracy, the military is subordinated, the executive is constrained, the constitution is supreme, due process is respected, civil society is autonomous and free, citizens are politically equal, women and minorities have access to power, and individuals have real freedom to speak and publish and organize and protest. I do not call this "full democracy" because liberal democracy is also no more than a threshold, and "the democratic invention" is a never-ending quest. Democracy can always become deeper and more liberal—more inclusive, more politically egalitarian and just, more accountable, more accessible and responsive. And since human nature is inclined toward the abuse of power—which is why we have laws and constitutions—democracies are not immune from the tendency of all forms of government toward corruption, favoritism, narrowing of access, and arbitrary exercise of power, even if they are less vulnerable to such pathologies than other types of regimes.

If we look carefully at the quality of democracy and the trends with respect to liberal democracy over the past decade, we have cause both for gratitude and concern. The elements of liberal democracy are roughly

TABLE 3—TRENDS IN OVERALL FREEDOM LEVELS, 1974–96

Year	Number of Declining Freedom Scores	Number of Improving Freedom Scores	Median Freedom Score	Average Freedom Score
1974	16	16	5.0	4.47
1980	24	25	5.0	4.26
1985	12	9	5.0	4.29
1990	18	36	4.0	3.84
1991	17	41	3.5	3.68
1992	31	39	3.5	3.61
1993	43	18	3.5	3.72
1994	23	22	3.5	3.69
1995	11	29	3.5	3.63
1996	13	31	3.5	3.58
1997	9	13	3.5	3.58
1998	11	32	3.5	3.56

Sources: See Table 2.

represented by the ranking of "Free" that Freedom House gives annually to those states which have an annual score of 2.5 or better on its two combined scales of political rights and civil liberties. (On these scales, which are averaged for this purpose, a score of 1 indicates the most free or democratic and 7 the least free or most repressive.)[6]

On the one hand, liberal democracy has expanded dramatically during the third wave (though not as dramatically as electoral democracy). Both the number of countries and the proportion of countries in the world rated "Free" by Freedom House have significantly increased. From the beginning of the Freedom House survey in 1972 until 1980, the number of "Free" states increased by only ten (and the proportion of "Free" states in the world rose only slightly, from 29 percent to 32 percent). Moreover, change was not only in one direction, as five states suffered breakdowns or erosions of democracy that cost them their "Free" status by the end of the decade.

In the latter half of the 1980s and beginning of the 1990s, freedom took its biggest jump during the third wave. Between 1985 and 1991, the number of "Free" states jumped from 56 to 76, and the proportion of "Free" states in the world increased from a third to over 40 percent. Moreover, the proportion of blatantly authoritarian, "Not Free" states declined to a historic low of 23 percent in 1991, falling further to just over 20 percent in 1992. By contrast, in 1972 almost half the independent states in the world were rated "Not Free" (Table 2).

Until 1998, the 1991–92 period was the high-water mark for freedom in the world. After 1991, the proportion of "Free" states declined slightly, and even with the modest net increase of three "Free" states during 1996, in proportional terms liberal democracies were no more common than they were in 1991.[7] Gains in freedom were generally offset by losses in these five years. Although 1996 was a better year for freedom in the world (with country gains in freedom outstripping setbacks 31 to 13), the overall level of freedom in the world in 1996 was virtually identical to what it had been in 1992 (Table 3).[8] As we see in Tables 2 and 3, the overall level of freedom in the world has steadily improved since the mid-1990s. The number and proportion of "Free" states have increased, and the average freedom score has steadily improved. The former trend is more striking than the latter, however. Although the dominant trend in the second half of this decade has been for countries to improve their levels of freedom, these improvements have tended to be very modest. The increase during 1998 in the number of "Free" states to 88 is particularly noteworthy, but this encompasses a number of states with many illiberal features that are just over the threshold of "Free" (with an average Freedom House score of 2.5), and a number of these countries have moved in and out of the "Free" category during the past decade.[9] Moreover, despite the positive overall trend, freedom (or the quality of democracy) was seen to be slipping in some influential third-wave democracies, such as Russia and Argentina.

Contradictory Trends

The first half of the 1990s witnessed two contradictory trends: continued growth in electoral democracy, but stagnation in liberal democracy. Juxtaposed, these trends signaled the increasing shallowness of democratization in the late period of the third wave. During the first six years of the 1990s, the gap between formal (electoral) and liberal democracy in the world steadily widened. As a proportion of all the world's democracies, "Free" states declined from 85 percent in 1990 to 65 percent in 1995 (Table 4). The proportion rose back up to 69 percent in 1997, and then quite significantly to 74 percent in 1998. But it remains to be seen whether this is a harbinger of a new trend of democratic deepening and maturation or just oscillation within a new equilibrium. During the first half of the 1990s, the quality of democracy (as measured by the levels of political rights and civil liberties) eroded in a number of the most important and influential new democracies of the third wave—Russia, Turkey, Brazil, and Pakistan—while an expected transition to democracy in Nigeria, Africa's most populous country, imploded. At the same time, political freedom has deteriorated in several of the longest-surviving democ-racies in the developing world, including India, Sri Lanka, Colombia, and Venezuela.

In Latin America, where historic progress has been made toward the creation of a community of democratic states, the deterioration of democ-racy or persistence of illiberal democracy has been a major feature of the third wave.[10] By 1993 there were significantly fewer "Free" countries (eight) than there had been in 1987 (13) among the 22 countries below the Rio Grande with populations over one million. By the end of 1998,

TABLE 4—FORMAL AND LIBERAL DEMOCRACIES, 1990–96

Year	Formal Democracies (N, %)	Free States– Liberal Democracies (N, %)	Free States as a % of Formal Democracies	Total
1990	76 (46.1)	65 (39.4)	85.5	165
1991	91 (49.7)	76 (41.5)	83.5	183
1992	99 (53.2)	75 (40.3)	75.8	186
1993	108 (56.8)	72 (37.9)	66.7	190
1994	114 (59.7)	76 (39.8)	66.7	191
1995	117 (61.3)	76 (39.8)	65.0	191
1996	118 (61.8)	79 (41.4)	67.0	191
1997	117 (61.3)	81 (42.4)	69.2	191
1998	117 (61.3)	88 (46.1)	75.2	191

Sources: See Table 1.

all of Central America had moved at least slightly over the threshold into "Free" status, and there were 14 countries in all that were rated "Free" by Freedom House, but freedom levels had declined in five countries, including Argentina, and 10 of the 14 "Free" countries had levels of civil liberties (3 on the 7-point scale) that still allowed for serious deficiencies in the rule of law. By one assessment, the retreat of harsh and blatant authoritarian rule throughout the region has not yet brought the triumph of liberal democracy but rather a "convergence" toward "more mixed kinds of semidemocratic regimes."[11]

Some consider it remarkable that Latin American democracies have survived at all under the enormous stresses of the past decade—dramatic economic downturns and increases in poverty (only recently being reversed in some countries), the mushrooming drug trade, and the violence and corruption that flourish in its wake. Since the redemocratization of Latin America began in the early 1980s, the response to severe adversity and political crisis—including scandals that have forced presidential resignations in several countries—has primarily been adherence to constitutional process and electoral alternation in office. In the practice of voting incumbents out of office rather than mobilizing against democracy itself, Latin American publics have given many observers cause to discern a normalization and maturation of democratic politics unlike previous eras.[12] Indeed, a number of democratic governments (in Southern and Eastern Europe as well as Latin America) have been able to make some considerable progress in economic reform during the third wave. This adherence to constitutionalism provides grounds for hope. So do recent reforms that have decentralized power and opened up the electoral process in Venezuela, Colombia, and Bolivia, instituted an independent electoral commission in Panama, and improved judicial functioning in several countries. But these positive signs and steps have been counterbalanced and in many countries outweighed by conditions that render electoral democracy hollow, illiberal, delegative, and afflicted. These trends, evident in the growth of authoritarian practices under elected civilian presidents in countries such as Peru and Venezuela, the persistence of human rights violations, military and police impunity, judicial corruption and inefficacy, and the decimation of the rule of law under pressure from the drug trade, highlight the very substantial gap between formal and liberal democracy. In Venezuela, the landslide election to the presidency in December 1998 of Hugo Chávez, the leader of a failed 1992 military coup attempt, is a chilling metaphor for the cynicism and frustration with which ordinary citizens view a corrupt, stale, and unresponsive democracy. The electoral breakthrough in April 1998 of the ultranationalist, right-wing Nationalist Action Party in Turkey is a similar sign of broad popular disaffection with the established political class, and of a democracy that is simply not working to deliver the effective governance that citizens expect.

The poor performance of new democracies is a major obstacle to their consolidation. Outside of Southern and Central Europe, most new democracies of the past two decades have yet to garner widespread and enduring public support and satisfaction.[13] Instead, from Turkey to Thailand, from South Africa to South America, from Pakistan to Russia, there is widespread disaffection with rising levels of corruption, crime, violence, and inequality.[14] Indeed, mounting evidence from public opinion surveys, journalistic accounts, and qualitative research suggests that the *political* performance of the regime in delivering transparent, accountable, responsive, orderly government, with a rule of law that ensures freedom and predictability, is as important as economic performance—if not more so—in shaping popular commitment to the legitimacy of new democracies.[15] With the coming to power of a reformist government following the economic crisis of late 1997, Thailand has turned a corner on constitutional reform and is showing interesting signs of progress toward the deepening and revitalization of democracy. On a continent where democracy has generally flickered and faded, South Africa's constitutional regime continues to exhibit broad popular support and stability, as evidenced in the huge voter turnout and peaceful conduct of the country's second post-transition national elections in June 1999. Some postcommunist states have large margins of support for democracy in principle, but even in the relatively prosperous new democracies of Korea and Taiwan there is still considerable public ambivalence about the inherent desirability of democracy.[16] When large numbers of ordinary people are suffering, these perceived policy failings can aggravate feelings of injustice and risk, inspiring (as in Venezuela in the early 1990s) efforts to overthrow or suspend democratic institutions.

The deterioration or hollowness of democracy has been evident in every region touched by the third wave. Indeed, as one moves toward the former Soviet Union, Africa, parts of Asia, and the Middle East, elections themselves are increasingly hollow and uncompetitive, a thin disguise for the

authoritarian hegemony of despots and ruling parties. Human Rights
Watch recently observed: "As recognition grows of the right freely to
elect one's governmental representatives, more governments [feel]
compelled to hold elections in order to gain [international] legitimacy."[17]
But in Central Asia and much of Africa, these contests have descended
into "an electoral charade" because of intimidation, rigging, and
constriction (or in the extreme, utter obliteration) of the right of opposition
forces to organize and contest.[18] Since the recent wave of democratization
began its sweep through Africa in early 1991, 16 (formally) civilian
regimes have held multiparty elections so flawed that they do not meet
the minimal criteria for electoral democracy. In 1996 alone, fraud and
intimidation negated the promise of electoral democracy in 11 of these
countries, including Zambia, which lost its democratic status as a result.[19]

We thus have not only a gap between liberal democracy and electoral
democracy but an even wider gap between liberal democracy and its
pale (and in many countries barely discernible) shadow of pseudodemocracy. Perhaps the most stunning feature of the third wave of
democratization is how few regimes are left in the world (less than 20
percent) that do not fit into one of these three categories of civilian,
multiparty, electoral regimes.[20] This contradiction—expansion of the
form of electoral democracy (and even more widely, of multiparty
elections) while levels of actual freedom and democratic performance
within many of these regimes stagnate or diminish—signals not only
the ideological hegemony of "democracy" in the post–Cold War world
system but also the superficial nature of that hegemony. In Latin
America and the Caribbean, the United States and the international
community demand real electoral democracy, but they have been less
insistent about adherence to high standards of human rights and the
rule of law. For Africa, a lower standard is set by the major Western
powers: opposition parties that can contest for office, even if they are
to be manipulated, hounded, and blatantly rigged into defeat at election
time.

Even when chicanery is prevented on election day, how free, fair,
and meaningful can elections be when the civil liberties of individuals
and associations are routinely violated; when the legislatures that are
elected have little or no power over public policy; when state power
remains heavily centralized and people have virtually no control over
policy and resources at the local level; when the judiciary is corrupt,
ineffective, and unable to provide a rule of law; and when elites who are
not accountable to any elected authority—the military, the bureaucracy,
local political bosses—exercise substantial veto power or direct control
over public policy? In these circumstances, elections—however much
they freely and accurately reflect the preferences between given options
of those who turn out to vote on election day—cannot in themselves
signal the presence of liberal democracy.

Huntington has defined a "wave" of democratization as a group of transitions to democracy within a specified time period "that significantly outnumber transitions in the opposite direction during that period of time."[21] In this sense of continued expansion of the number of democracies, the period of time of the third wave has ended. The second wave of democratization lasted about two decades. There is no intrinsic reason why the third wave should last longer.

If my analysis is correct, the key question now is: Will there be a "third reverse wave"? This past pattern of Huntington's wave thesis need not unfold again, if the new democracies of the past two decades can sink deep roots of popular commitment and institutional effectiveness. To date, two factors have been primarily responsible for preventing a third reverse wave: the absence of any authoritarian ideological alternative or model capable of mobilizing wide support across nations and the pressure from the international community against blatant authoritarian reversals. This latter pressure has been instrumental in deterring military coups and in reversing or containing executive coups in such countries as Pakistan, Turkey, Guatemala, Peru, Venezuela, and Paraguay. But as I have argued, it has not halted the hollowing out of democracy in several of these countries and in many other post-Soviet, Asian, and African states, where the political power and intrusiveness of the military has palpably expanded, where presidents have marginalized the legislatures and stacked the courts and bureaucracy to do their bidding, and where ruling parties have colonized neutral centers of power and distorted the electoral process. Moreover, we should not assume that democracy will indefinitely maintain its current global ideological hegemony, particularly if it fails to meet people's expectations for just and decent governance and an eventual improvement in material conditions.

If a third reverse wave is to be avoided, the overriding challenge is to consolidate those democracies that have come into being during the third wave and to revitalize those others that have fallen into crisis and disrepair. So far, only a handful of third-wave democracies have achieved such consolidation. What is necessary for this broader stabilization to occur?

First, democracy must become deeper, more inclusive, more accountable, and more rigorously constitutional and law-abiding. The essence of consolidation is legitimation: the growth—among elites and citizens of every major party, interest, ethnicity, and ideology—of the belief that democracy is the best form of government and that its rules provide the only acceptable means to compete for power. Even where economic performance is painfully disappointing, surveys in country after country show that citizens value more than their immediate material situation. They value freedom and democracy in and for themselves. One thing that the formal structures of a new democracy can and must deliver is

democracy. In most third-wave democracies, this requires a sweeping
agenda of institutionalization and reform:
  • to widen citizen access to the judicial system and to develop a true
rule of law;
  • to control the proliferating political corruption that fans cynicism,
alienation, and disengagement from the political process;
  • to strengthen the law-making and investigative power of the legislature as a serious, professional, and independent branch of government;
  • to decentralize state authority and empower provincial and local
government, so that democracy can be responsive and meaningful to
citizens throughout the country at levels they can directly engage;
  • to create political parties that mobilize and represent enduring
interests in society, not just personal leaders and cliques of politicians;
  • to build up the independent associations and media in civil society
that nurture social capital, deepen civic participation, and limit but also
affirm the constitutional authority of the state;
  • and to launch, both in and outside the school system (as the new
international CIVITAS network seeks to do), new programs of civic
education that cultivate the skills of informed participation and the values
of tolerance, reason, moderation, and compromise, which are the
hallmark of democratic citizenship.
  This is an ambitious agenda that will require passing new laws,
building new institutions, and strengthening the capacities of existing
institutions in the state, the party system, and civil society. A growing
number of public and private agencies in the established democracies
are now trying to meet these challenges of political assistance. This is
an endeavor of vital importance not only for democracy but for development as well. In much of the world, corrupt, predatory governance—
with no foundation in law and no constraint upon the arbitrary exercise
of power—has been a major impediment to economic growth. Strengthening the legal and civic institutions of democracy and helping to edu-
cate mass publics about how market economies work and why liberalizing economic reforms are necessary for growth are crucial to fostering
sustainable economic development.
  If the established democracies can help fledgling democracies meet
the challenges of reform, deepening, and consolidation, we can avert a
third reverse wave. In the next 10 to 15 years, we can transform the world
yet again—into a global system in which the predominant type of regime
is not just a minimal, electoral democracy but a stable, liberal democracy.

A Fourth Wave

  Democrats throughout the world increasingly share a vision of a world
system that is democratic in two senses: one that is composed of free

societies and democratic states, and one in which relations between states and among peoples are constrained by law and by common principles of decency and justice.

At the international level, the norms, expectations, and institutions of such a world are continuing to evolve. In the next generation, we have a historic opportunity to bring such a world into being. That quest encompasses three core challenges: first, as I have outlined above, to deepen and consolidate democracy where it has formally come into being and thus to preempt a third reverse wave; second, to continue to build and reinforce the cooperative structures and institutional rules of democracy at the level of regional and international organizations; and finally, to encourage the many disparate currents of change that could at some point in the future gather into a fourth wave of democratization.

None of this is inevitable. The most dangerous intellectual temptation for democrats is teleology—to think that the world is *necessarily* moving toward some natural democratic end state.[22] Too many international policy makers have taken electoral democracy as an end state in itself. Too many citizens blithely take the current state of their own established democracies as an end point of political evolution, the best that democracy can do, even though it leaves them increasingly cynical and detached. Some observers seem to assume that democratic consolidation is bound to follow democratic transition in much of the world. Finally, the statistical relationship between economic development and democracy is now so massive and irrefutable that some are now arguing that China is bound to become a democracy in about 20 years, once its per-capita income reaches the level of, say, South Korea in 1987.

All of these assumptions are false and even dangerous. Democratic progress is reversible at any point, and its quality and stability can never be taken for granted. No *deus ex machina*—economic or otherwise—will deliver democracy with some hidden hand. As Samuel Huntington observed in the last sentence of *The Third Wave:* "History . . . does not move forward in a straight line, but when skilled and determined leaders push, it does move forward."[23] What is necessary, then, to push democracy forward in the coming decades toward the kind of world we want to live in?

First, as the established democracies promote and support democratic change abroad, they have to worry about the quality of democracy in their own countries. The global expansion of democracy has always been driven partly by the diffusion of appealing models and ideas. It is wrong to think that democracy is the only model of governance with any power and legitimacy in the world today. Communism may be dead, but Leninism lives on. And even after the East Asian economic crisis tarnished its image, there is still an attraction in Asia (including among many Chinese communist elites) and elsewhere for what may be termed the "Singaporean" model—a form of pseudodemocracy that offers real economic freedom but only a thin veneer of electoral competition and constitutionalism, behind which a hegemonic state and ruling party firmly control and constrain political life. The Islamic fundamentalist model, even as it frays in Iran, is still alive in a crucial part of the world. Then there is the eternal danger of bigotry and intolerance. In the face of social and economic stress, democracy will always struggle against one or another form of ethnic or nationalist chauvinism, which exalts some defined "we" by demonizing and persecuting some perceived "other."

If democratic progress is to continue in the next century, it must continue at the core, in the most economically advanced countries. As Philippe Schmitter has observed, the ability of these countries "to adjust their well-entrenched rules and practices to accommodate the growing disaffection of their citizenries will determine the prospects for democracy worldwide."[24] As Mário Soares notes in his contribution to this volume, democracy, even when consolidated, cannot be taken for granted. Once invented, it must be reinvented, rejuvenated, and reformed by each succeeding generation in the face of new problems and challenges. Many political scientists agree with Soares' appeal: We need renewed and more vigorous engagement of citizens in public life. We need to nurture and revitalize the associational structures through which citizens participate and cooperate directly as political equals, and which breed the cultural foundations of a healthy democracy: trust, tolerance, efficacy, reciprocity, honesty, and respect for law.[25] In the United States especially—the most radically individualist of all major democracies—the culture of rights must be tempered by rejuvenating the spirit of civic obligation to the community.

There is a large agenda of democratic reform in the established democracies. Access to power must continue to expand to women and minorities. Political parties must find new ways to elicit commitment and engagement from citizens. Many systems of party and campaign finance must be reformed to level the playing field, curb the raw purchase of political influence, and restore a sense of political ownership of the process on the part of ordinary citizens. Continued economic dynamism must be secured through needed economic reforms, including the restructuring of welfare and social-security systems that are fiscally unsustainable. Yet at the same time, democracies everywhere in the world need to worry about the yawning gaps between rich and poor and to make the investments in human capital that are needed to narrow them.

A second imperative is to help create the economic conditions that will not only consolidate the third wave but also help bring into being a fourth. New democracies have survived in the third wave in the face of economic hardships that many believed they could not endure. Now, after painful economic reforms, a number of postcommunist, Latin American, and even African states are experiencing real, even vigorous growth. International assistance can help to foster the market-oriented reforms that are driving this growth and are necessary to quicken and sustain it. Ultimately, however, the most powerful initiative for fostering growth in these emerging democracies is to open advanced-country markets to the goods they produce and to compel them to open theirs, while observing international standards of trade and labor rights. Open economies are the institutional companion of open societies and free political systems. As communities of nations liberalize and eliminate their barriers to trade, they draw closer politically and culturally as well. The European Union is the single greatest and most important community of democracies in the history of the world. Two of the highest strategic priorities for the advance of democracy in the world are to expand that union to incorporate the postcommunist states and to bring about a true common market in the Americas.

The latter is a feasible and urgently important goal for the next decade. We have in the Americas a growing network of free-trade agreements, anchored by NAFTA (the North American Free Trade Agreement) in the North and Mercosur in the South. The goal of an enduringly democratic Western Hemisphere could be powerfully boosted by the construction of a free-trade community uniting North, Central, and South America and by conditioning membership—as does the EU—on democracy and respect for fundamental human rights. Already, we have an evolving political architecture for such a system in the Organization of American States and its increasingly explicit readiness, as in Guatemala, Peru, Haiti, and Paraguay, to take action to collectively to defend democracy.

Asian and African Frontiers

If there is to be a fourth wave, it must encompass authoritarian Asia, and it will have to involve democratic change in the world's next superpower, China. Dealing with China is likely to be the most formidable international challenge that the established democracies (and certainly the United States) will face in the next decade or two. It is vitally important that China continue to develop economically, and nothing would be gained for democracy by using trade as a weapon to punish China for its reprehensible record on human rights. Relations with China must recognize contradictory trends and therefore move on multiple tracks. On the one hand, China is not only rapidly growing richer, as a result of dramatic (albeit still partial) market reforms; at a slower pace, it is also making some significant political reforms. There is a brewing experimentation with competitive elections at the village level, which may represent "an embryonic form of grassroots democratization." Legislative bodies at all levels, including the National People's Congress, are beginning to assert themselves as more independent centers of deliberation and authority. Gradually a system of law (and of lawyers) is beginning to emerge that constrains some aspects of state administrative functioning and even enables citizens to sue the government for certain types of abuses of power. In addition, economic growth and the transition away from a totalitarian system are fostering a rapid expansion in the number of associations, many of which are independent from the state and have civic, if not yet overtly political, concerns.[26] Finally, "in the 1990s, China's elite political culture has begun to change. Democracy has begun to be enshrined as an ultimate goal for China."[27]

These trends should not be exaggerated, nor should they diminish or obscure ugly parallel realities: the brutal suppression of political dissent; the persecution of religious belief and practice; the systematic repression of independent labor organization; the torture and mistreatment of prisoners and political activists; the continual efforts to control and restrict the flow of information; and the genocidal campaign, through terror, domination, and inward migration, to erase the independent identity of the Tibetan people. These grave violations of human rights must be exposed and condemned. And moral and diplomatic pressure must be mounted through a variety of means and fora to persuade China to improve this abysmal record.

However, international moral outrage will not change China. If it is not balanced by engagement and dialogue it could provoke a nationalist reaction that would set back the prospects for political reform in the country. While protesting abuses in the short term, international democrats must encourage the longer-term processes of social and political change in China. That involves working with reformist elements in various state and semi-official institutions to provide technical assistance and support quietly for the types of political reforms mentioned above. It involves exchanges to broaden contact between various types of organizations and professionals in China and their counterparts in Western democracies. It involves support for Chinese organizations and intellectuals abroad who are providing various actors in China with ideas, strategies, information, and tools for democratic change. And it involves the investment and trade that, by accelerating economic growth in China, are creating a more sophisticated, pluralistic, informed, and organized society—one which will be increasingly difficult to manage by purely authoritarian means.

These same principles of democratic pressure, engagement, and assistance apply to other parts of authoritarian Asia, such as Vietnam. In Indonesia, however, where the quest for a genuine electoral democracy is now alive, much more urgent international engagement is needed to build up democratic capacities and norms among political parties, representative institutions, and civil-society organizations and media, while keeping the pressure on the Indonesian military and political establishment to allow the process of democratization—which speaks to broad, manifest popular aspirations for freedom and more accountable government—to move forward.

Although it is even poorer and weaker in its state structures, Africa is another major frontier for democratic expansion in the next generation. Since the "second liberation" began in Africa in 1990, more than a dozen African countries have made a transition to electoral democracy. The successful completion in 1999 of Nigeria's democratic transition (after more than a decade of cynical manipulation and false starts) is particularly significant, because Nigeria's vast population, cultural dynamism, political weight, and potential wealth give it great potential to serve as a point of leadership and diffusion not only for West Africa but for the entire continent. Many other African countries have liberalized politically to some degree. Today, most of Africa is in a political flux. A great opportunity for democracy derives from the profound discredit that has befallen all forms of authoritarianism—military, personal, and one-party. Increasingly, Africans attribute the calamities of the postindependence era—economic destitution, humanitarian crisis, ethnic violence, civil war, and state decay—to the absence of the constitutionalism and accountability that democracy provides. A growing array of elites and organizations recognize that economic development and political stability require good governance, which in turn encompasses political choice and inclusion, freedom of expression and organization, and a rule of law—in essence, some form of democracy.

The dependence of African states on international aid, finance, and investment makes it possible to provide tangible incentives for liberalizing reforms and to impose penalties on those regimes that cling to corrupt and abusive practices. Concerted international pressure on authoritarian elites could reinforce domestic pressures and persuade authoritarian elites that the costs of resisting demands for democracy exceed the benefits they expect to reap. At a minimum, international pressure can narrow the base of support for an authoritarian regime and induce it to negotiate with the opposition for a new democratic framework, as happened in South Africa, Zambia, and Malawi. But international sanctions and inducements can work only if they are consistently applied and broadly adhered to by the major powers.

A new bargain is needed between Africa and the West, swapping debt for democracy and development for good governance. Aid should be conditioned on economic liberalization, political freedom and accountability, and redirection of budgetary priorities away from military and other unproductive spending and toward human and physical capital. Particularly important are concrete institutional steps to strengthen the rule of law and control corruption, and this should be a litmus test for assistance to endemically corrupt states like Nigeria. Those governments that are serious about development and good governance deserve more aid, including debt relief, as a transitional boost to sustainable development. Those that are not should be denied international aid and loans. Even in the most authoritarian situations, however, the international community needs to seek out and support civil-society groups that are serious about development, democratization, and accountability. If international actors are to promote democratization, they must affect the domestic political context; this means strengthening prodemocratic forces from below and giving wavering and divided regime elites incentives to tilt toward democracy.

Political Leadership and Vision

The possibilities for democracy are shaped by many grand historical and social forces: the failure of empires, the diffusion of models, the movement of peoples, the change of generations, and the transformation of values and class structures that comes with economic development. But in the end, democracy is won or lost, invented or squandered, perfected or perverted, by individuals and groups and their choices and actions. If democracy globally is to continue its forward motion—if a third reverse wave is to be averted in the near term and the ground laid for a fourth wave of democratization at some (unpredictable) point in the future—the same political courage, leadership, vision, and generosity that brought democracy to Portugal will be sorely needed on the international stage.

More and more democracies in the world are becoming involved in assisting and encouraging the development of democracy in other countries. Official development assistance agencies are incorporating democratic development not just as a goal but as a major current of their grants and programs abroad. And more countries are establishing with public funding the kind of nongovernmental organizations—like the German party foundations, the National Endowment for Democracy, and the Westminster Foundation—that have a distinctive ability to render political and civic assistance and to respond rapidly and flexibly to new democratic appeals and opportunities. As the most powerful democracy in the world, the United States must play a major role in promoting democracy abroad. But it cannot be successful if its role is a solitary or dominant one. As more of the established democracies become engaged, through their state agencies and through a wide variety of their own civil-society organizations, in fostering and encouraging democracy abroad, the international legitimacy of democracy and the global solidarity of democrats will be strengthened. Moreover, there is great value in a rich diversity of democracy-promotion activities and approaches. Democratizing countries benefit when they see in the political assistance efforts of the international community the same pluralism that they are being encouraged to institutionalize in their own political systems.

If the established democracies of the world have the patience and vision to stay the course of democratic international engagement, democracy in the world will likely take root and ultimately resume its historic expansion. The most remarkable feature of the third wave of democratization is that, even a quarter-century after its inception, no ideological or regime alternative has emerged to rival democracy on a global level. Vigorous diplomatic pressure and insistence on international norms and conventions have narrowed the room for maneuver of authoritarian elites. Diverse forms of international assistance and cooperation have given democratic political leaders, parties, civic organizations, and mass media in emerging regimes confidence, skills, ideas, and resources. Moreover, as they integrate capital, technology, and information across national borders with breathtaking speed and momentum, the impersonal forces of globalization are further undermining authoritarian forms of government. They press instead for the openness, lawfulness, flexibility, legitimacy, and durability that come with liberal democracy.[28] If the growing number of established and prosperous democracies press *with* these forces, pressure on the remaining dictatorships will continue to grow, while many new democracies make their way toward deepening and consolidation. To be sure, not all efforts at democratic change will succeed, especially not the first or even second time. But with sustained international engagement, democratic pressures and progress will someday cumulate to launch a fourth wave of democratization, spreading political and civil freedom around the world to a degree that no one would have dared imagine a quarter century ago, when the third wave began.

NOTES

1. Samuel P. Huntington, *The Third Wave: Democratization in the Late Twentieth Century* (Norman: University of Oklahoma Press, 1991), 25–26.

2. Richard L. Sklar, "Towards a Theory of Developmental Democracy," in Adrian Leftwich, ed., *Democracy and Development: Theory and Practice* (Cambridge: Polity, 1996), 25–44.

3. Both the term "developmental" and my emphasis on the continuous and open-ended nature of change in the character, degree, and depth of democratic institutions owe heavily to the work of Richard L. Sklar: "Developmental Democracy," *Comparative Studies in Society and History* 29 (1987): 686–714, and "Towards a Theory of Developmental Democracy." Readers will nevertheless note important differences in our perspectives.

4. Obviously, the independent power of the legislature to "check and balance" executive power will differ markedly between presidential and parliamentary regimes. However, even in parliamentary regimes, democratic vigor requires striking a balance between disciplined parliamentary support for the governing party and independent capacity to scrutinize and question the actions of cabinet ministers and executive agencies. For the political quality of democracy, the most important additional mechanism of horizontal accountability is an autonomous judiciary, but crucial as well are institutionalized means (often in a separate, autonomous agency) to monitor, investigate, and punish government corruption at all levels. On the concept of "lateral" or "horizontal" accountability and its importance, see the two essays by Sklar above

and the essays by Andreas Schedler, Guillermo O'Donnell, and others in Andreas Schedler, Larry Diamond, and Marc F. Plattner, eds., *The Self-Restraining State: Power and Accountability in New Democracies* (Boulder, Colo.: Lynne Rienner, 1999).

5. This emphasis on the nonelectoral dimensions of democracy in the continuing play of interests in politics figures especially prominently in the work of Philippe Schmitter and Terry Karl. See, for example, their "What Democracy Is . . . and Is Not," *Journal of Democracy* 2 (Summer 1991): 75–88.

6. For a full explanation of the survey methodology, see Freedom House, *Freedom in the World: The Annual Survey of Political Rights and Civil Liberties, 1994–1995* (New York: Freedom House, 1995), 672–77, or *Freedom in The World, 1997–1998*, 592–99.

7. During 1996, five states crossed the threshold to "Free" status (the Philippines, Taiwan, Romania, Bolivia, and Venezuela) while two slipped from it (Slovakia and Ecuador). The developments in Taiwan and Romania may be seen as especially significant since they marked the first time in history that either country had reached what could be termed liberal democracy. *Freedom Review* 28 (January–February 1997): 6–7.

8. On the average combined scale for political rights and civil liberties (varying from 1 to 7), the average score of all countries was 3.61 in 1992 and 3.58 in 1996.

9. The oscillators include India and several Latin American countries, such as Venezuela, the Dominican Republic, and Ecuador.

10. Larry Diamond, "Democracy in Latin America: Degrees, Illusions, and Directions for Consolidation," in Tom Farer, ed., *Beyond Sovereignty: Collectively Defending Democracy in the Americas* (Baltimore: Johns Hopkins University Press, 1996), 52–104.

11. Jonathan Hartlyn, "Democracies in Contemporary South America: Convergences and Diversities," in Joseph Tulchin and Allison M. Garland, eds., *Argentina: The Challenges of Modernization* (Wilmington, Del.: Scholarly Resources, 1997), 90.

12. See in particular Karen L. Remmer, "Democracy and Economic Crisis: The Latin American Experience," *World Politics* 42 (April 1990): 315–35; "The Political Impact of Economic Crisis in Latin America," *American Political Science Review* 85 (September 1991): 777–800; and "Democratization in Latin America," in Robert O. Slater, Barry M. Schutz, and Steven R. Dorr, eds., *Global Transformation and the Third World* (Boulder, Colo.: Lynne Rienner, 1993), 91–111.

13. For the evidence from various public opinion surveys, see Larry Diamond, *Developing Democracy: Toward Consolidation* (Baltimore: Johns Hopkins University Press), ch. 5.

14. Robin Wright, "Democracy: Challenges and Innovations in the 1990s," *The Washington Quarterly* 20 (Summer 1997): 23–36.

15. This is a major conclusion of Diamond, *Developing Democracy*. For evidence from the postcommunist states, see Richard Rose, William Mishler, and Christian Haerpfer, *Democracy and Its Alternatives: Understanding Post-Communist Societies* (Baltimore: Johns Hopkins University Press, 1998).

16. See the essays on public opinion in new democracies by Richard Rose on postcommunist Europe, Doh C. Shin and Huoyan Shyu on Korea and Taiwan, and Marta Lagos on Latin America in the July 1997 issue of the *Journal of Democracy*.

17. *Human Rights Watch World Report 1996*, xxv.

18. Ibid.

19. The countries are Senegal, Cote d'Ivoire, Burkina Faso, Ghana (in 1992 but not 1996), Togo, Cameroon, Gabon, Zimbabwe, Kenya, Ethiopia, Chad, Equatorial Guinea, Gambia, Mauritania, Niger, and Zambia. Particularly significant has been the recent trend toward subversion of the electoral process (in Chad, the Gambia, and Niger) "to clothe army coup-makers in civilian legitimacy that places little restraint on repressive rule." Thomas R. Lasner, "Africa: Between Failure and Opportunity," *Freedom Review* 28 (January–February 1997): 133.

20. Although regimes can be difficult to classify (in the thinness of their tolerance for political opposition), I calculate that only about 35 regimes in the world do not allow at least one or more opposition parties to contest elections, at least superficially. This is only about 18 percent of the world's regimes.

21. Samuel P. Huntington, *The Third Wave*, 15.

22. Although I do not agree with his rejection of consolidation as a useful concept (and theoretical approach), Guillermo O'Donnell presents a forceful warning of the danger of teleological thinking about democratic development. See his "Illusions about Consolidation," *Journal of Democracy* 7 (April 1996): 34–51.

23. Samuel P. Huntington, *The Third Wave*, 316.

24. Philippe C. Schmitter, "Democracy's Future: More Liberal, Preliberal, or Postliberal?" *Journal of Democracy* 6 (January 1995): 14–22.

25. Robert Putnam, with Roberto Leonardi and Raffaella Y. Nanetti, *Making Democracy Work: Civic Traditions in Italy* (Princeton, N.J.: Princeton University Press, 1993).

26. Minxin Pei, "Creeping Democratization in China," *Journal of Democracy* 6 (October 1995): 65–79, quote on p. 76; Pei, "Is China Democratizing?" *Foreign Affairs* 77 (January–February 1998): 68–82; Pei, "Citizens v. Mandarins: Administrative Litigation in China," *The China Quarterly* 152 (December 1997): 832–62; Pei, "Chinese Civic Associations: An Empirical Analysis," *Modern China* (July 1998); Pei, *From Reform to Revolution: The Demise of Communism in China and the Soviet Union* (Cambridge, Mass.: Harvard University Press, 1994), ch. 5; Chih-Yu Shih, "The Institutionalization of China's People's Congress System: The Views of People's Deputies," *International Politics* 33 (June 1996): 145–62; Yingyi Qian and Barry R. Weingast, *China's Transition to Markets: Market-Preserving Federalism, Chinese Style* (Stanford, Calif.: Hoover Institution, 1995).

27. Michel Oksenberg, "Will China Democratize? Confronting a Classic Dilemma," *Journal of Democracy* 9 (January 1998): 27–40, quote on p. 30.

28. Thomas L. Friedman, *The Lexus and the Olive Tree: Understanding Globalization* (New York: Farrar, Straus and Giroux, 1999).

3

THE DEMOCRATIC INVENTION

Mário Soares

Mário Soares, a leader of the struggle for democracy in Portugal, served as prime minister and later as president (1986–96) of his country. A lawyer by training, he defended political prisoners and was a leader of the democratic opposition before being forced into exile in France in 1970, where he was a professor at Vincennes and at the Sorbonne. Returning to Portugal after the April 1974 revolution, he led the Socialist Party and became minister of foreign affairs in the first three provisional governments. He now heads the Mário Soares Foundation in Lisbon.

On 25 April 1999, Portuguese democracy will commemorate its twenty-fifth anniversary. Our country accomplished a successful transition to democracy whose importance has been recognized worldwide. According to Samuel P. Huntington's famous formulation, it was the Portuguese revolution that set in motion the third wave of democratization that subsequently spread to every corner of the globe. Portugal managed to pass through the initial revolutionary stage of its transition without shedding any blood, and eventually to abide by the people's will as expressed through free elections. Although the preceding dictatorship had lasted for almost 50 years and was often ruthless and merciless, retaliation and political trials were avoided. The need for a policy of "national reconciliation" was widely recognized, and it yielded the best possible results. Today Portugal has a fully developed democracy that enjoys political and social stability and broad popular support. The Portuguese democratic transition had a positive impact on Spain, on Latin America, and on the Portuguese-speaking African countries, with whom our country has particularly friendly relations today.

Portugal is currently a full and active member of the European Union (EU). Though it still bears some marks of its longtime structural backwardness, the country has largely managed to catch up with its neighbors in terms of development, while preserving the social and human dimensions of economic life. Our current priority is education. The path on which Portugal is moving today is unprecedented in the centuries-old history of our country.

As an old fighter against dictatorship, I belong to a generation that learned from experience the value of democracy and the importance of liberty, a generation that knows what it means to be subject to dictatorship and deprived of basic human rights. We internalized the terrible experience of decades of random violence, imposed colonial wars, arrests and deportation to concentration camps, censorship and thought control, and discrimination and persecution of every kind, with all possible pathways of personal fulfillment utterly closed to citizens who did not align themselves with official policy.

This painful experience of almost half a century makes it a moral imperative for us to fight, day after day, to perfect our democracy. We view democracy as a frail and precious flower that needs care and permanent vigilance. We feel compelled to share our experience with the younger generations, so that they can understand that life without freedom makes no sense.

Democracy requires civic education and the possession of knowledge, for it needs free and aware citizens at every level of decision making. That is why we have been trying to convey to the generations born after the end of dictatorship the importance of civic participation. It is not sufficient to repeat the ritual of elections and to ensure that they are freely held, freely contested, and freely supervised. Voting constitutes a civic duty, but democracy requires more. Respect for the rights of minorities must be ensured, along with the rule of law. The laws must be obeyed by everyone, but above all by those who are temporarily entrusted with public office by their fellow citizens. Only if it meets these requirements can democracy preserve pluralism, secure alternation in power, and enable civil society to breathe freely. Democratic political institutions should include checks and balances, leaving room for citizens to play an active role through political parties, trade unions, and employers' associations, while encouraging their participation in every possible form of association.

Democracy also requires a prestigious, independent justice system, administered with despatch and discretion, whose honesty and impartiality are acknowledged by the people. A word of warning, however, must be addressed to those who seek to promote a "Republic of Magistrates" (as was attempted in Italy) to punish the corrupt without eliminating corruption. They should realize that to hinder the exercise of legitimate political power is also to impair the functioning of democracy.

Freedom of the press, in the broadest possible sense, is a *sine qua non* of democracy. A controlled press means the absence of democratic pluralism. But as a rule-based regime, democracy demands a high sense of responsibility and strict standards; otherwise it is in danger of becoming a regime of impunity where everything is permitted—even the most inquisitorial investigations. Legal protections must be created against illegitimate violations of privacy (regardless of who commits them) and, especially, against the power of money. Let us never forget that in a democracy economic power must yield to political power and the rule of law—not the other way around. Only political power has the legitimacy that derives from the people's suffrage and from respect for the laws and the constitution.

Does Democracy Have a Future?

The title of this essay, "The Democratic Invention," is borrowed from a book of the same name written by French political scientist Claude Lefort, director of the Ecole des Hautes Etudes in Paris. When it was published in 1981, Lefort's book had a strong impact, at least in Europe. In the contemporary context, when almost no one openly questions the universal value of democracy, the phrase may sound a bit ambiguous. Its main purpose, however, is to emphasize democracy's need for continuous and progressive improvement with a view to perfecting democratic institutions in all their aspects and practical applications (though these will of course differ from country to country and from continent to continent, based on the lessons of experience). This title also helps to stress that any democratic construction will constantly generate problems and remains incomplete by definition. In other words, democracy cannot be taken for granted as something established once and for all, nor can it be viewed as a single static model applicable to any country, as if it were a finished and unchangeable work. On the contrary, democracy is an evolving system that is gradually enriched and fine-tuned in each country that adopts it in response to the socio-economic, technological, and cultural changes to which today's open and dynamic societies are exposed.

To better illustrate my point, I want to discuss a very stimulating article by Arthur Schlesinger, Jr., published in *Foreign Affairs* in October 1997 and entitled "Has Democracy a Future?" This apparently innocent and harmless question contains within itself the explosive charge of a true provocation. After all, the end of the Cold War seemingly marked the triumph of liberal democracy, which is now perceived both as a universal value in itself and as intimately connected to the (almost indispensable) adoption of a market economy. Especially now, after the implosion of the international communist movement and the more or less successful attempts by the so-called people's democracies to transform themselves into liberal democracies and market economies, it may seem misplaced to question whether democracy has a future.

Nonetheless, Schlesinger's question remains a pertinent one. I shall try to demonstrate why. Citing the late Isaiah Berlin, who wrote that the twentieth century was the most terrible and troubled of Western history,

Schlesinger notes that "this terrible century has—or appears to be having—a happy ending." Is this true? Concurring with this thesis, U.S. President Bill Clinton stated in the first speech of his second term of office, "For the first time in the history of our planet, more people live in democracy than in dictatorships." Similarly, the *New York Times* published an interesting estimate: "3.1 billion people live in democracy, while 2.6 billion are ruled by nondemocratic regimes." These figures are indeed encouraging, especially if we bear in mind that in 1941 there were only 12 democratic countries in the whole world. The increase in the number of nations considered democratic is quite impressive and suggests that liberal democracy may be becoming universalized as a final template of human governance. Perhaps this is what Francis Fukuyama had in mind when he claimed that we are nearing the "end of history."

But when Schlesinger asks if democracy has a future, he is thinking back to the context of the early twentieth century, when people also believed that the spread of democracy and the inevitability of progress would bring about a world ruled by rationality and the universal yearning for peace. President Wilson embodied this optimism. Before World War I, he proclaimed that "the world—and peace—would be saved by democracy."

Today we know what followed President Wilson's prophecy: the carnage of World War I; the Russian revolution; the fall of Europe's remaining empires; the iniquitous Treaty of Versailles; the powerlessness of the League of Nations; American isolationism; the advent of communist, fascist, and Nazi totalitarianism; the great economic crisis of 1929; the Japanese invasion of China; the Spanish civil war; the Nazi-Soviet pact; World War II, with all its horrors; the Holocaust; the atom bomb; the iron curtain; the Korean war; regional wars; colonial wars; Vietnam; peasant, urban, and religious guerrillas; terrorism; the implosion of communism; the resurgence of nationalism and ethnic prejudice; the intolerable poverty in which two-thirds of human beings live, with no access to knowledge or minimum levels of welfare; social exclusion; constant ecological threats; international organized crime; religious fundamentalism; and the irrationality of a divided and deregulated world, clinging to a precarious international order that the United Nations and its specialized agencies can barely maintain in spite of their essential services on behalf of peace and development.

Hence the pertinence of the questions: Does democracy have a future? What kind of democracy? In view of the uncertainties and challenges that the future will bring (only partially foreseeable today in a present that itself is not at all tranquil), who is prepared to assure us that the next century will bring about the universal triumph of democracy—even in its merely formal version?

Let me return to Schlesinger's article. He lucidly writes that liberal democracy "could fail in the twenty-first century, as it failed in the twentieth." Unfortunately, this is a possibility that we cannot afford to ignore, for a number of reasons that Schlesinger suggests and that I would synthesize and update as follows: ethnic feuds; a wave of insidious new forms of racism and social exclusion; and the new interactiveness made possible by the computer revolution, which allows communication and the spread of information to be virtually instantaneous. In this regard, nothing permits us to assume that cybernetics and cyberdemocracy are necessarily a good thing; in fact, we see them short-circuit representative democracy with their opinion polls and computer-assisted direct inquiries, while managing to avoid any government control. Finally, let me refer to the new forms of international speculative capitalism—faceless, subject to no consistent international regulations, and capable of undermining government authority and destroying national economies. We recently witnessed its consequences when the economies of the formerly applauded "Asian tigers" began to crumble, followed by Japan, then the Russian Federation, and most recently Brazil and other South American countries.

Democracy and Development

With respect to the clearly disheartening picture painted above, two clarifications are necessary. First, it is not legitimate to identify democracy with a market economy, or even to establish a necessary link between them. They are entirely different things. Although it is true that history does not give us any examples of fully developed democracies without a market economy, the reverse assertion does not apply. In fact, a number of dictatorships have managed to generate high rates of economic growth—at least in the short run. This was the case, for example, in Pinochet's Chile, but at the expense of terrible burdens imposed on the Chilean people. Moreover, the market produces inevitable inequalities that democracy—if it is to be more than merely formal—should endeavor to correct by means of reform policies aimed at sustaining socially and politically stable societies.

The second clarification stems in part from the first. In order to function in the best possible way, democracy cannot be merely formal. In other words, democracy should not focus exclusively on its political, legal, and institutional requisites—the choice of rulers through free elections; alternation in office; the separation of state powers and their interdependence; protection of the rights and liberties of citizens; respect for minorities; the rule of law; the independence of the judiciary; and the like. Democracy must do more. It cannot ignore the basic economic, social, and cultural conditions in which people live, as these necessarily have a profound influence on the functioning of democratic institutions.

There is actually a very close relationship between the sustainable development of a society (that is, a development that takes stock both of the actual welfare of the population and of ecological balances) and the functioning of democracy. Disregarding this interrelationship and mutual influence may prove fatal to the future of democracy, especially in the less developed regions of the planet. So-called liberal democracy, however, frequently ignores the social, economic, and cultural dimensions that must be incorporated into a democratic system in order for it to be deeply rooted in the hearts of the people. Human rights—one of the major achievements of our century—cannot be imposed *urbi et orbi* as an ideology, while overlooking the economic, social, and cultural constraints present in each nation, including its indicators of relative poverty, its inability to master certain technologies, and its lack of access to information and scientific knowledge. Unless the civilizational attributes, the idiosyncrasies, the customs, and the mindset of each nation are fully taken into account, it is very difficult to make an accurate assessment of the extent to which it respects human rights and of the character of its democracy.

In his most recent book, Huntington refers to a "clash of civilizations" as the reason for today's major conflicts. In my view, however, virtually all these conflicts are attributable to the very serious economic and social imbalances that cause divisions between countries, regions, and continents and also generate antagonism between segments of the population within individual countries.

In much of the world, levels of welfare and consumption are abysmally low and discrepancies between rich and poor are alarmingly high. What is even more worrying is that these discrepancies are being exacerbated every year, especially due to differing capabilities to access new technologies, knowledge, and information (the real sources of power in today's world). This gap is a new kind of "wall of shame" like the "Berlin Wall" before it. It separates rich from poor, job holders from the unemployed, and people who have access to education from those who are hopelessly doomed to intellectual underdevelopment. This gap is the source of multiple conflicts, of increased levels of crime, violence, and drug addiction, of expanding prison populations, of social marginality, and even of the insecurity felt by the rich in over-policed societies. In my view, we urgently need to develop programs aimed at uprooting poverty, as has been repeatedly advocated by Pope John Paul II. If the political will to do so exists, and the resources allocated to international organizations (especially the international financial institutions) are better used, science and technology can certainly help us to design such programs.

The Global Dimension

We live in an era of increasing globalization, not only as regards our economies but also in terms of knowledge and information. Today issues related to democracy have a global dimension that cannot and must not be ignored. States are losing some of their authority to emerging new transnational powers—multinational corporations, global media groups, and today's dynamic and mobile financial capitalism, which is exempt from any international control and only weakly linked to individual nations. This requires a rethinking of the nature, powers, and resources of international organizations (like the United Nations and its specialized agencies) and of regional organizations (like the EU and Mercosur), with a view to rendering them more democratic.

The globalization of the world's economies and the nature of the major challenges that the planet faces today—for example, the preservation of ecological balances, crime and terrorism, underdevelopment, and the struggle against poverty—suggest that some kind of global governance is required. This governance should rely essentially on the UN, not on an informal directory of the most developed countries like the G7.

At the same time, the information and telecommunications revolutions, and especially the widespread use of the Internet, are now generating what could be the beginnings of a global public opinion. It is not only customs, fashions, commercial products, and music that are becoming universal. There is also an emerging feeling of individual responsibility concerning global issues that may be viewed as the embryo of a citizenship related not only to a particular state but also to the earth, our common home.

This feeling of belonging to a larger whole is becoming widespread within the EU. As of January 1999, the Euro became the single reference currency for our 15 member states. Even for those countries that have decided not to adopt it immediately, the Euro is a huge step toward the actual integration of the member states into the EU. It requires a supranational institutional reform that gives new powers to the European Parliament and the European Commission, thereby limiting to some extent the sovereign powers of each member state. (The expansion of the EU to include new entrants will not be possible until this process is completed.) This change in the status quo logically demands the strengthening of European citizenship and of democratic control mechanisms over the institutions of the Union—in other words, an increased participation of citizens at the European level, irrespective of their national background.

As president of the European Movement, created 50 years ago at the Hague Congress to secure peace in Europe and promote cooperation and solidarity in reconstructing a shattered continent, I believe that the EU is a pioneering model of regional organization, one that stems from free and open societies and relies on the values of representative democracy, including participation and solidarity. An active and vigilant civil society is no less important to democracy than the existence of public institutions subject to democratic control. Although I hesitate to run the risks of predicting the future, I anticipate that over the coming decades, civil societies (and the nongovernmental organizations that partly voice their views) will play a paramount role in the affairs of democratic states and will gradually help to build a global civic awareness with an increased impact on international decision making. Thus I believe that civil societies will provide the needed counterweight to globalization, and that is a reason for hope amid the uncertainty facing us at the end of this century.

Let me conclude by returning to a point that seems to me critical to the fate of democracy in the decades ahead: I am referring to the economic, social, and cultural inequalities that separate people within nations and from country to country. Inequalities and injustices often render people insensitive and indifferent to the (always important) formal rules of democracy. Freedom, say the demagogues, does not provide food to the starving, nor does it meet the social and cultural requirements of those in need. That is correct. But we should also realize that those wishing to attack democracy try to use the exposure of existing injustices to discredit the system and destroy the politicians who serve it. In recent years we have witnessed a series of media operations aimed at accomplishing this goal. We must not ignore them. That is why it is so decisively important for us to realize that democracy is not merely a political system but also a socioeconomic and cultural system that becomes more developed and more profound in the struggle against inequalities. As a just regime in whose sight every citizen is equal, democracy should also be concerned with social justice. If it fails to demonstrate such concern, democracy stands to lose much of its vigor and substance.

II

Transitions to Democracy

4

GEORGE WASHINGTON AND THE FOUNDING OF DEMOCRACY

Seymour Martin Lipset

Seymour Martin Lipset, Hazel Professor of Public Policy at George Mason University and senior fellow at the Hoover Institution, is the author of more than 20 books, including Political Man (1960). The essay that follows is reprinted (with added material and revisions) from Extensions (Spring 1998) and is excerpted from the Julian J. Rothbaum Distinguished Lecture in Representative Government. Copyright ©1998, Carl Albert Congressional Research and Studies Center, University of Oklahoma. All rights reserved.

George Washington is an underestimated figure. Abraham Lincoln, Thomas Jefferson, and Benjamin Franklin are seen as real people with lives and emotions; Washington is a painting on the wall. Yet I believe that he is the most important single figure in American history. Without him, the Revolution might have failed. This is not because of his military ability; he lost many of the battles he fought, and only French intervention brought victory. His first enormous achievement was to build and maintain the morale of the Continental Army's troops and the loyalty of its officers under depressing conditions. Later, during the Newburgh crisis of 1783, he secured their obedience to civilian authority at a time when they were sorely tempted to do otherwise. He exemplified the ultimate in self-sacrificing heroism.

Another George, King George III of England, who was Washington's enemy, acknowledged his significance. The king asked the painter Jonathan Trumbull, freshly arrived from America, what he thought Washington would do when the war ended. "Go back to his farm," Trumbull replied. "If he does that, he will be the greatest man in the world," rejoined the king.[1] And that *is* what Washington did, twice— first when the war ended, and later after his second term as president of the United States. Following this second withdrawal, King George reiterated his opinion, saying that these actions "placed [Washington] in a light the most distinguished of any man living," and made him "the greatest character of the age."[2] The Duke of Wellington, Britain's foremost soldier and the victor at Waterloo, described Washington as "perhaps the purest and noblest character of modern times."[3]

Like almost all successful people, Washington was very ambitious. But his ambition was not for power and money—both of which he had—but for his repute, for what people thought of him. To be seen as a man of integrity and virtue was the reward he sought. Both as commander-in-chief and as president, he refused to accept any salary, and he eagerly looked forward to giving up military and political power and going home to his plantation at Mount Vernon on the Virginia shore of the Potomac River. And yet, when he was selected as a member of the Continental Congress in 1775, he entered it wearing the uniform (his own design) of a colonel in the Virginia militia. The only member of Congress to report so attired, he caused some to think, at the time and later, that he was offering to assume command of the Continental Army then forming in the siege works hemming in the British garrison of Boston. Some scholars reject this conclusion, however, noting that when his name was broached, Washington withdrew from the session after asking a friend to speak against the idea.

Little need be said here about Washington the general, or of what he did prior to the closing years of the Revolution, as important as such aspects of his career undoubtedly are.[4] Instead, I will discuss Washington as a founder, the man who helped the United States to formulate an identity and to institutionalize a competitive electoral democracy—or, to put it in terms that Washington himself would have found more familiar, to establish a republic.

The relevance of individual greatness to history has been much debated.[5] In ironic contrast to the theoretical determinism of Marxism, the history of twentieth-century communist regimes underlines the importance of the leader. It may be strongly argued that if Lenin had not been able to return to Russia in April 1917, or if he had been killed or imprisoned, the October Revolution would never have occurred. Prior to Lenin's arrival at the Finland Station (courtesy of the German General Staff) and his bold proposal that the Bolsheviks plan to seize power, no left-wing factional leader had favored such a move. Everyone adhered instead to the Marxist assumption that the next stage of Russia's development had to be a bourgeois revolution, with capitalism and industrialization preceding any move toward "workers' power." Only Trotsky thought otherwise, but he was not one of the Bolsheviks and had no influence on them or any other organized faction. Lenin, despite objections from other Bolshevik leaders, carried the day because of his leadership position and ability to dominate in organization and debate. Hence one may conclude: No Lenin, no Russian Revolution.

One cannot say, with comparable conviction and evidence: No Washington, no American democratic republic. The United States would in all probability have eventually become a democracy, even had Washington not been on the scene. Elections predated independence in the British colonies, and as historian William Chambers noted, the new nation possessed many of the other "prerequisites for full democratic participation and practice."[6] Yet Washington played a necessary role because of the charisma that flowed from his personality and his military leadership (which was something different from his generalship in a narrower sense). He inspired incredible trust and facilitated—as no one else alive at the time probably could have—the formation of the culture and institutions needed for a stable, legitimate, and effective democratic system. Washington, in short, was one of those "great men" without whom history would be very different.[7]

The Problem of Weak Legitimacy

The postindependence experience of the entire non-British-ruled ex-colonial world, and much of the former British Empire as well, is a story of secessions, military coups, and dictatorships. The history of postcoup, postrevolutionary regimes is largely one of democratic failure. It is rare for all the major players, including the military, economic, and political elites, to accept the need to conform to the rules of the new system. New political regimes inherently have weak or low legitimacy.

Max Weber suggested there are basically three ways in which authority may possess legitimacy. The first is *traditional,* as in a monarchy where kings have seemingly "always" ruled. *Rational-legal* authority exists in polities in which those in power are obeyed because of an acceptance of the system of rules under which they have won and hold office. It takes root as a result of prolonged periods of effectiveness, particularly in the economy. *Charismatic* authority rests upon faith in a leader who is believed to be endowed with great personal worth: This may come from God, as in the case of a religious prophet, or may arise from the display of extraordinary talents.

Old states possess traditional legitimacy, but where legitimacy is absent, it can be developed quickly only through charisma. Almost by definition, newly independent nations or revolutionary regimes begin with low legitimacy. Democratic norms require a willingness to accept political defeat: to leave office upon losing an election, to follow rules even when they work against one's interests. New democracies' weak legitimacy makes them unstable and potentially short-lived. For illustrations, one can turn to the history of Latin America, of much of Europe before 1945, and of most of Africa and Asia since that date.

The postrevolutionary United States, also marked by weak legitimacy, faced recurrent crises of authority as important "players" rejected the "rules of the game." The years from 1800 to the Civil War saw a number of attempts at secession, some in the North, some in the South, one in the West. Washington was privately pessimistic about the fledgling Union's prospects for survival, expecting a rupture between free and slave states during his lifetime. Even before the end of the War of Independence, he had to overcome a projected military coup. Soon after he left the presidency in 1797, the declining Federalist majority in Congress passed the Alien and Sedition Acts, curtailing free speech in hopes of suppressing their opponents.

Three years later, shortly after Washington's own death in December 1799, the leaders of the defeated Federalists tried to overturn the results of the 1800 presidential election, which had brought their enemy Thomas Jefferson to power. The intended victims of the Federalists, Jefferson and his own party, the Democratic-Republicans, behaved in a similar manner after they took office.[8] Aaron Burr, Jefferson's rival and first vice-president, upon leaving office hatched a conspiracy to split the trans-Appalachian West from the rest of the country. Clearly, the conditions conducive to the breakdown of postrevolutionary regimes and new states were present in the early United States. But unlike almost all of Latin America and many latter-day "new nations," the United States was able to survive its first three-quarters of a century with its competitive electoral democracy intact. During this time, political parties became institutionalized, the suffrage was expanded to include all white male citizens, and the republic enlarged rapidly in population, productive wealth, and geographical extent, settling and adding new states as it grew. How was it able to do so? The answer in part is a form of charismatic legitimacy.

To understand why this happened we must examine the role of Washington, who consciously employed his status as military leader and hero of the Revolution to create respect for national authority and to bolster the legitimacy of the new nation. Unlike most leaders of new postcolonial regimes, Washington was committed to a free polity and understood the problem posed by weak legitimacy. The record suggests that he was the only person who could have created or sustained allegiance, building respect for the new nation.

The mandate to obey newly created legal structures is necessarily a weak source of authority in societies in which law and government have been identified with the interests of an imperial power or a previous autocratic regime. Charismatic authority, by contrast, is well-suited to the needs of such polities. A charismatic leader plays several roles. He is first of all the symbol of the new nation or political system, a hero who embodies its values and aspirations. But more than merely symbolizing the polity, he, like the monarch in a traditional system, legitimizes the government by endowing it with his "gift of grace." Charismatic authority can be seen as a transitional phenomenon inducing citizens to observe the requirements for national stability out of trust in the leader until they learn to do so out of a more impersonal sense of loyalty to or satisfaction with the regime.

Charisma with Moderation

Because it is so personalized, charismatic leadership is inherently unstable. Unlike traditional authority, new charismatic authority admits of little or no distinction between itself and its agents. (In a monarchy, by contrast, "the king can do no wrong"—fault is never imputed to the crown, but only to its ministers.) Under charismatic authority, dissatisfaction with particular policies or officials can easily produce generalized disaffection with the system and with the source of authority, who is also seen as the responsible agent. A charismatic leader, therefore, must either make public opposition or criticism impermissible, or he must transcend partisan conflict by playing the role of a constitutional monarch, who symbolizes the system but remains above the ordinary political fray. Even where opposition to specific policies on an individual or informal factional basis may be tolerated, there must not be organized opposition to the charismatic leader.

The difference between these options is fateful. Authoritarian regimes often break down because the charismatic head, inherently a policy actor, is blamed for adverse outcomes. Conversely, it may be argued that revolutionary dictatorships require efforts at charismatic legitimation, since the only alternative is the costly and difficult one of absolute repression. Communist states take as their legitimating doctrine Marxism, which, as noted, explicitly rejects any "great man" theory of history. Yet such states have been notorious for creating "personality cults" around rulers like Lenin, Stalin, Tito, Mao, Ho Chi Minh, Kim Il-sung, Enver Hoxha, Nicolae Ceaușescu, and Fidel Castro. This, as the Marxists say, was no accident. The imputation of quasi-divine virtues to the heads of regimes that were supposedly based on the "scientific laws of history," strange as it seems, was the only way to avoid having to base the system entirely on terror and force. Other dictatorial systems, including those of Adolf Hitler, Benito Mussolini, and Idi Amin, behaved similarly.

The republic that emerged from the American Revolution was legitimized by charisma. To a degree that we today often do not appreciate, Washington was idolized; his name, image, and person were held in almost sacred regard. He understood this role and, his biographers have stressed, cultivated a profound concern with acting properly, doing what was right, and setting a good example in matters large and small. His "great gifts to the presidency and to the Republic," as Clinton Rossiter put it, "were dignity, authority and constitutionalism."[9] His self-consciousness about being a model began with the way he performed his role as commander of the Continental Army. To secure respect as head of a rebel force (as later, of a new government), he had to be aloof, to discourage familiarity, to demand deference. Although privately he enjoyed humor and conviviality (including dancing), publicly he practiced a studied reserve. Charles de Gaulle, who faced challenges similar to Washington's almost two centuries later, is reputed to have deliberately modeled himself on the Virginian. Washington has been a hero to the French since the American Revolution stimulated theirs.

As commander of an army whose men were not accustomed to military hierarchy, which had limited resources, and which won few battles, Washington's greatest contribution was to keep it viable, to command respect, and to maintain morale. He showed no personal weakness and never gave his soldiers any reason to lose faith in him. He lived with his troops, drew no pay, and rejected opportunities to take even the briefest leave to visit Mount Vernon.

In 1783, when the fighting was almost over but before the peace treaty had been signed, Washington was called on to affirm the principle of civilian supremacy by heading off a possible coup by nearly all his officers (then in camp at Newburgh, New York) against the Congress in Philadelphia. They were concerned that Congress would not keep its promises about their pay. Certain politicians, led by Robert Morris and Washington's former aide Alexander Hamilton, sought to encourage these grievances to generate support for a stronger, executive-led central government. Washington shared their goal but rejected their tactics, warning sternly that "the Army . . . is a dangerous instrument to play with."[10]

How Washington used his personal standing to put down the embryonic mutiny at Newburgh has frequently been recounted. He called his own meeting of the officer corps, at which he treated the unsigned list of grievances that had been circulating as the work of an outsider, implying that it was beneath the honor of those assembled before him. His prepared address expressed his confidence that his comrades would show themselves capable of "rising superior to the pressure of the most complicated sufferings" and setting a "glorious example" for posterity. His ability to handle people was never as dramatically exhibited as when, toward the end of his talk, he took out a new pair of spectacles and put them on in order to read from a letter. Letting his officers learn for the first time that his eyesight had been declining, he said, "I have grown gray in your service and now find myself growing blind."[11] Washington then put away his eyeglasses and left the hall. Many wept.

The meeting continued with a vote to thank General Washington for his intervention. The officers then passed a motion expressing their grievances to Congress, which Washington forwarded under a double-edged covering letter that both shamed and praised them. Writing of Washington's actions at Newburgh, Thomas Jefferson observed, "The moderation of a single character probably prevented this revolution from being closed, as most others have been, by a subversion of that liberty it was intended to establish."[12]

Always deferential to civilian authorities, Washington let them be the first to return to New York City after the British evacuated it. He then gave a series of farewell addresses, in most of which he stated his intention to withdraw from public life. His returning to his farm revived the legend of Cincinnatus, the Roman hero whose plowing had been interrupted by a call to save the republic from invaders, and who had gone back to his lands when the job was done. (Washington's behavior inspired the founding of the Order of Cincinnatus by former officers of the Revolutionary army; its name symbolizes that their greatest action was to return to being ordinary citizens again.) In retiring, Washington exhibited a disdain for office and power that only enhanced his charisma and increased his influence. He made it clear that he had no interest in any public position, certainly not as king, which many wanted him to become, but equally not as head of the republic. A disdain for office did not mean a lack of interest in the shape of the new nation. Washington understood that to have one nation, it would be necessary to have a central government with an executive—something not provided for in the Articles of Confederation. His resignation address to the Continental Congress had included a strong argument for such a government.

Washington feared that the opponents of the experiment in democratic government, who had predicted that the new polity would dissolve, might turn out to be right. The Congress-dominated government under the Articles of Confederation had revealed itself all too clearly as unequal to the challenges of handling either domestic or foreign affairs. Distressed by repeated crises, he wrote frequently to friends in different states urging that the Articles be revised.

Legitimizing the New System

Changes of the type that he advocated were adopted at the Constitutional Convention, held in Philadelphia during the summer of 1787. The meeting was called to propose revisions to the Articles, but soon took up the work of drafting a new fundamental law. Washington had been reluctant to attend it, worrying that he might be appearing to renege on his pledge to stay out of public life. But Shays' Rebellion, an armed uprising by western Massachusetts farmers in the fall of 1786, shocked him and convinced him to take part. Critics' predictions that the new nation would not be able to govern itself seemed to be coming true. Washington went to the Philadelphia Convention, and as everyone expected, was chosen as its presiding officer.

As chairman, he never spoke or voted. In typical Washingtonian fashion, he set an example for the delegates by never missing a session or arriving late. His greatest influence, however, was exerted off the convention floor.[13] Everyone knew that he favored what became the Convention's basic outcome: a more powerful central government led by a president, albeit one subject to elaborate checks and balances. It has been agreed, both then and since, that the expectation that Washington would be the first incumbent played a large role in the creation of this office and in securing approval for the Constitution generally. No one feared that he would misuse power. As noted earlier, his genuine hesitancy, his reluctance to assume the position only served to reinforce the almost universal desire that he do so.

In any case, it was agreed before, during, and after the Philadelphia Convention that Washington's presence at the sessions, and his subsequent public approval of the Constitution, were necessary to secure its passage. The opponents of the Constitution, who feared a more powerful executive, were quite numerous in many states, including New York and Virginia, without whose approval the new Constitution would have been inoperative. Writing of the subsequent deliberations to secure Virginia's ratification, James Monroe wrote privately to Jefferson, "Be assured, his influence carried the government."

Washington assumed the presidency in 1789 knowing that his task was to create respect for the office so that the new polity might survive. In ways large and small, therefore, Washington sought to have his position recognized as supreme, as a symbol of national unity. When he visited Massachusetts, for instance, he insisted that the state's governor, John Hancock, recognize the precedence of the federal government by calling on him, holding that adherence to such "rules of proceeding" would be "prudent for a young state."[14]

If ever there was an example of charismatic legitimization of a polity, it was the way in which respect and veneration for Washington sanctified the new Republic. The man who would not be king, who was genuinely reluctant to take part in politics, who resisted and feared becoming president, was able to legitimate the new system.

Washington knew what he was doing. He never used the phrase "charismatic legitimacy"—a modern coinage—but he understood that a stable and free polity required a set of values, a national character that subsumed the rule of law, respect for authority, and a willingness to subordinate private interest and factional conflict for the sake of the larger good. His task was to set an example, to be a model of "public virtue," to awe the politicians and the public into doing right. But he understood, as he noted in his Farewell Address, that "[t]ime and habit are at least as necessary to fix the true character of government as of other human institutions."[15]

Washington's concern for inculcating virtue in the citizens and leaders of the young republic was evident in his effort to create a national university in the nation's capital. For Washington, "the guarantee that the American government would never degenerate into despotism lay in the ultimate virtue of the American people," and first-rate higher education contributed to that end.[16] He believed that a "national university would help form the characters of future leaders by breaking down local attachments and state prejudices" and teaching them to understand "the principles of the Constitution [and] the laws."[17] His first and last messages to Congress recommended its establishment,[18] and in his last will and testament, which included a bequest for the university, he described the proposal as a "matter of infinite importance in my judgment."

Washington was capable of mistakes—for instance, in his belief that parties are intrinsically bad for democracy. He was distressed by factional strife, and by public pursuit of individual or group self-interest. Though he obviously knew he could not prevent interest-driven conflict, he was able during the first years of the Republic to keep it within bounds, to coax opponents to cooperate, to sustain among strong partisans allegiance to the nation and obedience to policies they opposed.[19] But he was never reconciled to partisan struggles, and the outbreak of a maritime quasi-war with Revolutionary France seemingly pushed him to drop his initial opposition to the repressive Alien and Sedition Acts.

Alexander Hamilton and Thomas Jefferson, the leaders of the factions that would become the first parties, served in Washington's cabinet for most of his presidency and never let their antagonism break completely into the open. Privately, Washington sided with Treasury Secretary Hamilton and the Federalists, who favored a strong central government and the use of public resources to build up the economy, against Secretary of State Jefferson and his Democratic-Republicans, who tended to favor localism and agrarianism. In public, as we have seen, Washington was careful to stand above the fray and appear nonpartisan. Throughout the often bitter controversies of the 1790s, nearly all Americans continued to revere him.

Religion and Race

Washington tried to demonstrate by word and deed how to deal with religion in a pluralistic society. He clearly believed in God and formally belonged to the Episcopal Church for most of his life, but was not strongly committed to any particular creed. The evidence seems clear that he was a deist. But he set a model that all future presidents have followed by adding "so help me God" to the inaugural oath.[20]

More important were his efforts to integrate minority religions and to command respect for them. His famous 1791 letter to the Touro Synagogue in Rhode Island stated his pleasure that Judaism was among the American creeds. He went on to criticize the idea of tolerance as invidious, saying, "It is now no more that toleration is spoken of, as if it was by the indulgence of one class of people, that another enjoyed the exercise of their inherent natural rights." Jews were not merely to be tolerated; they were Americans. During the Revolution, he forbade a New England festivity called "Pope's Day" as offensive to his Catholic soldiers. After the war, he opposed the continued "establishment" of the Episcopal Church in Virginia, urging that members of all religious groups should instead pay legally required assessments to their respective religious bodies, while nonbelievers paid levies to charity.

Barry Schwartz notes how Washington reached out to the various religious minorities:

> The Baptists, for example, were delighted when the nation's hero urged them to be persuaded that "no one would be more zealous than myself to establish effectual barriers against the horrors of spiritual tyranny, and every species of religious persecution." The Quakers rejoiced to know that the new President considered them "exemplary and useful citizens," despite their refusal to aid him in war. Catholics, who were in many respects the most despised of the religious minorities, saw an end to persecution when the chief magistrate assured them that all citizens "are equally entitled to the protection of civil government. . . . And I presume that your fellow-citizens will not forget the patriotic part which you took in the accomplishment of the revolution, and the establishment of their government." Jews found in Washington's policy an unprecedented expression of friendship from a head of state. . . . The Universalists, disdained by the pious for their liberal religious views, were congratulated by Washington for their "political professions and practices," which were "almost universally friendly to the order and happiness of our civil institutions." Acknowledging in each instance that respect for diversity was a fair price for commitment to the nation and its regime, Washington abolished deep-rooted fears that would have otherwise alienated a large part of the population from the nation-building process. For this large minority, he embodied not the ideal of union, nor even that of liberty, but rather the reconciliation of union and liberty.[21]

Discussion of Washington's liberality as regards religious minorities leads inevitably to the subject of Washington as a slave owner.[22] Virginia in his time contained about two-fifths of all the slaves in the original 13 states, and Washington himself owned more than a hundred slaves to maintain the several farms, numerous outbuildings, and gracious riverfront mansion that made up Mount Vernon. As Washington matured, he faced up to the immorality of slavery, with opinions that put him squarely on the liberal side of the Southern spectrum regarding "the peculiar institution" and its future. He appears to have begun thinking about the problem with great seriousness during the War of Independence. Foreign and domestic friends raised the obvious question of how slavery could be reconciled with a war for freedom.

Washington considered ways of freeing the slaves, but expressed concern over the prospects awaiting largely unskilled and uneducated people who also would face discrimination. After the war, he tried to enhance the skills of his slaves and to collect enough money to support them after manumission. His personal situation was difficult because the many slaves that his wife Martha had brought into their marriage had belonged to a previous husband who had died without a will. Under the laws of Virginia, these so-called "dower" slaves belonged neither to Washington nor his wife, but to the estate of her first husband. Washington could have freed his own slaves during his lifetime, but neither Martha nor he could have freed hers.

Washington saved enough money to free his own and his wife's slaves after he died and to provide a fund for their support. Their children were to be educated. Washington's estate made payments to former Mount Vernon slaves until 1833, a third of a century after his death. A hint as to the depth of his feelings shows through in conversations he had early in his presidency, when he privately expressed fears that the new nation would break up along North-South lines. At that time, this proud Virginian told friends, including fellow Virginian Edmund Randolph, that such an event would force him to move to the North.[23] Washington exceeded Jefferson and almost all his fellow southern Founders in the generosity with which he dealt with his slaves.

Institutionalizing Democracy

Washington wished to retire after one term in office, but the conflict between Hamilton and Jefferson would not permit it. At the urging of these two principal lieutenants and of many others, he agreed to serve another term. As much as he regretted the emergence of embryonic parties, he was thereby unwittingly permitting the further peaceful extension of factional conflict under his administration. Yet the decision to stay on turned out to be a crucial one. His second term saw the country badly torn by conflicting attitudes toward the French Revolution, and also faced with a Western antitax uprising, the so-called Whiskey Rebellion, that required the dispatch of federal troops to the Allegheny Mountains of Pennsylvania.

In sum, it is clear that Washington was an indispensable charismatic leader. Yet there can be no doubt that he pushed the United States toward a legal-rational system of authority by his firm refusal to take advantage of his status. He rejected all suggestions that he assume autocratic powers or become president-for-life. He retired while still in good health, identifying himself to the end with the laws and spirit of the nation. His brand of charismatic leadership had a critical stabilizing effect on the society's evolution. The first succession contest, between Jefferson and Vice-President John Adams, took place while Washington still held office, enabling him to set a precedent as the first head of a modern state to hand over the reins to a duly elected successor (Adams). Had Washington continued in office until his death, it is quite possible that subsequent presidential successions would have been more difficult, with efforts by the defeated to contest the results, or by later presidents to retain office indefinitely, much as was to happen in Latin America. But Washington never even entertained the possibility of staying in office, for he knew that he had to set an example and step down, lest people think that "having tasted the sweets of office, he could not do without them."[24] His reputation and his understanding of the requirements for a stable republic required that he withdraw.

The charismatic aspects of Washington's appeal were consciously used by U.S. political leaders to create a character, an identity for the young nation. In 1800, shortly after Washington's death, the British ambassador to the United States discussed the functions of tributes to Washington in a report to the Foreign Office:

> The leading men in the United States appear to be of the opinion that these ceremonies tend to elevate the spirit of the people, and contribute to the formation of a *national character,* which they consider as much wanting in this country. And assuredly, if self-opinion is (as perhaps it is) an essential ingredient in that character which promotes the prosperity and dignity of a nation, the Americans will be the gainers by the periodical recital of the feats of their Revolutionary War, and the repetition of the praises of Washington. The hyperbolical amplifications, the Panegyricks in question have an evident effect especially among the younger parts of the community, in fomenting the growth of that vanity, which to the feelings of a stranger have already arrived at a sufficient height.[25]

The "near-apotheosis" of Washington characterized almost all that was written and said about him for the first few generations of the new nation.[26]

The importance of Washington's role for the institutionalization of democracy in the early United States can be summarized as follows:

1) In a small, fragile, and new political entity riven by serious cleavages, he singlehandedly provided a basis for unity. His enormous prestige commanded the loyalty of the leaders of the different factions as well as of the general populace.

2) He was strongly committed to constitutional government in both principle and practice, and provided paternal guidance to those involved in developing the machinery of deliberation and administration. He stayed in power long enough to permit the crystallization of factions into embryonic parties, a development that dismayed him greatly.

3) By voluntarily retiring from office, he set a precedent exemplifying a proper republican approach to the problem of succession.

In most new nations that have had them, charismatic leaders have only fulfilled the first of these tasks, acting as symbols to help prolong the feelings of unity that develop prior to the achievement of independence. The neglect of the other two results in "charismatic personalities . . . [who do] not ordinarily build . . . the institutions which are indispensable for carrying on the life of a political society."[27] And when such personalities leave the scene, there arises again, as there did after the achievement of independence, the difficult problem of maintaining national unity among a conglomeration of groups and interests.[28] Jefferson, even as he worried that Washington's prestige would undermine efforts to develop an opposition party, understood what Washington was doing by epitomizing virtue. As Jefferson emphasized, Washington had been "scrupulously obeying the laws through the whole of his career, civil and military," a model "of which the history of the world furnishes no other example."[29] The first president's great biographer, James Flexner, concludes: "Washington had given the United States an unheard-of boon: charisma with hardly any cost."[30]

NOTES

The author would like to thank the Woodrow Wilson Center for International Scholars in Washington, D.C. and the Hoover Institution of Stanford University for their institutional support, and Amy Bunger Pool of the American University for her considerable intellectual contribution.

1. Gordon S. Wood, *The Radicalism of the American Revolution* (New York: Vintage, 1993), 206.

2. Richard Brookhiser, *Founding Father: Rediscovering George Washington* (New York: Free Press, 1996), 103.

3. Nort Callahan, *George Washington: Soldier and Man* (New York: William Morris, 1972), 278.

4. On Washington as a military commander, see Dave R. Palmer, *The Way of the Fox: American Strategy in the War for America, 1775–1783* (Westport, Conn.: Greenwood, 1975).

5. For a treatment of this debate, see Sidney Hook, *The Hero in History: A Study in Limitation and Possibility* (New Brunswick, N.J.: Transaction, 1991).

6. William Chambers, *Political Parties in a New Nation* (New York: Oxford University Press, 1963), 99–100. This conclusion was also that of my own early research on the subject. See Seymour Martin Lipset, *The First New Nation: The United States in Comparative and Historical Perspective* (New York: Basic Books, 1963), esp. 18–23.

7. See Forrest McDonald, *The Presidency of George Washington* (Lawrence: University Press of Kansas, 1974), 25.

8. See Leonard Levy, *Jefferson and Civil Liberties: The Darker Side* (Cambridge: Harvard University Press, 1963), 302–5.

9. Clinton Rossiter, *The American Presidency* (New York: Harcourt, Brace, 1960), 1–88. Other notable accounts of Washington include Marcus Cunliffe, *George Washington: Man and Monument* (Boston: Little, Brown, 1958); Edmund S. Morgan, *The Genius of George Washington* (Washington, D.C.: Society of the Cincinnati, 1980); Gordon S. Wood, "The Greatness of George Washington," *Virginia Quarterly Review* 68 (Spring 1992): 189–207; Woodrow Wilson, *George Washington* (New York: Schocken, 1969); Richard Norton Smith, *Patriarch: George Washington and the New American Nation* (Boston: Houghton Mifflin, 1993); and John R. Alden, *George Washington: A Biography* (Baton Rouge: Louisiana State University Press, 1984).

10. A detailed description of this still somewhat murky episode and a bibliography of earlier works on it may be found in Richard H. Kohn, "The Inside Story of the Newburgh

Conspiracy: America and the Coup d'Etat," *William and Mary Quarterly*, 27 (April 1970): 187–220. See also C. Edward Skeen, "The Newburgh Conspiracy Reconsidered," with Kohn's "Rebuttal," *William and Mary Quarterly* 30 (April 1974): 273–98.

11. John E. Ferling, *The First of Men: The Life of General Washington* (Knoxville: University of Tennessee Press, 1988), 321.

12. Kohn, "The Inside Story of the Newburgh Conspiracy," 220.

13. James Thomas Flexner, *George Washington and the New Nation, 1783–1793* (Boston: Little, Brown, 1970), 423.

14. Wilson, *George Washington*, 276.

15. William B. Allen, ed., *George Washington: A Collection* (Indianapolis: Liberty Classics, 1988), 519.

16. Bernard Bailyn, *The Ideological Origins of the American Revolution* (Cambridge, Mass: Belknap, 1992), 369–70.

17. Richard Loss, "The Political Thought of President George Washington," *Presidential Studies Quarterly* 19 (Summer 1989): 480; Smith, *Patriarch*, 287.

18. Leonard C. Helderman, *George Washington: Patron of Learning* (New York: The Century Co., 1932), 27–31.

19. Glenn A. Phelps, "George Washington and the Paradox of Party," *Presidential Studies Quarterly* 19 (Fall 1989): 733–45.

20. Paul F. Boller, Jr., *George Washington and Religion* (Dallas: Southern Methodist University Press, 1963), 75.

21. Barry Schwartz, *George Washington: The Making of an American Symbol* (New York: Free Press, 1987), 121.

22. See Walter H. Mazyck, *George Washington and the Negro* (Washington, D.C.: Associated Publishers, 1932).

23. Flexner, *George Washington and the New Nation*, 40.

24. Smith, *Patriarch*, 121.

25. Quoted in Joseph Charles, *The Origin of the American Party System* (New York: Harper Torch, 1961), 52. (Emphasis in original.)

26. See the 84 evaluations collected in W.S. Baker, ed., *Character Portraits of Washington* (Philadelphia: Robert McLindsay, 1887).

27. Edward Shils, "Political Development in the New States," *Comparative Studies in Society and History* 2 (1960): 288.

28. Among the founders of third-wave democracies, it is probably only Nelson Mandela whose charisma, role, and accomplishments give him some claim to be the George Washington of his country. The issue remains, however, whether South Africa has the social structure to support democratic institutions—i.e., to sustain a stable game of "ins" and "outs" by preserving the rights of the opposition so as to make possible turnovers in office.

29. Thomas Jefferson to Dr. Walter Jones, 2 January 1814, in Adrienne Koch and William Peden, eds., *The Life and Selected Writings of Thomas Jefferson* (New York: Random House, 1944), 175.

30. Flexner, *George Washington and the New Nation*, 423.

5

REFLECTIONS ON THE PORTUGUESE REVOLUTION

Diogo Freitas do Amaral

Diego Freitas do Amaral, a professor at the University of Lisbon's School of Law, has had a long and distinguished political career in Portugal. As a founder and leader of the Social Democratic Center party, he played an instrumental role in establishing democracy in his country. He served in Parliament in 1975–83 and again in 1992–93, and his governmental posts included minister of foreign affairs and of defense as well as deputy prime minister and interim prime minister. In 1986 he was narrowly defeated in presidential elections by Mário Soares. In 1995–96 he served as president of the United Nations General Assembly.

According to Samuel P. Huntington, Portugal in 1974–75 carried out a successful democratic transition that initiated the global third wave of transitions from dictatorships to democracies.[1] If one looks solely at the final result, it is hard to deny the success of the Portuguese transition: At the start of 1974, Portugal was a dictatorship; by the middle of 1976, it had been transformed into a young pluralist democracy. Nonetheless, the Portuguese transition was not a peaceful one, and I do not believe that it provides a model worthy of emulation by other countries.

Portugal's democratic transition occurred far later and far less peacefully than it could have. During the years from 1968 to 1974–75, the Portuguese people were twice deprived of the possibility of enjoying a peaceful democratic transition, first due to the influence of the extreme right during the final years of the dictatorship under Marcello Caetano, and again during the period when the totalitarian left dominated the revolution. These two missed opportunities had damaging consequences for the country.

When António de Salazar, who had ruled Portugal with an iron fist since 1932, became incapacitated in 1968, Marcello Caetano was chosen to succeed him as prime minister. Formerly a close associate of Salazar, Caetano permitted a measure of limited liberalization, including some relaxation of secret police activity and the return from exile of Socialist Party leader Mário Soares. Some observers believe that most Portuguese citizens were satisfied at the time with this partial opening up of their country: with the "continuity and evolution" program; the policy of giving priority to economic development rather than political liberalization; the high rates of growth; and the improvements in education and social security. In this view, it was only military discontent over the ongoing wars that Portugal was waging to hold on to its colonies in Angola, Mozambique, and Guinea-Bissau that hastened the downfall of the regime. While I do not share this opinion (I believe that by the end of his days in office, Caetano found himself without significant support on either the left or the right), I admit that the early days of Caetano's rule constituted a sort of "political spring," a period in which the majority of the Portuguese population, while not entirely satisfied with the status quo, had hopes for economic development, political liberalization, and the reform of their regime.

Two public-opinion surveys are interesting in this regard. The first was carried out in Spain in 1980 and reprinted by the Spanish newspaper *El País* in 1997. According to this survey, on the day that their dictator Francisco Franco died, the political attitudes of the Spanish were as follows: those in favor of retaining the regime unaltered, 13 percent; those in favor of a complete political and economic break (in other words, a socialist revolution), 17 percent; those in favor of gradual transformation, 47 percent. No such poll seems to have been carried out in Portugal at the time of Salazar's incapacitation, but a survey in 1984 conducted by "Norma-Semanário" on the tenth anniversary of Portugal's April 25 revolution showed that only 7 percent of the Portuguese people longed for the Salazar regime, while more than 80 percent were satisfied with the freedom that they had won. (We also know that in the April 1975 elections for the Constituent Assembly, the Communists and the extreme left obtained only 20 percent of the total vote, while the three main democratic parties—the Portuguese Socialist Party, the Popular Democratic Party [subsequently renamed the Social Democratic Party], and the Social Democratic Center—won approximately 70 percent.) Given these survey results and the considerable similarity of the two Iberian countries in their political structures and the mentalities of their peoples, it seems reasonable to estimate that during the "Marcello spring," 10–20 percent of the Portuguese population were in favor of maintaining the status quo, 20–25 percent wanted a socialist revolution, and between 45 and 60 percent supported a peaceful transition to democracy.

Aware of this popular sentiment, Marcello Caetano began to implement "political decompression" measures, introducing into the National Assembly a "liberal wing" that affirmed the need for a change in regime. Unfortunately, however, the people's hopes for such a change were dashed. A group of old influential Salazar associates, including the country's president Admiral Américo Tomás, some senior military officers, and the heads of prominent financial corporations, opposed Caetano's attempts at reform and prevented any fundamental change from taking place. The regime closed in on itself and hardened. The government's decision to continue the wars in its African colonies further precluded the possibility of political change. The liberal wing became marginalized and finally dissolved. Under the guise of "prior examination," censorship continued unabated. The secret police continued to function, albeit under the new label of General Directorate of Security. Mário Soares, who had come to represent democratic socialism, was deported to the far-off island of São Tomé. And Marcello Caetano's own prospects for gaining the presidency—perhaps the only way he could have freed himself of the constant veto power of President Américo Tomás—first floundered, and then finally disappeared with the reelection of Tomás, the representative of the extreme right.

Had Caetano learned from Charles de Gaulle how to deal with overseas colonies and had he anticipated the uncommon adroitness of Adolfo Suarez (Spain's prime minister from 1975 to 1980) in managing a democratic transition, Portugal would have been spared the devastating economic costs of the revolution and faced the difficult decade of the 1970s with its full economic potential intact. Instead, the evolution of the regime was interrupted, and reform halted. Soon, the sense began to grow among all groups in society that only a revolution could produce the kinds of changes that Portugal sorely needed. As President John F. Kennedy had lucidly stated years earlier: "Those who make peace-ful evolution impossible will make violent revolution inevitable."

The April 1974 Revolution

The hour of liberation finally arrived at dawn on 25 April 1974, when a group of mainly left-wing military officers calling themselves the Armed Forces Movement (Movimento das Forças Armadas—MFA) seized power in a bloodless coup. Unlike most coups, particularly those in Latin America, that tend to overthrow civilian democratic regimes and replace them with military dictatorships, Portugal's April 1974 revolution was a military coup aimed at replacing a civilian dictatorship with a democracy.

The leader of the "Junta of National Salvation," General António de Spínola, emerged as the titular head of the new regime. In public declarations by the Junta and the MFA following the coup, the promise was clear: Rather than embark on any sort of revolutionary or radical adventure, Portugal would set about creating political structures that would allow a Constituent Assembly to be elected. This body, in turn, would decide on the reforms to be carried out in the country.

The Portuguese people applauded this proposal and looked forward to the opportunity to express their will in the elections for the Constituent Assembly. For the second time in five years—and now with even stronger reasons—the country believed that it would undergo a gradual transformation from dictatorship to democracy, from an antiquated economy to a developed one, and from a poor and unjust society to a fairer, more prosperous, and more united society.

The political scene, however, was not yet conducive to peaceful democratization. The Portuguese Communist Party (PCP) and the radical left, in alliance with extremists within the MFA, were determined to pursue the revolutionary path regardless of how the people would express their will at the ballot box.

The struggle between the democratic camp and the revolutionary communist camp lasted for nearly a year. In 1974, after the PCP managed to replace a moderate, civilian prime minister (Palma Carlos) with a militant Communist prime minister (Vasco Gonçalves), and a right-wing president (General Spínola) with a left-wing president (General Costa Gomes), the Communists dominated the MFA. This led the Communist Party to conceive and implement a plan to seize power through revolutionary means. There is evidence suggesting that this plan had direct support from Moscow.

The Communist Party demonstrated its strength by (illegally) preventing a pro-Spínola demonstration from taking place in the streets of Lisbon. The government, the police authorities, and the armed forces refrained from intervening, allowing the Communist Party to overpower Spínola and force him to resign on September 28. In November, the heads of major private corporations were arrested on the order of Prime Minister Gonçalves, and charged with sabotaging the national economy. In January 1975, when discussions were underway over whether to create a single central trade union or to authorize multiple trade unions, the MFA went against the wishes of the main political parties by recognizing only one central trade union, Intersindical, which was loyal to the Communists.

On 11 March 1975, using the pretext of a countercoup launched by General Spínola, and in violation of the constitutional law, the MFA created the Council of the Revolution, a body of 20 military officers that sought to govern the country. The Council of the Revolution nationalized banks, insurance companies, and the country's main industrial enterprises. Simultaneously, it announced a land reform program aimed at expropriating large properties from their rightful owners and handing them over to workers' cooperatives.

Thus unfolded the socialist revolution. The Council of the Revolution (which by then had a communist majority) decided—in the middle of the campaign for the April 25 Constituent Assembly elections—that Portugal would become a socialist country engaged in a revolution that would hand power to the working class.

It may be worth recalling that in the *Communist Manifesto,* Marx and Engels presented ten measures to bring about the socialist revolution: Measure number one was the abolition of private property; measure number five was the centralization of credit in the hands of the state; and measures six and seven entailed the nationalization of other basic sectors of the economy.[2] The leader of the Portuguese Communists, Alvaro Cunhal, set out to realize these objectives. Loyal to the teachings of Lenin, as expressed in the book *Two Tactics of Social-Democracy in the Democratic Revolution,*[3] Cunhal believed that in Portugal, as in Russia, the passage from dictatorship to democracy required not merely a single revolution (the democratic revolution) but rather two revolutions—first, a *liberal* revolution that would move the country from autocracy to bourgeois parliamentarism, and then a *socialist* revolution that would guide the transition from bourgeois parliamentarism to proletarian republicanism.

In Russia, these two revolutions took place in February and October of 1917, respectively. In Portugal, the liberal revolution took place in April 1974 and the socialist revolution was attempted between September 1974 and November 1975.

The "Hot Summer of 1975"

The struggle between Portugal's communists and democrats was a hotly contested one. In the weeks leading up to the Constituent Assembly elections of 25 April 1975, the PCP and the extreme left mounted a strong political campaign and the Council of the Revolution issued a decree proclaiming the "option for socialism." Nevertheless, on election day, it was the democratic parties that won: The Socialists, led by Mário Soares, secured 37.9 percent of the vote; the Popular Democrats, led by Francisco Sá Carneiro, obtained 26.4 percent; and my own Social Democratic Center party received 7.6 percent. On the communist side, the PCP, led by Alvaro Cunhal, obtained less than 13 percent, while its sister party, the Portuguese Democratic Movement, took a mere 4.1 percent. The Constituent Assembly elections marked a clear victory for the democrats, showing that the overwhelming majority of the Portuguese people (over 70 percent of the electorate) wished for a peaceful transition to democracy.

Although the Socialists and the Popular Democrats won most of the votes, the MFA stubbornly held on to power, refusing to draw any conclusions from the results of the election. Had the MFA shown greater democratic spirit and had the Communists not plunged the country into turmoil, Portugal's postelection political scene would have been quite different. Two scenarios could have arisen, one predominantly military in nature, led by the MFA, the other primarily civilian, guided by the parties that received the most votes in the Constituent

Assembly elections. In the first scenario, the MFA would have retained the Council of the Revolution in some form, but without the subordination of political parties, and it would have probably implemented the so-called Melo Antunes Plan, an economic program based on a model of in-depth intervention from the top, but one that did not include nationalization, land reform, or worker control (the PCP's three principal themes at the time). The second scenario would probably have seen Mário Soares, leader of the Socialist Party, which had received the most votes in the election, at the head of the new government. This would certainly have been a government of the center, with Soares as prime minister, handling political reform and decolonization, and Sá Carneiro as deputy prime minister coordinating economic affairs.

In either case, the political development of the country would have followed the will of the people, as expressed in the Constituent Assembly elections. Business owners would not have been imprisoned, senior and middle managers would not have fled, and the country's production structure would not have been dismantled. In short, the economic and social costs of a revolution led by a minority moving rapidly toward the collectivization of the main means of production would not have been as high.

The period between March and November 1975, the most difficult phase in the Portuguese transition to democracy, was dubbed the "hot summer of 1975." Throughout these months, the Communists employed all their familiar tactics to subdue opponents—control of the state apparatus, police, and armed forces; domination of the press, radio, and television; management of public and private companies by workers' committees; and street disturbances and massive demonstrations. On the democratic side, however, no one succumbed to intimidation; instead, everyone took to the streets. During the "hot summer of 1975," Portugal was the site of huge demonstrations, with the threat of civil war looming dangerously on the horizon.

The Communists refused to give in. In keeping with their nature, they immediately declared that the "socialist revolution" was more important than "bourgeois elections." In September, they felt that the time was right for the final coup. Contrary to Leninist theory and tradition, they made an alliance with the radical left, the Revolutionary Unity Front (Frente de Unidade Revolucionária, or FUR), and mounted street demonstrations and strikes. They surrounded the Constituent Assembly, demanding its immediate dissolution (as had happened in Russia), and on 25 November 1975 they launched a military coup in Lisbon, with the aim of putting power in the hands of totalitarian socialism.

But history did not repeat itself. The domestic and international contexts were vastly different in 1975 than they had been in 1917. In Russia, the Bolsheviks prevailed; in Portugal, it was the democrats who defeated the communists. Led by General Ramalho Eanes, military officers loyal to the democratic enterprise put down the coup and averted civil war.

This is what I call "the Portuguese miracle": Our country managed to halt a communist revolution while avoiding civil war and military dictatorship. Many people fought anonymously for freedom—in the political parties, at the workplace, and in the media. Yet there is one man who courageously personified and triumphantly led the democratic struggle against totalitarianism. His name is Mário Soares.

Counting the Costs

After the communist coup of 25 November 1975 was suppressed, victory fell to the democrats. The storm abated; the waters calmed. Nonetheless, the normalization of democratic life did not take place overnight. Although Portugal had a democratically elected president and government by the summer of 1976, it took until the end of 1982 for the Council of the Revolution to be disbanded and for the armed forces to be brought under the control of the civilian authorities. Portugal joined the European Union (EU) in 1985. Only in 1989, in a third constitutional revision, was the economic part of the Constitution revised, eliminating the principle of the collectivization of the main means of production, which had been introduced during the "hot summer of 1975." In this respect, democratic normalization in Portugal took no less than 14 years. This may seem an abnormally long time, but that is how it was.

Some might say that the historical processes of postrevolutionary normalization are necessarily slow and that, in spite of everything, the essential measures were carried out in Portugal as quickly as could be expected. While this is mostly true, one must bear in mind the huge costs that this slowness entailed. For example, although Portugal's banking sector has been restructured and is thriving today, it had to endure nationalization and poor management for more than 10 years. Although the Sá Carneiro government (January–December 1980) tried on three occasions to privatize banks and insurance companies, its plans were rejected each time by the Council of the Revolution and vetoed by President Ramalho Eanes. It was only in 1984, under the center-left government of Mário Soares, that this highly important economic measure—the opening up of the banking and insurance sectors to private initiative—was passed. Under this center-left government, and later, under the government of Aníbal Cavaco Silva (1987–95), privatizations were carried out, and a healthier equilibrium was reestablished between the public sector and the private sector, reducing the role of the state in the national economy.

Nevertheless, Portugal's tumultuous transition to democracy proved costly to its people. For 10 to 15 years, once prosperous and profitable companies became chronically indebted, accumulating billions of escudos in losses. The most important economic groups were broken up, centers of economic rationality and investment capacity disappearing with them. Hundreds of competent and motivated senior and middle managers were let go; many spent 10 to 15 years abroad before returning. The state intervened hundreds of times in the management of private companies facing financial difficulties, which in many cases merely served to worsen their situation. Land reform was implemented and then undone, without visible benefit to farmers or agriculture in Alentejo Province. To top it all off, at the very moment when Portugal's membership in the single European market was bringing it face to face with the fundamental problem of international competitiveness, the state paid belated, unfair, and in some cases, even risible compensation to the owners of nationalized companies. Thus, contrary to both its obligations and interests, it failed to contribute to the strengthening of Portuguese enterprises.

In other words, Portugal's failure to achieve a prompt and peaceful transition to democracy has had a very high price. We are still footing the bill for it today—for a public debt that grew too high; for privatizations that have yet to be carried out successfully; for privatizations that cannot be implemented because companies are too poor; and for the time that everything takes when one starts so many years late.

Let us consider Spain for a moment. While we Portuguese implemented a policy of nationalization and then privatization, it is Spain, not Portugal, that has profoundly restructured its industry and production. While we implemented and then abandoned land reform, it is Spain, not Portugal, that has a modern, prosperous, and competitive agricultural sector. While we took 13 years to agree on a constitution, Spain adopted one from the outset. This is a tough lesson for our nation's dreamers, and it poses a tough task for our leaders. Rather than waste time blaming the extremists for twice depriving us of the democratization to which we were entitled, let us instead ask what is to be done now to make up for lost time.

Reforming the State

Permit me to recount a small parable. Imagine a German, Swedish, or British tourist visiting Portugal during the summer. He knows little about Portugal beyond the fact that, like his own country, it is a member of the European Union. Perhaps he also knows that Portugal is one of the poorest countries in the EU, but that its per-capita income clearly places it within the upper third of the world. He may even be aware that, thanks to the continued efforts of different governments, Portugal met all the Maastricht criteria and has become a founding member of the "Euro." At the end of a two-week vacation in Portugal, what conclusions would our northern European tourist draw about this small, friendly country in the south of Europe?

The first conclusion would undoubtedly be the beauty of the sea and the beaches, the radiance of the sun, and the pleasantly temperate climate, factors that he will tend to attribute to the work of God, if he is a religious person, or to the work of nature, if he is not. Next, our curious visitor would be pleasantly surprised at the number of very good things provided by the Portuguese—high-quality food and wine, fine hotels and nightclubs, varied commerce, exquisite handicrafts, well-stocked bookstores, and numerous efficient banking establishments.

At the end of his stay, our visitor might well conclude, "Portugal is a first-rate country and fully deserves to be a part of the European Union, just like my own country." This would be the conclusion reached by someone whose experience in Portugal involved only its private sector. The little he would have seen of the public sector—one or two airports, highways, main trunk routes—would merely have confirmed the excellent impression that the visit had made.

Let us suppose, however, that in the middle of his stay, our friendly tourist is unlucky enough to fall off a bicycle in the Lisbon suburb of Estoril and break his arm. Upon arriving at Cascais Hospital, he would not believe that he is in the same country, for his surroundings would now be reminiscent of a Third World country.

Our tourist would gain a similarly negative impression if he were to visit other state hospitals, enter most of the public schools, pass through the slums that abound in Lisbon, drive along the roads in the interior of the country, or have contact with a court, registry office, or real-estate registration office. If, attracted by the favorable aspects of the country, our tourist decided to set up a company in Portugal—something that would take less than 24 hours in his own country—he would be appalled to learn that in Portugal this simple venture would probably take about six months and would cost him the highest fees in the entire EU.

Our tourist's final conclusion might well be that Portugal is an excellent country in which to spend one's summer vacation, but a dreadful one in which to do business or to get assistance from the government. He might also conclude that, while the private sector makes Portugal look like a European country, the public sector makes it seem like a member of the Third World.

In my opinion, the greatest question facing us today is this: Why is the Portuguese state so deficient? And shouldn't our first priority be reforming the state?

I firmly believe that, although reform of the Portuguese state has been a priority for many years, our turbulent transition to democracy has prevented such reform from being carried out successfully. The explosion of social demands (most of them justifiable) in the wake of the April 1974 revolution contributed directly to the fact that within a few years we had *more state involvement and a less efficient state*. A few figures will serve to illustrate this fact:

Civil Servants. In 1970, there were 200,000 civil servants. In 1984, that figure had risen to 650,000, more than tripling in 15 years.

Administrative public-sector expenses. These expenses made up 21.7 percent of Portugal's GDP in 1972 and 43.3 percent of the GDP by 1983. In other words, administrative public-sector expenses doubled in ten years.

Foreign debt. This stood at 91,600 billion escudos in 1973. By 1983, it had risen to 1,623,000 billion escudos. In other words, it grew 17-fold in ten years.

It is clear that, as a result of the revolution, the Portuguese state grew much larger, more cumbersome, and more expensive than it would have been if Portugal had undergone a peaceful transition to democracy. The harm done was not just in terms of size, but also in terms of quality. In addition to having greater state involvement, we have a less efficient state.

Anyone who pays attention to Portugal's parliamentary debates or to the media is aware that tax evasion is widespread; the judicial system is in turmoil; the education and health systems leave a lot to be desired; social security is seriously threatened in the medium term; public housing is insufficient for a majority of the neediest; and in general, the quality and efficiency of our public administration are sorely lacking. What is urgently needed in Portugal, therefore, is a profound reform of the state, and in particular, a comprehensive reform of public admini-stration and the judicial system.

It should not be forgotten that in the second half of the twentieth century, Portugal was the only European country—perhaps the only country in the world—that had to suffer a year of leftist revolution, seven years of rule by a military junta, and 13 years of an imposed Marxist constitution that divided its people. This weakened and impoverished the country and delayed its progress. At the same time, it sharpened and developed our wits. The progress we have made since 1974–75 has been substantial.

Our constitution has been revised and agreed upon. The armed forces have been praised for their act of liberation and have returned to their barracks. The problem of decolonization has been overcome, and a policy of friendly cooperation with Portuguese-speaking countries has been implemented and consolidated. Half a million expatriates have been reintegrated into Portuguese society. The island territories of the Azores and Madeira enjoy autonomy within the framework of a unified state. Political stability has been achieved. Local power has flourished.

Public finance is balanced and in line with the top countries in the EU. European integration has proven a success and promises to continue on the right course. Portugal has begun to play a more prominent and effective role in world affairs.

Our generation has done its duty to the country. Naturally, it is not the fault of the democratic parties and leaders who have governed us since 1976 that, prior to that time, peaceful evolution toward democracy had twice been blocked, and that a revolution with a profound impact and long-term consequences made their task far more difficult than it otherwise would have been. We may perhaps conclude that we have arrived where we are today because, after the revolution, we worked harder than any of our European partners. As a result, we can firmly state that a people that has achieved what we have achieved over the last two decades, despite our difficult starting point, can clearly achieve much more and do much better in the next 20 years. All it takes is the will to achieve it.

NOTES

1. Samuel P. Huntington, *The Third Wave: Democratization in the Late Twentieth Century* (Norman: University of Oklahoma Press, 1991), 3.

2. Karl Marx and Friedrich Engels, *The Communist Manifesto* (New York: International Publishers, 1948), 30.

3. V.I. Lenin, *Two Tactics of Social-Democracy in the Democratic Revolution* (New York: International Publishers, 1935).

6

THE TRANSFORMATION OF CENTRAL EUROPE

Bronisław Geremek

Bronisław Geremek *is foreign minister of Poland. A medieval historian by training, he was a key advisor to Lech Wałęsa from the earliest days of Solidarity and spent over a year in prison during the period of martial law. He chaired the Committee for Political Reform during Solidarity's 1989 "roundtable" talks with the leaders of Poland's communist regime. From 1989 until his appointment as foreign minister in 1997, he was chairman of the parliament's Foreign Affairs Committee.*

Only ten years ago, the political world that we live in today would have been considered a bold, futuristic vision. The reality of those bygone years had been shaped by many decades of the Cold War, during which a huge part of Europe had been ruled by communist regimes. Central and Eastern Europe was separated from an integrating Western Europe by the "Iron Curtain," and both the economic gap and the civilization gap between the two halves of Europe continually widened. Although the weaknesses of the so-called people's democracies were clearly visible, almost no Western experts were predicting the rapid downfall of the entire Soviet system.

Against this backdrop, ten years ago representatives of Poland's democratic opposition sat down at a negotiating table in Warsaw with the hierarchy of the country's communist regime. Within that same year there followed the fall of the Berlin Wall and the Velvet Revolution in Czechoslovakia. Soon other societies awoke—and that was the end of communism in Europe.

Central European societies paid the price of their struggle for freedom on the streets of Budapest in 1956, in Czechoslovakia in 1968, and in Poland in 1956, 1968, 1970, and 1981. In 1989, however, Poles chose dialogue instead of confrontation as a means to overcome a political deadlock. The "roundtable" talks, sometimes called the "negotiated revolution," marked the beginning of the end of the struggle against communism for Poles and other peoples of Central and Eastern Europe.

I would like to present some thoughts on our transition to democracy and a free market, but I also wish to call attention to some of the hazards of that process. I believe that today we are at a very particular moment in European history. Our perception of the successes and failures of the last 10 years is heavily influenced right now by pictures from Yugoslavia, pictures that call into question the view that Europe is becoming a single entity. This view has been advanced for the past few years by Central Europeans contending that the notion of a separate and distinct Central and Eastern Europe had lost its validity.

The term "Central Europe" has sometimes been considered an expression of nostalgia for the old Austro-Hungarian Empire. The term also implied a special intellectual atmosphere, which was often seen as a privilege for those born there. In the 1960s, 1970s, and 1980s, the notion of Central Europe could also be associated with the dream of freedom and the aspiration to membership in a community of free nations.

Nowadays the notion of Central Europe is associated with rapid economic and social transformation, albeit not without high social costs. This transformation, firmly based on the premises of democracy and human rights, allowed many nations in our region to claim that we belong to a single European family. The crisis in Kosovo is a severe test for that family and, at the same time, proof that the ghosts of nationalism are still alive in parts of Central and Eastern Europe.

The roots of the nationalism that has destroyed so many lives in the Balkans over the last eight years are not to be found only in remote history. Those roots grew very quickly during the decadent phase of communism. When I think about the success of Poland, I now can see very clearly that in Yugoslavia the postcommunist elites rejected democratic change and that the Central European model of transformation was not applied there. This is a painful lesson for those of us involved in democratic change in the region, as well as for the entire European family of nations.

Everyone now acknowledges that communism was economic nonsense. By wasting capital reserves and human resources, by overburdening society with arms production, and by suppressing the spirit of entrepreneurship and innovation, it finally bankrupted itself. On a philosophical level, however, communism inflicted upon itself an even greater defeat. Unable to convince society to believe in their ideology, communist leaders restricted the rights of their citizens and built their empires on a foundation of violence, terror, and lies.

But these pillars of power proved inadequate to the task. Alexis de Tocqueville was correct in stating, "There is no end which the human will despairs of attaining through the combined power of individuals united into a society." The power and the will of the Polish nation were welded together by the spirit of Solidarity. This spirit united proponents of diverse ideological views in a fight for the rights of the oppressed, a call for human dignity, and a drive to remind those in power of their role as servants to the people.

The core of the great Solidarity movement was the dream of freedom and democracy, understood as an innate right of every human being to decide his or her own fate and to share responsibility for the fate of the nation. Thus the opposition movement in Poland was not just a rebellion against a constraining system but a positive force shaping an attractive new alternative in the form of democracy, free markets, and a bond with European and Euro-Atlantic structures. As a result, Poles, at the brink of regaining their independence, knew not only what they rejected but also what they wanted. This was a critical factor in the transition.

At the beginning of our transition, we introduced as the basis of our democracy the principles of human rights, constituent-oriented government, legally based means of conflict resolution, and guarantees of the right of ethnic minorities to their identity. We quickly established good relations with our neighbors, making our borders open and friendly. We made a historic effort at reconciliation with Germany, which is not only our largest economic partner but also an important ally in promoting European unity. We have opened a new chapter in relations with Ukraine—we were the first country to recognize its statehood. In the past, our relationship with Ukraine had often been beset with conflicts. Today, however, Ukraine is our strategic partner, and we share a community of interests. Our countries and peoples have understood that only together can they be independent and secure: One cannot imagine an independent Poland without an independent Ukraine, and vice versa. Partnership between these two countries is a cornerstone of peace and stability in Europe. We have continually supported Lithuania and the other Baltic States in their efforts to integrate with Western structures. Another example of our commitment to regional cooperation is the Višegrad Group, composed of Poland, Hungary, Slovakia, and the Czech Republic, which has overcome some past animosities in favor of a close partnership. We are building relations with Russia in a spirit of mutual respect, and we hope that Russia will become a member of the European community of democratic states.

We are committed to our role as a friendly and reliable partner in the region, for we are determined that new walls should not be raised in Europe. Now that the "Iron Curtain" has vanished, we cannot let another curtain descend, one that would divide peoples not by political beliefs but by economic performance. This kind of curtain might not be made of iron, yet it could be as cruel as the old one. We think that regional cooperation will help prevent such an evolution. This outlook is also a legacy of the Solidarity movement.

I have enumerated with some pride these accomplishments on the international scene. Thanks to them, Poland is looked upon as a country that plays a vital stabilizing role in the region. This also helps to explain why we have exceptionally good relations with the United States, with which we share many political interests and a common view of the values that are essential to the proper functioning of the international community.

Overcoming the Past

During the last 10 years, Poland has laid the foundations for a stable free market economy. A large portion of our GDP—70 percent—is produced by the private sector, and by the year 2005 we intend to raise this ratio up to 92 percent. Despite the unfavorable global economic environment generated by the effects of the recent crises in Asia, Latin America, and Russia, the Polish economy is still expanding. Politicians might be suspected of exaggerating Poland's economic success, but nearly $30 billion in Western investment is an irrefutable testimonial to the confidence of the global market in Poland's stability and prospects for future growth.

The accomplishments that I have noted were possible only through the hard work of the Polish people. To achieve these results, we had to overcome the fear of the unknown future that lay ahead of us, such as life under a free, competitive market. We also have had to discard the burden of historical prejudices and stereotypes. It was essential to get used to criticism and to plurality of thought and ideas, and also to leave behind our nostalgic attachment to the illusory benefits of a *paternalistic* socialist state. Although echoes of the past are still with us, I am certain that they will not deter us from reaching our destination.

We are delighted that other Central European states besides Poland have also been successful in their transformations. This can be easily confirmed by noting their participation in the process of integration with European and Transatlantic structures. Unfortunately, however, some countries in Eastern and Southeastern Europe are still bedeviled by problems characteristic of the transition period.

The emergence of democratic political, social, and economic institutions is initially marked by the coexistence of old and new elements. The process of reform frequently suspends society between the expiration of the old system and the genesis of the new. It is a time of uncertainty and frustration, with a shortage of quick answers to pressing questions. Sometimes the sheer magnitude of the necessary changes is so great that a temptation arises to find a "third way" that can offer a panacea for current problems. Yielding to this temptation often leads to delays in reform—an ideal situation for influential interest groups that seek to turn the process of change to their own advantage. This can produce understandable bitterness in transitional societies, which have a tendency to accept the false explanation that the free market is the *cause* of the negative social and economic phenomena that appear. The real truth is that it is precisely the absence of stable institutions and of honest and fair free-market rules that is responsible for the impoverishment of some societies in transition.

The bankruptcy of communist ideology and the downfall of its power have produced a moral vacuum that can pose a clear and present danger to democracy. Sometimes advocates of primitive and shallow slogans use fear as a tool to promote nationalism. If they obtain power, they use it for destruction, not creation. Their unhappy countries, instead of participating in integration processes, often drift into alienation, increasing the risk that they will develop an aggressive policy toward internal and external enemies (many of whom are totally imaginary).

The only countries in Central Europe that have succeeded in their transformation are those which have shown determination in pushing through free-market reforms and which have built their public institutions on strong democratic foundations. Democracy and the free market are complementary: There is no lasting democracy if the economy is in chaos, and corruption can hinder the development of truly democratic institutions. It is also impossible to build a free-market economy in the long run unless the government has the support of the people. Otherwise, the fear of an uncontrolled display of popular dissatisfaction frequently forces regimes to impose costly economic restrictions. Some may argue that the compromises required in modern democracies are too time-consuming and inefficient for building a modern economy, but Poland has proven that this is not the case.

I look forward to the twenty-first century with optimism. Central Europe is becoming a part of the transatlantic zone of security and prosperity. NATO has already embraced new members from our region, and soon the European Union will also be enlarged. Thus there is now an expanding area that Zbigniew Brzezinski has called the "bridgehead of democracy" in Eurasia. I believe that this process marks a new policy direction for the entire Euro-Atlantic community during the coming century, a period in which Poland and the entire Central European region will have a vital role to play in further extending the bridgehead of democracy.

For this to happen, a united Europe must develop a common vision for the future of the continent, including the parameters within which the Euro-Atlantic community will function. The continuation of NATO expansion is a vital element of this process. The "Open Door" policy must provide concrete opportunities for those Central and Eastern countries that have expressed the desire and possess the capabilities to join the Treaty. As a Treaty member, Poland will be an active advocate for these countries. We know the price of freedom, and we know how valuable security is in a region that suffered more than any other as a result of this century's wars.

The European Union needs vision and courage. Those two elements have been the cornerstones of its success since the beginning of European integration in the 1950s. We in the candidate countries may feel that those elements are sometimes lacking. Discussion of the future of a united Europe cannot be limited to functional matters, no matter how important these may be. There must also be room for a deeper debate on the shared values that are the philosophical basis of European integration. The Union must not be like Tarzan, with strong muscles but problems in communication. It must enlarge and promote a community of values, which include democracy, free markets, the rule of law, and the centrality of human rights. Only such a Union, fully conscious of its identity and its goals, can fulfill its role as the agent of stability, peace, and prosperity in Europe.

In some Central and Eastern European countries, one may hear doubts about whether the difficulties of the transition period can be overcome. Many look back nostalgically to the "good old days" and doubt that the future will be as good. We hope that NATO and the European Union will support the process of transformation. The readiness of these organizations to include new members will motivate the countries of our region to work harder. Our common goal should be to counteract the threat of a new wall dividing the democratic and affluent countries of Europe from those sunk in political chaos and economic stagnation.

In closing, let me once again quote Tocqueville: "It cannot be repeated too often that nothing is more fertile in prodigies than the art of being free; but there is nothing more arduous than the apprenticeship of liberty. . . . Liberty [unlike despotism] is generally established with difficulty in the midst of storms; it is perfected by civil discord; and its benefits cannot be appreciated until it is already old." We accept these words with humility, but we cannot wait for the fruits of freedom to age. On this point, at least, we hope to prove this great visionary wrong.

III

Beyond and Below the Nation

7

DEMOCRACY AND THE NATION

Jean Daniel

Jean Daniel *is the founder, editor, and director of the French weekly*
Le Nouvel Observateur *and a member of the High Council of the French
Language. He served as president of the Council of Ministers in the
cabinet of provisional president Felix Gouin in 1946 and was the editor-
in-chief of* L'Express *from 1955 to 1964. He is the author of more than
ten books.*

On 2 May 1998, a historic event took place in Europe that is equally
significant for the invention of democracy and for the survival of nations: 15 European nations decided to adopt a single currency. Many
experts in the United States were convinced that such an agreement
would never come to pass; some even went so far as to say that if it
were by some miracle to happen, it would lead to a series of upheavals
and perhaps even to conflict between France and Germany. I remember
a study by an American academic that concluded, "Europe, born out of
France and Germany's determination to put an end to their wars, will
bring about a return to bellicose attitudes; not unlike Israel, born out of
the determination to put an end to antisemitism, which has succeeded
in breeding in the Arab people the same antisemitism as existed among
Christians."

Although the State Department, Wall Street, and leading American
academics do not agree with this rash prediction, it does reflect the
widespread American belief, not infrequently borne out by fact, that
Europeans are unable to solve the slightest problem without U.S.
assistance, arbitration, or intervention. Furthermore, it reflects a feeling
of discomfort over the rebirth of an old continent that was supposed
to evoke feelings of nostalgia, not to become a real rival to the New
World.

These events are being compared to the Treaties of Westphalia of
1648 that put an end to the Thirty Years' War. Even this comparison,
however, is inadequate, for those treaties were the product of a tradition
that held that the only way any portion of sovereignty could be

sacrificed was as an outcome of violent conflict. In fact, one can say that these events are truly unprecedented; never before in the history of nations had a country relinquished any part of its power in peacetime.

The 11 nations that signed the agreement on the Euro are all democracies. To become a pioneering member of the Euro club, candidates, in addition to having the proper democratic credentials, had to meet certain economic criteria, such as controlling their budget deficits. These 11 nations, which had already composed a community of neighboring democracies before forming a union, decided that they could do something together that none of them could do on their own. The question therefore arises: Is democracy possible outside the framework of the nation-state? Are there factors other than democracy and proximity—or more generally, political regimes and geography—that can explain this decision to come together?

The emerging Europe is a laboratory for experimenting with a new form of postnational citizenship that will pave the way for the advent of an actual supranational government.

Politics and geography aside, history compels us to look backward: Europe has existed before. In the Middle Ages, scholars moved freely from Montpelier to Salamanca and from Heidelberg to Padua. Even after Latin ceased to be the common language, songs of love and ambition were still sung in a similar manner; suffering and death were feared alike; fate and God were discussed in the works of Shakespeare, Cervantes, Erasmus, and Montaigne; and everyone agreed on the preeminence of Dante Alighieri.

We are in the throes of a revolution. Yet Germany, not France, is the nation most profoundly affected by these changes. In France, we have failed to understand the extent to which, for Germany, the Deutschemark, like all currencies a symbol of sovereignty, has also been a guarantee not only of economic recovery but of national unity. The mark has gradually become the strongest and most stable currency in the world, leaving behind the dollar and the yen. In fact, the mark has served as the currency of choice for all neighboring countries, whether German-speaking or not. It is a strong currency, and its strength has created a mark zone. Five of the 11 signatory countries of the Euro agreement are more or less in the mark zone: Germany, Austria, Luxembourg, Finland, and the Netherlands (although one might dispute the inclusion of the latter). In effect, the mark zone also already includes the Czech Republic, Slovakia, Hungary, Slovenia, Croatia, and, to a certain extent, Romania and Poland.

In this light, Germany might understandably have feared that it stood to lose everything with the integration of Europe and especially with the adoption of the Euro. Had it not been for the guilt complex tied to the memory of Nazism, Germans would never have been such ardent advocates of a united Europe. This complex has been revived as a result of German reunification and the increased power of the mark zone, two phenomena that cause the old Prussian temptation to reappear and make the return of the old demons more dangerous. In other words, it is a secret desire to be less German that has made the Germans more European.

It was, in fact, largely to make the Germans less German that the French took the initiative and set about building Europe. As long as Germans were held in check by their feelings of guilt, there was no need to fear the German economic powerhouse, since France was needed to vouch for Germany politically and to provide it with international legitimacy. France played the part of the blameless soul, while her partner had to be content with material achievements. Yet today all has changed in Bonn and Paris; some of the current "Euroskeptics" now believe that France may no longer be able to control the process that it set in motion.

Under such circumstances, the months and years immediately following the Euro agreement are likely to be marked by dangerous disruptions. It should come as no surprise if the resurgence of nationalism spreads beyond the French and German pro-Nazi movements. The anthropologist Ernest Gellner has stated that nationalism must always precede the emergence of the nation. Yet nationalism can resurface in an exaggerated form if the nation is declared to be "in danger" or, as was the case in Poland, when it simply ceases to exist.

Most certainly, as Jacques Delors has said, in the beginning the Europe to be built is that of nation-states. In accordance with the principle of subsidiarity, only those things that cannot be done by a single nation are to be shared. But one must also understand that once a single currency is adopted (and sovereignty is thus conferred upon a new entity), if Europe also chooses to head toward a common defense structure serving a common foreign policy, the importance of this new European entity will far outweigh that of its constituent nation-states.

Are European nations then headed toward a federation similar to the United States? In the long run, this is their likely destiny. Let us remember that the European Union (EU) has institutions in the economic and legal fields that are truly federal in character. The problem posed by the multiplicity of languages is undeniable, yet it is mitigated by an overall harmonization of values in civil society. All of these nations, for example, have abolished the death penalty, legalized contraception and abortion, and regulated immigration. One might even say that the emerging Europe is a laboratory for experimenting with a new form of postnational citizenship that will pave the way for the advent of an actual supranational government.

In the future entity, a foreign resident who is not a citizen of an EU member state will have almost all the same rights as a citizen. In fact, discussion is still going on over whether all rights should be granted, without exception. To be absolutely clear on this point, at issue is whether noncitizens should be given the right to vote. Thanks to the process of European integration, we are finding a way to solve the problem of separating citizenship and nationality.

Universality and Uniqueness

The universality of democracy makes it possible for democracy to transcend its historical roots. Can the triumph of democracy over nationality be radical, and should it be? This issue calls for a review of the origins—or perhaps less ambitiously, of the past—of democracy. The great modern scholars of ancient Greece have taught us that the search for democracy started very early and actually preceded the forming of nations. After considerable debate, all now agree that the ancient Greeks, in spite of the existence of slavery, were the fathers of the idea of democratic relations among the citizen body.

But what does this mean? Democracy implies two concepts: freedom and the individual. This definition can be refined. Here is a definition that is reduced to its barest elements: Democracy is that system which, in a given society, both protects its minorities and gives them an opportunity to form a majority and to take the place of those in power.

The primary principle of absolute monarchy was expressed as follows: The king is not subject to laws; the law is nothing other than the will of the sovereign. How did this definition change when the people became sovereign? A large part of the world was thrown into disarray when power was stripped away from anointed kings and turned over to the people.

When and how do the people become sovereign, and therefore the creator of laws? This is at the very crux of our problem. Many legal historians remind us that the sovereignty of the people, and indeed, that of monarchs, was geographically determined and had territorial limits. In other words, the search for democracy preceded the establishment of nations, but until now, it could be fully exercised only after national self-determination. The geographer Michel Foucher has even defined a civilization as the development of a social system within national borders. It is as if we have been dealing with twin concepts that could not be dissociated: the territorial nation and the sovereignty of the people.

This leads me to my next observation: Democracy, as a concept, comes from a universal wellspring but, at the same time, it is a way of thinking determined by territory and tradition, which can be summarized by the expression "national will." The word "will" connotes the freedom of democracy, and the word "national" provides for the limitation of its exercise.

All this is another way of saying that, with the construction of a united Europe under way, it is entirely possible to believe that the new entity will be democratic while, at the same time, fearing that the exercise of this democracy may be carried out at the expense of national uniqueness. Thus the answer to our original question is that democracy is conceivable in a framework other than the nation-state, but the organization of such a democracy must take national sovereignty into account.

We must therefore reexamine the concept of nationhood. The fears that integration would pose a threat to uniqueness appeared not only before the establishment of nation-states but perhaps even before the advent of nations themselves. One can see from the history of the unifications of Germany and Italy that such arguments were made to resist unity, both in Tuscany and in Bavaria. At the opposite end of the spectrum, the United States is cited as an example of a nation-state where democratic universality serves as a unifying factor, both politically and culturally, although the latter is increasingly being questioned. And then there is Israel, which, by bringing Ethiopian and Russian Jews back onto its territory, has achieved a sort of messianic holy empire, in which the collective will overlaps with predestined territory.

Inventing and Exporting Democracy

It is often said that the invention of democracy took hold in fertile soil in France and the United States and that these are the only two nations that have sought to export the universal features of democracy. Yet although the U.S. Declaration of Independence undoubtedly inspired some of the people who drafted the French Declaration of the Rights of Man, it would be an overstatement to say that the American Revolution, a very regional and peculiar movement, was exported to Europe. In fact, it was an anticolonial national-liberation movement, not an endeavor of universal scope.

Why was it that only France was successful in exporting its revolution? After 1688 Great Britain had a parliamentary monarchy, a regime upon which Montesquieu and Voltaire lavished praise. The idea of extending this democratic monarchy to other countries, however, was declared to be impossible, since other countries had neither an enlightened nobility nor a powerful bourgeoisie. Great Britain soon realized that, as a great nation in Europe and the world at large, its interests could only be impeded if the system it had adopted were to spread beyond the British

Isles. Paradoxically, the first constitutional monarchy was to become the greatest ally of absolute monarchies overseas. Indeed it became a sanctuary of counterrevolutionary ideas, initially for reasons of foreign policy, and later for colonial reasons. It was on these grounds that Great Britain opposed the independence of the United States, even though Edmund Burke, who has not been given the credit he deserves for this, took the side of the American rebels.

Recently, American foreign-policy heavyweights like Henry Kissinger, Zbigniew Brzezinski, Strobe Talbott, and Samuel P. Huntington have been at loggerheads over issues such as Somalia, Bosnia, the Gulf crisis, and whether the United States or the United Nations should take responsibility for dealing with these hot spots. At the root of their debate is the same issue: that of exporting democracy.

Henry Kissinger has argued vigorously that the United States cannot have a "civilizing mission"; that such a mission would be as arrogant as it would be unrealistic; and that U.S. foreign policy should concentrate on areas where its interests are in jeopardy. He states his faith in Theodore Roosevelt, not Woodrow Wilson. In international relations, he places as much emphasis on the balance of power as on forms of government. The United States must show the way rather than intervene or, as Roosevelt used to say, must be a "lighthouse rather than a messiah." But having said that, Kissinger ends up approving virtually every U.S. intervention abroad.

In an article in the November–December 1996 issue of *Foreign Affairs,*[1] Samuel Huntington expresses his own opinion on the "balance of power." In his view, the traditional British position of aiding the weaker party to a conflict in the belief that every victor poses a threat (a stance that continues to be taken in the Middle East by Hafez el-Assad) has become obsolete. According to Huntington, the danger of weakening the ties among Western nations should be a cause of much greater concern than the goal of obliging the entire planet to adopt a democratic system, particularly as he contends that democratic values are not universal. He is outraged by the tendency to believe that people need only to like McDonald's and Coca-Cola to become "Westernized," "modern," or quite simply, democratic.[2]

Most importantly, he claims that non-Western nations, and especially China, know how to play Western nations like France and the United States off against one another over issues relating to human rights, the proliferation of nuclear weapons, and trade with Iran or Cuba.[3] Like Kissinger, Huntington believes that it takes centuries for a country to develop ways of democratic thinking and that the endeavor to make non-Western nations adopt human rights, the separation of church and state, multiparty systems, and the like can only lead to dangerous utopianism.[4]

In the same issue of *Foreign Affairs,* U.S. deputy secretary of state

Strobe Talbott answers these views.[5] He notes that President Bill Clinton has pressed Congress to fund programs promoting democracy and the rule of law throughout the world. In 1994, Clinton sent 21,000 U.S. troops to Haiti to impose this ideal. In December 1995, he sent a 20,000-strong contingent to enforce democracy in Bosnia. And in 1996, he brought considerable pressure to bear on Russia to have it organize its first free presidential election.[6]

Even allies of the United States question the wisdom of allowing a single nation, albeit an imperial power, to determine the criteria of democracy and to specify where it should flourish.

In none of these three countries did democracy ultimately triumph. This is one of the reasons why crusades for democracy have been condemned, not just by isolationists, but also by the partisans of *realpolitik*. Talbott, however, argues that the entire debate on this issue is an anachronism in an age when the shortening of distances, the opening up of borders, and the interpenetration of cultures and economies are creating an unprecedented situation.[7] Like goods and services, ideas travel from country to country and from one continent to another just as fast as epidemics, drugs, criminality, and terrorism. Clinton's foreign policy, like those of Woodrow Wilson and Franklin D. Roosevelt, is based on the conviction that "the larger and more close-knit the community of nations that choose democratic forms of government, the safer and more prosperous Americans will be."[8] According to Talbott, "the United States is uniquely and self-consciously a country founded on a set of ideas, and ideals, applicable to people everywhere."[9]

Talbott cites the examples of Thailand, Nicaragua, Cambodia, Kuwait, Yemen, Jordan, and the Palestinians, who elected their first parliament in January 1996.[10] He concludes that the idea of democracy is viable virtually everywhere, even in countries suffering from underdevelopment, though he recognizes that the process of establishing democracy may be long and difficult. He concedes that the so-called third wave of democratization has suffered serious relapses[11] and admits that in certain cases true democracies—like Germany in the 1930s—may elect a dictator and be ushered into war.[12] Yet he argues that this is no reason for denying the universality of democracy; rather, it shows that there is more to democracy than simply elections.

According to Talbott, "America's own experience should make us patient, persistent, and respectful with those who are in the early stages of the transition from colonialism and autocracy. After the United States became a 'new independent state' in 1776, it took 11 years to draft a constitution, 89 to abolish slavery, 144 to give women the vote, 188 to extend full constitutional protections to all citizens."[13] In the new lyrical manner of the White House, he concludes that "the world continues to look to the United States for leadership not just because of our economic and military might, but also because we are at our best when promoting and defending the same political principles abroad that we live by at home."[14]

Yet not only nations that see themselves as the victims of Western interference, but even allies of the United States question the wisdom of allowing a single nation, albeit an imperial power, to determine the criteria of democracy and to specify where it should flourish. General de Gaulle declared that France could not accept such a situation without demeaning itself and without relinquishing its ideals.

This issue is of particular importance to us in our endeavor to understand the democratic invention and its development through modern times. We can see that it is no longer an issue merely of isolationism versus interventionism, but of analyzing new concepts in foreign policy and political philosophy. On the one hand, there is the question of whether the most powerful nation on earth has the duty to provide assistance and the right to intervene unilaterally on foreign soil. On the other hand, people are beginning to question the usual definitions of democracy and whether they are universally applicable. Zbigniew Brzezinski, former national security advisor to President Jimmy Carter, categorically claims that the United States will have incomparable and unassailable supremacy for a very long time in all areas and that this de facto leadership confers duties, not rights. In his view, the concern about the balance of power is a thing of the past; the destiny of the planet is now at stake. Yet Brzezinski seems to overlook that the intervention of a single nation, especially when that nation is the world's only superpower, is never perceived as disinterested. Such intervention not only gives rise to anti-NATO and anti-American feelings but also serves to unite powers such as China, Russia, the Third World, and perhaps very soon Europe as well. President George Bush was well aware that the United States ought not to move against Saddam Hussein without UN approval and active participation on the part of the Arab world. No nation, not even a superpower, is morally entitled to impose anything, even democracy, on another nation.

We Are All of One Stock

We must give Professor Huntington his due in underscoring the rising importance of traditionalist, irrational, and mythical sources of inspiration in our societies at the end of the century and the millennium. Democracy without roots implies the existence of an abstract individual with neither God nor king, a traveler with no luggage, master of his destiny and intoxicated by his freedom. In the real world, no such person exists; should circumstance bring such a being into existence, he would long for the warmth procured by the solidarity of the tribe and paternal authority.

Yet we must also acknowledge that it is not just Third World civilizations that are involved in a race at breakneck speed between the forces of loyalty to the past and those of the future. The dialectic between wandering and rootedness, between universality and identity, between the individual and the community—in short, between modernity and tradition—should be recognized as a feature inherent in each civilization rather than as a feature that sets civilizations apart. This dialectic is present in democracy; moreover, it is what brought down communism, which had failed the test of freedom.

This is yet another reason to oppose civilizational fatalism in the name of cultural voluntarism. I believe that there can be no harmony among the peoples of this planet unless we admit that they are of common stock, and I am convinced that they are. I believe that over and above the differences between civilizations and historical pasts, this common stock can serve as the basis upon which to build what I will call the "universal minimum"—what is common to the messages of all the main religions and revolutions. Ultimately, this will lead us to the Code of Hammurabi, the *Upanishads,* and the Egyptian *Book of the Dead,* which also contain the truths that are found in the Decalogue and the Sermon on the Mount. I also believe that, although intervention by a single power has every chance of being colonialist, assistance from a community of nations may sometimes be a duty, especially with reference to ensuring this "universal minimum."

We must therefore act on the assumption that the nation and democracy are able (indeed, that it is in their very nature) to be integrated into a larger entity without themselves dissolving. This is already the case, for the moment at any rate, with regard to the various confederations and nations that constitute the European entity. In fact, nothing is more exalting today than to watch Europe build itself up amidst trials, tribulations, vexations, and hesitations. Great achievements are never painless; giving birth is never devoid of risks. It is high time that we become aware of the period we are living in and learn to outgrow the blind belief that leads us to admire our political leaders only when they have won a war.

The great American journalist James Reston used to say that the greatest man of the century was Jean Monnet, who came up with the idea of Europe and got it successfully under way. I have not always agreed with Reston. I knew Jean Monnet well; he did not have what I found so compelling at the time, what Miguel de Unamuno called the "tragic sense of life." Yet I join with Monnet in favoring the federation of democratic nations because the nation is halfway between the individual and the universal, and as such only it can enable *the universal to take root.*

NOTES

1. Samuel P. Huntington, "The West: Unique, Not Universal," *Foreign Affairs* 75 (November–December 1996): 28–46.

2. Ibid., 28–29.

3. Ibid., 44.

4. Ibid., 41.

5. Strobe Talbott, "Democracy and the National Interest," *Foreign Affairs* 75 (November–December 1996): 47–63.

6. Ibid., 47.

7. Ibid., 48.

8. Ibid., 48.

9. Ibid., 49.

10. Ibid., 50, 53–54.

11. Ibid., 56.

12. Ibid., 59.

13. Ibid., 63.

14. Ibid., 63.

8

FEDERALISM AND DEMOCRACY

Alfred Stepan

Alfred Stepan, who was Gladstone Professor of Government at Oxford University in 1996–99, is now Wallace Sayre Professor of Government at Columbia University. His many books include Problems of Democratic Transition and Consolidation: Southern Europe, South America, and Post-Communist Europe *(with Juan J. Linz, 1996) and* Rethinking Military Politics: Brazil and the Southern Cone *(1988). A much fuller version of this essay will appear in his book* Arguing Comparative Politics, *which will be published by Oxford University Press in the spring of 2000. He is working with Juan Linz on a larger project on federalism that will culminate in a jointly authored book,* Federalism, Democracy and Nation.

For those of us interested in the spread and consolidation of democracy, whether as policy makers, human rights activists, political analysts, or democratic theorists, there is a greater need than ever to reconsider the potential risks and benefits of federalism. The greatest risk is that federal arrangements can offer opportunities for ethnic nationalists to mobilize their resources. This risk is especially grave when elections are introduced in the subunits of a formerly nondemocratic federal polity prior to democratic countrywide elections and in the absence of democratic countrywide parties. Of the nine states that once made up communist Europe, six were unitary and three were federal. The six unitary states are now five states (East Germany has reunited with the Federal Republic), while the three federal states—Yugoslavia, the USSR, and Czechoslovakia—are now 22 independent states. Most of post-communist Europe's ethnocracies and ethnic bloodshed have occurred within these postfederal states.

Yet in spite of these potential problems, federal rather than unitary states are the form most often associated with multinational democracies. Federal states are also associated with large populations, extensive territories, and democracies with territorially based linguistic fragmentation. In fact, every single longstanding democracy in a territorially based multilingual and multinational polity is a federal state.

Although there are many multinational polities in the world, few of them are democracies. Those multinational democracies that do exist, however (Switzerland, Canada, Belgium, Spain, and India), are *all* federal. Although all these democracies, except for Switzerland, have had problems managing their multinational polities (and even Switzerland had the Sonderbund War, the secession of the Catholic cantons in 1848), they remain reasonably stable. By contrast, Sri Lanka, a territorially based multilingual and multinational unitary state that feared the "slippery slope" of federalism, could not cope with its ethnic divisions and plunged headlong into a bloody civil war that has lasted more than 15 years.

In addition to the strong association between multinational democracies and federalism, the six longstanding democracies that score highest on an index of linguistic and ethnic diversity—India, Canada, Belgium, Switzerland, Spain, and the United States—are all federal states. The fact that these nations chose to adopt a federal system does not *prove* anything; it does, however, suggest that federalism may help these countries manage the problems that come with ethnic and linguistic diversity. In fact, in my judgment, if countries such as Indonesia, Russia, Nigeria, China, and Burma are ever to become stable democracies, they will have to craft workable federal systems that allow cultural diversity, a robust capacity for socioeconomic development, and a general standard of equality among their citizens.

Consider the case of Indonesia, for example. It seems to meet all the indicators for a federal state. It has a population of over 200 million, and its territory is spread across more than 2,000 inhabited islands. It has great linguistic and ethnic fragmentation and many religions. Thus it is near the top in virtually all the categories associated with federalism. If Indonesia is to become a democracy, one would think that it would have to address the question of federalism or decentralization. Yet at a meeting of Indonesian political, military, religious, and intellectual leaders that I attended after the fall of Suharto, most of the participants (especially those from the military) rejected federalism out of hand because of secessionist conflicts at the end of Dutch colonial rule. Indonesia should at least consider what I call a *federacy* to deal with special jurisdictions like Aceh or Irian Jaya. A federacy is the only variation *between* unitary states and federal states. It is a political system in which an otherwise unitary state develops a federal relationship with a territorially, ethnically, or culturally distinct community while all the other parts of the state remain under unitary rule. Denmark has such a relationship with Greenland, and Finland with the Aaland Islands.

A Misleading Picture of Federalism

In seeking to understand why some countries are reluctant to adopt federal systems, it is helpful to examine what political science has had to say about federalism. Unfortunately, some of the most influential works in political science today offer incomplete or insufficiently broad definitions of federalism and thereby suggest that the range of choices facing newly democratizing states is narrower than it actually is. In large part, this stems from their focusing too exclusively on the model offered by the United States, the oldest and certainly one of the most successful federal democracies.

> *American-style federalism embodies some values that would be very inappropriate for many democratizing countries, especially multinational polities.*

One of the most influential political scientists to write about federalism in the last half-century, the late William H. Riker, stresses three factors present in the U.S. form of federalism that he claims to be true for federalism in general.[1] First, Riker assumes that every longstanding federation, democratic or not, is the result of a bargain whereby previously sovereign polities agree to give up part of their sovereignty in order to pool their resources to increase their collective security and to achieve other goals, including economic ones. I call this type of federalism *coming-together federalism*. For Riker, it is the only type of federalism in the world.

Second, Riker and many other U.S. scholars assume that one of the goals of federalism is to protect individual rights against encroachments on the part of the central government (or even against the "tyranny of the majority") by a number of institutional devices, such as a bicameral legislature in which one house is elected on the basis of population, while in the other house the subunits are represented equally. In addition, many competences are permanently granted to the subunits instead of to the center. If we can call all of the citizens in the polity taken as a whole the *demos,* we may say that these devices, although democratic, are *"demos-constraining."*

Third, as a result of the federal bargain that created the United States, each of the states was accorded the *same* constitutional competences. U.S. federalism is thus considered to be constitutionally *symmetrical.* By contrast, *asymmetrical* arrangements that grant different competencies and group-specific rights to some states, which are not now part of the U.S. model of federalism, are seen as incompatible with the principled equality of the states and with equality of citizens' rights in the postsegregation era.

Yet although these three points are a reasonably accurate depiction of the political structures and normative values associated with U.S. federalism, most democratic countries that have adopted federal systems have chosen not to follow the U.S. model. Indeed, American-style federalism embodies some values that would be very inappropriate for many democratizing countries, especially multinational polities. To explain what I mean by this, let me review each of these three points in turn.

"Coming-Together" vs. "Holding-Together"

First of all, we need to ask: How are democratic federal systems actually formed? Riker has to engage in some "concept-stretching" to include all the federal systems in the world in one model. For example, he contends that the Soviet Union meets his definition of a federal system that came about as the result of a "federal bargain." Yet it is clearly a distortion of history, language, and theory to call what happened in Georgia, Azerbaijan, and Armenia, for example, a "federal bargain." These three previously independent countries were conquered by the 11th Red Army. In Azerbaijan, the former nationalist prime minister and the former head of the army were executed just one week after accepting the "bargain."

Many democratic federations, however, emerge from a completely different historical and political logic, which I call *holding-together federalism*. India in late 1948, Belgium in 1969, and Spain in 1975 were all political systems with strong unitary features. Nevertheless, political leaders in these three multicultural polities came to the decision that the best way—indeed, the only way—to hold their countries together in a democracy would be to devolve power constitutionally and turn their threatened polities into federations. The 1950 Indian Constitution, the 1978 Spanish Constitution, and the 1993 Belgian Constitution are all federal.

Let us briefly examine the "holding-together" characteristics of the creation of federalism in India to show how they differ from the "coming-together" characteristics correctly associated with the creation of American-style federalism. When he presented India's draft constitution for the consideration of the members of the constituent assembly, the chairman of the drafting committee, B.R. Ambedkar, said explicitly that it was designed to maintain the unity of India—in short, to hold it together. He argued that the constitution was guided by principles and mechanisms that were fundamentally different from those found in the United States, in that the Indian subunits had much less prior sovereignty than did the American states. Since they had less sovereignty, they therefore had much less bargaining power. Ambedkar told the assembly that although India was to be a federation, this federation was created not as the result of an agreement among the states, but by an act of the constituent assembly.[2] As Mohit Bhattacharya, in a careful review of the constituent assembly, points out, by the time Ambedkar had presented the draft in November 1948, both the partition between Pakistan and India and the somewhat reluctant and occasionally even coerced integration of virtually all of the 568 princely states had already occurred.[3] Therefore, bargaining conditions between relatively sovereign units, crucial to Riker's view of how and why enduring federations are created, in essence no longer existed.

Thus one may see the formation of democratic federal systems as fitting into a sort of continuum. On one end, closest to the pure model of a largely voluntary bargain, are the relatively autonomous units that "come together" to pool their sovereignty while retaining their individual identities. The United States, Switzerland, and Australia are examples of such states. At the other end of the democratic continuum, we have India, Belgium, and Spain as examples of "holding-together" federalism. And then there is what I call "putting-together" federalism, a heavily coercive effort by a nondemocratic centralizing power to put together a multinational state, some of the components of which had previously been independent states. The USSR was an example of this type of federalism. Since federal systems have been formed for different reasons and to achieve different goals, it is no surprise that their founders created fundamentally different structures. This leads us to our next point.

"*Demos*-Constraining" vs. "*Demos*-Enabling"

Earlier, I described American-style federalism as "*demos*-constraining." In some respects, all democratic federations are more "*demos*-constraining" than unitary democracies. There are three reasons for this. First, unitary democracies have an open agenda, as Adam Przeworski points out, while in a federal democracy the agenda of the *demos* is somewhat restricted because many policy areas have been constitutionally assigned to the exclusive competence of the states.[4] Second, even at the center there are two legislative chambers, one (in theory) representing the one person–one vote principle, and the other representing the territorial principle. Third, because jurisdictional disputes are a more difficult and persistent issue in federal than in unitary systems, the judiciary, which is not responsible to the *demos,* is necessarily more salient and powerful.

Riker sees the *demos*-constraining aspect of federalism (and the weak politywide political parties normally associated with federalism) as basically good, because it can help protect individual rights from being infringed by the central government's potential for producing populist majorities.[5] But when examined from the point of view of equality and efficacy, both of which are as important to the consolidation of democracy as is liberty, the picture becomes more complicated. The deviation from the one citizen–one vote principle that federalism necessarily implies may be seen as a violation of the principle of equality. Overrepresentation in the upper house, combined with constitutional provisions requiring a supermajority to pass certain kinds of legislation, could, in certain extreme cases, lead to a situation in which legislators representing less than 10 percent of the electorate are able to thwart the wishes of the vast majority. This raises serious questions for the efficacious and legitimate functioning of democracy. If one were interested only in creating a system that best reflects the *demos* and that functions as an effective democracy, a case could be made that the democratic values of participation, decentralization, and equality would be better addressed in a unitary system that has decentralized participation than in a federal system. But if a polity has great linguistic diversity, is multinational, and is very large, its chances of being a democracy are much better if it adopts a federal system.

If federal systems were forced to adhere to the Rikerian model, multinational democracies would be faced with a stark choice: If they wished to adopt a federal system to reduce ethnic, religious, or linguistic tensions, they could do so only at the risk of severely constraining majority rule. But if we look at the federal systems that actually exist in the world, we see that not all federal systems are *demos*-constraining to the same degree. American-style federalism is *demos*-constraining, and Brazil is the most *demos*-constraining federation in the world. Yet the German federal system is much more *demos*-enabling than that of the United States, and India's is even more *demos*-enabling than Germany's. We can, in fact, construct a continuum, ranging from federal systems that are *demos*-constraining to those that are *demos*-enabling. Where a particular federal system lies on this continuum is largely determined by the nature of the party system, which I discuss elsewhere, and by three constitutionally embedded variables: 1) the degree of overrepresentation in the upper chamber; 2) the policy scope of the territorial chamber; and 3) the sorts of policy issues that are off the policy agenda of the *demos* because they have been allocated to the states or subunits.

1) Overrepresentation in the territorial chamber. I think it is fair to argue that the greater the representation of the less populous states (and therefore the underrepresentation of the more populous states), the greater the *demos*-constraining potential of the upper house will be. The United States and Brazil follow the same format: In both countries, each state gets the same number of senators. Since Wyoming had a population of 453,000 and California had a population of 30 million in 1990, this meant that one vote for a senator in Wyoming was worth 66 votes in California. In Brazil, the overrepresentation is even more extreme. One vote cast for senator in Roraima has 144 times as much weight as a vote for senator in São Paulo. Moreover, Brazil and Argentina are the only democratic federations in the world that replicate a version of this overrepresentation in the lower house. With perfect proportional representation, São Paulo should have 114 seats. It actually has 70. With perfect representation, Roraima should have one seat. It actually has eight. The Brazilian Constitution, inspired by the ideology of territorial representation, specifies that no state can have more than 70 seats in the lower house (thereby partially disenfranchising São Paulo) and that no state can have fewer than eight.

Yet the principle of equal representation of each state in the upper house is not democratically necessary and may even prove to be a disincentive to multinational polities that contemplate adopting a federal system.

The principle of equal representation of each state in the upper house is not democratically necessary and may even prove to be a disincentive to multinational polities that contemplate adopting a federal system.

Many democratic federations have quite different formulas for constructing their upper houses. In Germany, the most populous states (or *Länder*) get six votes in the upper chamber, those of intermediate size get four, and the least populous get three. Austria, Belgium, and India are still closer to the one person–one vote end of the continuum. If multilingual India had followed the U.S. pattern, it would not have been able to do some things that were absolutely crucial for political stability. Between 1962 and 1987, India created six new culturally distinctive states in the northeast, mostly carved out of Assam, a conflict-ridden region bordering Burma and China. If India had followed the U.S. model, these new states, containing barely one percent of India's population, would have had to be given 25 percent of all the votes in the upper chamber. The other Indian states would never have allowed this. Thus something democratically useful—the creation of new states, some of which were demanding independence by violent means—would have been difficult or impossible under the U.S. principle of representing each state equally.

The range of variation among the world's federal democracies can be seen in Table 1 on the following page. This table also illustrates what I said above about most federal democracies choosing not to follow the U.S. model. The United States, along with Brazil and Argentina, which follow the same model, is an outlier on this continuum. The first line measures the degree of inequality of representation according to the Gini index. The values range from 0, which indicates perfect one person–one vote representation, to 1, which indicates that one subunit has all of the votes in the upper house. Belgium's upper house has a Gini-index value of close to 0. Austria's is not much higher. India's is .10. Spain's is .31. The U.S. Gini-index value is almost .50, and Brazil's is .52. This means that the best-represented decile in the United States has 39 percent of the votes in the Senate; in Brazil, the best-represented decile has 43 percent of the votes. In India, it only has 15 percent. The variations are

TABLE 1—A CONTINUUM OF THE DEGREE OF OVERREPRESENTATION IN THE UPPER HOUSES OF 12 MODERN FEDERAL DEMOCRACIES[1]

GINI INDEX OF INEQUALITY[2]	Belgium .015	Austria .05	India .10	Spain .31	Germany .32	Canada .34	Australia .36	Russia[3] .43	Switzerland .45	U.S.A. .49	Brazil .52	Argentina .61
RATIO OF BEST-REPRESENTED TO WORST-REPRESENTED FEDERAL UNIT (ON BASIS OF POPULATION)	Austria 1.5/1	Belgium 2/1	Spain 10/1	India 11/1	Germany 13/1	Australia 13/1	Canada 21/1	Switzerland 40/1	U.S.A. 66/1	Argentina 85/1	Brazil 144/1	Russia 370/1
PERCENTAGE OF SEATS OF BEST-REPRESENTED DECILE	Belgium 10.8	Austria 11.9	India 15.4	Spain 23.7	Germany 24.0	Australia 28.7	Canada 33.4	Russia 35.0	Switzerland 38.4	U.S.A. 39.7	Brazil 41.3	Argentina 44.8

1. Complete information on all federal countries is contained in the Alfred Stepan–Wilfrid Swenden federal data-bank. We are grateful to Cindy Skach and Jeff Kahn for having provided us with the data on India and Russia, respectively. Other data were taken from *Whitakers Almanac* (London: J. Whitaker, 1977); *The Europa World Year Book* (London: Europa, 1995); and Daniel J. Elazar, ed., *Federal Systems of the World*. For the constitutional provisions on second chambers, see S.E. Finer, Vernon Bogdanor, and Bernard Rudden, *Comparing Constitutions* and A.P. Blaustein and G.H. Flanz, *Constitutions of the Countries of the World* (Dobbs Ferry, New York: Oceana, 1991).

2. The Gini coefficient equals zero if the composition of the upper chamber is fully proportional and equals one if one subunit has all the votes in the second chamber. Arend Lijphart was among the first authors to use the Gini coefficient as a measure of inequality for the composition of second chambers. See Arend Lijphart, *Democracies: Patterns of Majoritarian and Consensus Government in Twenty-one Countries* (New Haven, Conn.: Yale University Press, 1984), 174.

3. The status of Russia as a democracy is the most questionable of the 12 countries in the table. The data are included for comparative purposes.

immense. On this indicator, the United States is clearly on the *demos-constraining* end of the continuum.

2) Policy scope of the territorial chamber. Now let us turn to our second variable, the competences of the territorially based chamber. My proposition is that the greater the competences of the territorial house, the more the *demos*—which is represented on a one person–one vote basis in the lower house—is constrained. In the United States, the lower house has a somewhat more important role than the Senate in budget initiation, but if one takes into account the Senate's constitutionally exclusive prerogatives to advise and consent on judicial, ambassadorial, and major administrative appointments, the two houses come fairly close to policy-making parity. On this variable, Brazil has the most *demos-constraining* system in the world. There is no area that the Brazilian Senate does not vote on, and there are 12 areas where it has exclusive competence, including authority to set limits on how much states can borrow.

As we can see in Table 2 on the following page, however, other federal democracies do not give the upper house as much policy scope as they give the lower house. The German, Spanish, and Indian systems are less *demos*-constraining, because their upper houses are less unrepresentative and less powerful. While in Brazil senators representing 13 percent of the total electorate can block ordinary legislation (and in the United States, a committee chairman alone can at times block important nominations), in Germany important bills are seldom vetoed by the upper chamber. How can we account for such a difference? First of all, the upper chamber cannot participate in the two most important legislative votes, those for government formation and government termination. This power is the exclusive competence of the lower chamber. Second, the upper chamber can delay, but not veto, bills that do not directly involve the *Länder*. Third, on the approximately 50 percent of the bills that the upper chamber can theoretically veto because they do relate directly to the *Länder*, it seldom does so after closed-door reconciliation meetings are held in the joint committee representing both houses.

In Spain, Belgium, India, and Austria, as well as in Germany, only the lower house participates in no-confidence votes. In many countries, the upper house is largely a revisionary chamber, although it has a major role in anything having to do with federal intervention. In Spain, for example, if the government wishes to take action against a regional government that is in contempt of the constitution, the decision must be approved by two-thirds of the upper house. This, in my view, is entirely appropriate.

3) The degree to which policy-making authority is constitutionally allocated to subunits. The third constitutionally embedded variable on

TABLE 2—A CONTINUUM OF THE UPPER CHAMBER'S CONSTITUTIONAL PREROGATIVES TO CONSTRAIN A MAJORITY AT THE CENTER

| Least Constraining ⟶ | | | | Most Constraining |
INDIA	SPAIN	GERMANY	UNITED STATES	BRAZIL
The territorial chamber has no constitutional powers to protect subunit autonomy against a 60-day central intervention. Upper chamber has capacity to review or deny "President's Rule" only after 60 days. Largely a revisionary chamber.	Major power is granted by Article 155 of the Constitution, which precludes intervention by the center unless it has received approval by an absolute majority of the upper house. Plays no role in constructive vote of no confidence or normal legislation. Largely a revisionary chamber.	Plays no role in constructive vote of no confidence. Can play a potential veto role only in that part of the legislative agenda that directly relates to center-subunit issues. Power has grown somewhat over the last 20 years. Conflicts between the two chambers are resolved in closed-door meetings.	Extensive capacity to block a democratic majority. Senate has the same voting rights on all legislation as the "one person–one vote" chamber. Has exclusive competence to confirm or deny all major judicial and administrative appointments. A committee chairman alone can at times block important nominations.	Excessive for the efficacious and legitimate functioning of democratic government. The extremely disproportional upper chamber must approve all legislation. The Senate has 12 areas of exclusive lawmaking prerogatives. Senators representing 13 percent of the total electorate can block ordinary legislation supported by senators representing 87 percent of the population.

which democratic federations differ greatly is the powers that are given to the *demos* at the center versus the powers that are constitutionally allocated to the states. The 1988 Brazilian Constitution is so extensively detailed that a great deal of ordinary legislation can be passed only by a supermajority. In Brazil, many specific provisions on state and municipal pensions, state banks (all the states have banks), and the right of states to tax exports were constitutionally embedded. This is extremely *demos*-constraining. When too many issues are constitutionally embedded, the result is profoundly undemocratic, because these issues cannot be decided by a normal majority. Almost everything of importance in Brazil is constitutionally embedded. In order to change the constitution, 60 percent of the members of both houses (both those present and those absent) must vote in favor of an amendment *twice*. In a country the size of a continent, with bad transportation, it is hard even to get 60 percent of the legislature to show up.

At the opposite end of the continuum (see Table 3 on the following page), India has a very *demos*-enabling constitution. At the time of its drafting, its authors were painfully aware that there were more than 15 languages spoken in the country that at least 20 million people could claim as their mother tongue. The boundaries of the states did not correspond with linguistic boundaries. To get the government closer to the people, the framers of the Indian Constitution had to respect the linguistic principle, so they decided (Article 3) that the lower house, by a simple majority vote, could eliminate any state, carve new states out of existing ones, or change their names. That is the sort of pro-vision that a "holding-together" federation can write. In a "states'-rights" federation like the United States, such a provision would be absolutely impossible. But if it had not been possible in India, the failure to realize the "imagined communities" of the country's hundreds of millions of non-Hindi speakers might have led to secession in a number of places.

The U.S. Constitution is even more difficult to amend than the Brazilian Constitution, but it is parsimonious, so the vast majority of legislation can be passed by ordinary majorities. In Spain, the main constraint on the majority at the center derives from the statutes of autonomy, which deal primarily with questions of culture and language. In Germany, many federal programs are administered by the *Länder*, but lawmaking and policy oversight remain the prerogative of the center.

Constitutionally Symmetrical vs. Asymmetrical

Let us now turn to a final point concerning the U.S. model. The U.S. Constitution, as discussed above, establishes a form of symmetrical federalism, which is bolstered by a certain normative disinclination on

TABLE 3—THE DEGREE TO WHICH POLICY MAKING IS CONSTITUTIONALLY ALLOCATED TO SUBUNITS OF THE FEDERATION

INDIA	GERMANY	SPAIN	UNITED STATES	BRAZIL
Does not constrain *demos*. Capacity to respond to minority desires by redrawing the boundaries of states. Probably should constrain the ease with which the majority can intervene in states. Since 1994 Supreme Court decisions give somewhat more protection to subunits from imposition of "President's Rule" from the center.	Federal Law explicitly given precedent over Land Law. Wide areas where lawmaking powers are either explicitly given to the center or are concurrent responsibilities. More tax money is spent by the *Länder* than by the center. Many federal programs are decentralized so as to be administered by the *Länder*, while lawmaking and policy oversight remains the prerogative of the center.	Major constraints on majority at the center derives from the statutes of autonomy. Occasional bargaining process if center needs votes of regional party during process of government formation.	Constitution is extremely difficult to amend but is parsimonious, so the vast majority of legislation can be passed as ordinary legislation. Power is horizontally shared at the center between three branches. Power is vertically devolved and shared in "marble-cake" federalism between the federal and the state governments.	1988 Constitution is so detailed about states' rights that much ordinary legislation can only be passed by exceptional majorities. States and municipalities had such extreme control over export taxes and banking that central government's fiscal and trade policy in 1989–96 was impeded. Some centralization of tax and bank policies in 1996–97 but extremely costly to the center.
Residual power with center.	Most powers are concurrent.	Residual power with center.	Residual power with states.	Residual power with states.

the part of Americans to accept the concept of collective rights. With the exception of Switzerland (where none of the political parties strictly represents any one linguistic or religious group), all of the multinational democracies are constitutionally asymmetrical: In order to hold the multinational polity together, they assign different linguistic, cultural, and legal competences to different states. Under the symmetrical American model, many of the things that are most essential in a multinational context cannot be accomplished. With the possible exception of the special case of Switzerland, *all* federations that are constitutionally symmetrical—Austria, Germany, Australia, the United States, Argentina, and Brazil—are mononational. India, Belgium, Canada, and Spain are multinational and their federations are all asymmetrical. (The Russian Federation is also asymmetrical, but, constitutionally, it does not yet work as a democratic federation.)

The concept of collective rights is in tension with the traditional American way of thinking about such matters, which is based on individual rights. It is true that a polity cannot be a democracy unless the individual rights of all citizens are enshrined in the constitution and a countrywide system of horizontal and vertical controls is credibly established to support these rights. Whatever rights the national subunits may possess, they cannot constitutionally or politically violate the rights of individual citizens. The enforcement of individual rights can be an obligation of both the center and the subunits, but the center cannot completely delegate responsibility for the establishment and maintenance of democratic rights and continue to be a democracy. Alexis de Tocqueville is very clear on this point. He admired the robust local associationalism of U.S. democracy but pointed out that the rule of law in the entire polity had to be guaranteed and enforced by the center.

In multinational polities, however, some groups may be able to participate fully as individual citizens only if they acquire, as a group, the right to have schooling, mass media, and religious or even legal structures that correspond to their language and culture. Some of these rights may be described as group-specific collective rights. Many thinkers in the liberal tradition assume that all rights are individual and universal and view any deviation from individualism and universalism with suspicion, but this assumption is open to question.

Let me conclude with four observations, partly drawn from studies of the historical development of democracy, about democratic group-specific rights (to use a term coined by the Canadian political philosopher Will Kymlicka).[6] First, individuals are indeed the primary bearers of rights, and no group rights should violate individual rights in a democratic polity. In democratic multinational federal states, this means that something like a bill of individual rights should be promulgated by the federal center, and any laws and social policies that violate it must fall outside the constitutionally guaranteed policy scope of the subunits.

Second, while individual rights are universal, it is simply bad history to argue that in actual democracies all rights have been universal. Frequently, the struggle to reconcile the imperatives of political integration with the legitimate imperatives of cultural difference has led countries to award certain minorities group-specific rights, such as those given to French-speaking Quebec in Canada, to cultural councils in Belgium, and to Muslim family courts in India. The key point is that it is the obligation of the democratic state to ensure that no group-specific right violates individual or universal rights.

Third, while individuals are the bearers of rights, there may well be concrete circumstances in which individuals cannot develop or exercise their full rights unless they are active members of a group that struggles for some collective goods common to most of its members. If, for example, the Catalans had not been given certain group-specific rights involving the public status of their own language, I doubt whether as individuals they could have become full democratic citizens of Spain. Similarly, I do not think Kurds will become full democratic citizens of Turkey unless they are granted certain group-specific rights (such as the right to Kurdish newspapers and radio stations in the southeast of Turkey, where Kurds are a majority).

Finally, although such group-specific rights may not be consistent with some nineteenth-century tenets of Anglo-Saxon liberal democracy or with the French idea of citizenship in a nation-state, they are consistent with a polity in which group rights do not violate individual rights, and they permit effective democratic citizenship and loyalty to be extended throughout the polity. They offer, in fact, one of the few ways to craft democracy successfully in the difficult and populous world of multi-national states.

The Limits of the U.S. Model

The U.S. model of federalism, in terms of the analytical categories developed in this article, is "coming-together" in its origin, "constitutionally symmetrical" in its structure, and "*demos*-constraining" in its political consequences. Despite the prestige of this U.S. model of federalism, it would seem to hold greater historical interest than contemporary attraction for other democracies.

Since the emergence of nation-states on the world stage in the aftermath of the French Revolution, *no* sovereign democratic nation-states have ever "come together" in an enduring federation. Three largely unitary states, however (Belgium, Spain, and India) have constructed "holding-together" federations. In contrast to the United States, these federations are constitutionally asymmetrical and more "*demos*-enabling" than "*demos*-constraining." Should the United Kingdom ever become a federation, it would also be "holding-together" in origin. Since it is extremely unlikely that Wales, Scotland, or Northern Ireland would have the same number of seats as England in the upper chamber of the new federation, or that the new upper chamber of the federation would be nearly equal in power to the lower chamber, the new federation would not be "*demos*-constraining" as I have defined that term. Finally, it would obviously defeat the purpose of such a new federation if it were constitutionally symmetrical. A U.K. federation, then, would not follow the U.S. model.

The fact that since the French Revolution no fully independent nation-states have come together to pool their sovereignty in a new and more powerful polity constructed in the form of a federation would seem to have implications for the future evolution of the European Union. The European Union is composed of independent states, most of which are nation-states. These states are indeed increasingly becoming "functionally federal." Were there to be a prolonged recession (or a depression), however, and were some EU member states to experience very high unemployment rates in comparison to others, member states could vote to dismantle some of the economic federal structures of the federation that were perceived as being "politically dysfunctional." Unlike most classic federations, such as the United States, the European Union will most likely continue to be marked by the presumption of freedom of exit.

Finally, many of the new federations that could emerge from the currently nondemocratic parts of the world would probably be territorially based, multilingual, and multinational. For the reasons spelled out in this article, very few, if any, such polities would attempt to consolidate democracy using the U.S. model of "coming-together," "*demos*-constraining," symmetrical federalism.[7]

NOTES

1. See William H. Riker, "Federalism," in Fred Greenstein and Nelson W. Polsby, eds., *Handbook of Political Science* (Reading, Mass.: Addison-Wesley, 1975) vol. 5: 93–172.

2. Ambedkar's speech is found in its entirety in: India. Constituent Assembly, *Debates: Official Report* (New Delhi: Manager of Publications, 1951) vol. II, 31–44.

3. Mohit Bhattacharya, "The Mind of the Founding Fathers," in Nirmal Mukarji and Balveer Arora, eds., *Federalism in India: Origins and Development* (New Delhi: Vikas, 1992), 81–102.

4. Adam Przeworski, "Some Problems in the Study of the Transition to Democracy," in Guillermo O'Donnell, Philippe C. Schmitter, and Laurence Whitehead, eds., *Transitions from Authoritarian Rule: Comparative Perspectives* (Baltimore: Johns Hopkins University Press, 1986), 47–63.

5. See William H. Riker, *Liberalism Against Populism: A Confrontation Between the Theory of Democracy and the Theory of Social Choice* (San Francisco: W.H. Freeman, 1982), 247–53. As Riker acknowledges, however, federalism may also give the majority in the subunits the power to limit the freedom of some of the citizens (as the history of the southern United States shows), making it difficult for the federal government to protect them.

6. See Will Kymlicka, *Multicultural Citizenship: A Liberal Theory of Minority-Rights* (Oxford: Clarendon, 1995). For a powerful argument by a distinguished legal theorist that group rights are often a precondition of individual rights, see Joseph Raz, *The Morality of Freedom* (Oxford: Clarendon, 1986), 193–216. For a political and philosophically acute discussion of these issues in India, see Rajeev Bhargava, "Secularism, Democracy, and Rights," in Mehdi Arslan and Jannaki Rajan, eds., *Communalism in India: Challenge and Response* (New Delhi: Manohar, 1994), 61–73.

7. The tentative arguments made in these concluding paragraphs will be developed analytically and empirically in much greater depth in *Federalism, Democracy and Nation,* a book being written by Juan J. Linz and myself.

9

DEMOCRATIZATION AND THE INTERNATIONAL COMMUNITY

Robert A. Pastor

Robert A. Pastor is professor of political science at Emory University and former director of the Latin American and Caribbean Program at the Carter Center in Atlanta (1985–98), where he organized international monitoring and mediating missions to more than 20 electoral processes in 15 countries in Latin America, the Caribbean, the Middle East, Africa, and Asia. The following essay is based on a lecture that he delivered on 4 July 1997 in Lisbon.

On this day, 221 years ago, the Continental Congress met in Philadelphia and approved Thomas Jefferson's draft of the Declaration of Independence. This historic document contains several features that are pertinent to the topic before us—the role of the world in national democracy. Due to their "decent respect for the opinions of mankind," the signers of the Declaration felt obliged to justify to the world their decision to "declare the causes which impel[led] them to the separation" from their mother country. The Founding Fathers of the United States understood that their freedom depended not only on their own struggle, but also on world support, or rather, on their ability to persuade other nations of the righteousness of their cause.

The Founding Fathers' defense was based not on national, cultural, or ethnocentric considerations, but on universal, inalienable, God-given rights: "We hold these truths to be self-evident: That all men are created equal; that they are endowed by their Creator with certain unalienable rights; that among these are life, liberty, and the pursuit of happiness." This was a declaration not just for Americans or the West; it was for all people. All human beings—whether Arab or European, Asian or African, rich or poor, educated or illiterate—know their interests, want to be free, and ought to be free.

The real thunderbolt in the Declaration followed: "To secure these [inalienable] rights, governments are instituted among men, deriving their just powers from the consent of the governed." This simple statement was as revolutionary as any ever written; it impugned the legitimacy of every government in the world because, with the partial exception of Great Britain (the country most threatened by the Declaration), all others were based on force, the divine right of kings, or "the mandate of heaven." None derived its powers from the people. The purpose of government, the Declaration said, was for the rulers to serve the people and not the other way around. The conscience of mankind was awakened that July 4, and monarchies everywhere were shaken.

Nearly one hundred years later, on the eve of America's most terrible war, Abraham Lincoln, pausing in Philadelphia en route to his inauguration, contemplated that day of independence and Jefferson's handiwork:

> It was not the mere matter of the separation of the colonies from the motherland; but something in that Declaration giving liberty, not alone to the people of this country, but hope to the world for all future time. It was that which gave promise that in due time the weights should be lifted from the shoulders of all men, and that all should have an equal chance. This is the sentiment embodied in that Declaration of Independence.[2]

The United States was born on 4 July 1776 of three simple, related ideas: 1) All the people of the world have the right to define their future; 2) we are all part of the human family; and 3) we depend on one another to secure these rights. That is why the Founding Fathers of the United States appealed to the opinions of mankind. That is why Jimmy Carter, in his inaugural address as president in 1977, declared: "Because we are free, we can never be indifferent to the fate of freedom elsewhere." Carter understood that freedom's power to shape the world derived from the nobility and the attractiveness of the idea: "The best way to enhance freedom in other lands is to demonstrate here that our democratic system is worthy of emulation."

Democracy does not arrive fully developed on a nation's doorstep. It is the result of struggle. Portugal is an example of a nation familiar with the struggle for democracy. Two decades ago, the people of this great nation, led by committed democrats such as Mário Soares, discarded centuries of authoritarianism and seized freedom.

Without diminishing the significance of the heroism of the Portuguese people, however, it is necessary to acknowledge—just as the Founding Fathers of the United States did in their own case—that part of the reason for democracy's success in Portugal was the support that the Portuguese received from abroad. In Germany, France, and Great Britain, social democrats lent their aid and support to democracy. The United States came late to this heroic endeavor, but in the end, U.S. Ambassador Frank Carlucci harnessed his country's true spirit to come to democracy's defense.

The issue before us today is the role and responsibility of the international community in the extension, preservation, and enhancement of democracy. Democracy is a national experiment, but if a people are denied their just rights by a dictator, what should the international community do?

The Conceptual Connection

The international community's legitimate role vis-à-vis national democracy has never been clearly defined. The charters of the United Nations and other international organizations offer conflicting guidance. On the one hand, the charters declare their support for democratic government as a universal right; on the other hand, they prohibit any intervention "in matters which are essentially within the domestic jurisdiction of any state." As national elections are undoubtedly a domestic matter, the combination of the two norms—the right of a people to have a democratic government and the right of a state to be free of outside intervention—made the democratic promise collectively unenforceable. Moreover, few governments were willing to support democracy abroad at the cost of other interests. Even Western democracies sometimes undermined democratic institutions when unfriendly governments came to power, as the United States did in Guatemala in 1954 and in Chile in 1970–73.

Only as the third wave of democratization waxed and the Cold War began to wane in the 1980s did the international community begin to find its voice on behalf of democracy. Foreign governments, nongovernmental organizations (NGOs), and intergovernmental organizations (IGOs) became increasingly important in facilitating democratic transitions and reversing unconstitutional coups.

Besides the obvious moral reason to defend democracy as the best system for securing human rights, there are two powerful security motives for doing so. First, democracy helps secure peace because, as we have learned, democracies rarely fight each other. It is worth noting that three authoritarian governments—South Africa, Brazil, and Argentina—all undertook deadly programs to develop weapons of mass destruction, even while denying that they were doing so. All three abandoned the programs when they became democracies. Whether the twenty-first century can avoid the scourges of war that marred the twentieth will depend to a great extent on whether the regimes in Russia and China, and to a lesser degree in Nigeria, Indonesia, Egypt, and Algeria, can make successful democratic transitions. If they succeed, they will have a positive effect on their neighbors and the world. If they fail, avoiding some form of regional or global conflict may prove difficult.

The second security reason for defending democracy is that it is the most powerful antidote to violence within states. There are three ways in which to handle ethnic and other divisions within states: 1) Divide up the state according to ethnic groups—an impractical option in most countries; 2) allow one ethnic group to dominate—a recipe for chronic instability; and 3) fashion a democratic formula that can ensure the rights of minorities and encourage coalitions across ethnic boundaries. Our collective minds must focus on making this third, democratic option a reality.

Most violent conflicts within nations do not involve ethnic differences. They tend to stem from a simple cause—the absence of popular suffrage. When people do not have the opportunity to change their governments peacefully, they use force. No less an authority than Che Guevara acknowledged that revolutions could not succeed against a government "which has come into power through some form of popular vote."[3] In short, democracy and peace are inextricably intertwined both within and among nations. The essential skills needed to manage a democratic government are compromise and negotiation, and these also help to manage relations among states. In contrast, authoritarian governments rely on force both internally and externally.

World peace and respect for human rights require the extension and preservation of democracy. The international community can achieve these goals in two ways: 1) by working within a state to facilitate and help consolidate a democratic transition; and 2) by forging among states a sturdy collective defense of democracy.

Facilitating Democratic Transitions

The first approach—facilitating democratic transitions within states— is a delicate one since transitions are primarily an internal challenge. For most countries, particularly those (like Russia, China, Nigeria, and Indonesia) whose transitions will affect the world's future, any attempt by the United States or other Western governments to try to "manage" a democratic process would undoubtedly evoke a negative, nationalistic response.

In the late 1980s, the international community found a way around the problem of sovereignty that had impeded earlier attempts to assist democracy from abroad. The breakthrough occurred in Nicaragua in August 1989 when the nationalistic Sandinista government invited the UN, the Organization of American States (OAS), the Carter Center, and dozens of other international organizations to observe Nicaragua's electoral process. The Sandinistas were so confident of their popularity and so fearful that the United States would not recognize their victory that they decided to invite trustworthy and credible international groups to monitor their country's elections.

Each invited group responded differently. The UN was quite hesitant initially, believing that election monitoring was beyond its mandate. The OAS had previously "observed" many elections, but had been passive in the face of transparent fraud. The Carter Center's Council of Freely Elected Heads of Government (a group of former and current presidents from the Americas) had observed Panama's election several months earlier, and when General Noriega had refused to explain the systematic pattern of irregularities, it had denounced the election as a fraud. Based on lessons it had learned from Panama, the Carter Center established a decisive precedent in Nicaragua.

Establishing fair rules for elections requires a certain level of trust among key political actors; in countries without a tradition of free elections, this trust is almost always lacking. In the case of Nicaragua before 1990, elections had always been manipulated by the incumbent regime, and the opposition's only path to power was violent revolution. When the incumbent Sandinistas announced elections in August 1989, the opposition united in a coalition called UNO, even though none of its members believed that the Sandinistas would permit free elections. For their part, the Sandinistas believed that the opposition would boycott the elections rather than risk losing. Left to themselves, the Nicaraguans would have been condemned to repeat their tragic past. Each side believed the worst of its opponents, and neither side had yet been disappointed.[4]

Beginning as "observers," the Council of Freely Elected Heads of Government gradually began to mediate the rules of the electoral game among Nicaraguans. The observers were able to surmount the problem of sovereignty because they did not represent states and because they had been invited. Their role was to listen, to distill the many complaints into specific problems, and to use their credibility and access to bring such problems to the attention of the authorities in a way that enhanced the prospects of their solution rather than the prospects of an election boycott. When problems are corrected, the opposition sees that the system can indeed respond to legitimate complaints. In Nicaragua, Haiti (in 1990), Guyana, and many other countries, this process of mediation kept all parties locked into the electoral process and ensured that all accepted the results in the end.

Today, there are many organizations playing different roles in facilitating democracy, and each group has distinct advantages. IGOs can mobilize vast resources, field large observation teams, and generate publicity, making it politically very costly for a government to try to rig an election. IGOs, however, have two liabilities. First, a country's government, one of the key players in an election, tends to be an IGO member, and the opposition often believes that the IGO is biased in favor of the incumbent. Mediation is difficult under such circumstances. Second, precisely because its members are states, IGOs tend to be very cautious about criticizing one of their own members. Although some IGOs have become more assertive, they rarely declare an election a fraud.

Party institutes are good at training political parties and civic groups in pollwatching and civic education. Other organizations, such as the International Foundation for Election Systems (IFES), provide election equip-ment and technical advice. By their presence, international monitors give confidence to voters that their vote will count and that voting will be safe because the world is watching. Since an opposition boycott can delegitimize the electoral process, international groups can increase the prospects for a genuine election if they mediate electoral reforms and level the electoral playing field. Monitors can deter fraud by credibly threatening to denounce it if it is detected, and, if they judge the election to be fair, they can encourage all sides to accept the results.[5] If local parties justifiably reject the results (as the opposition did in Haiti in June 1995, in Albania in May 1996, and in Algeria in 1997), the monitors should denounce the election as well (though few do so). A successful election is one in which the major parties accept and respect the results, which only occurs when they are convinced that the electoral process was fair. In transitional elections, such an outcome often requires a mediator.

Prodded by NGOs, the international community managed, through trial and error, to develop election-monitoring techniques that delegiti-mized leaders who rigged elections and assisted those who were demo-crats. NGOs have begun to play a critical role in advising local actors on the techniques of democracy, providing equipment, and mediating the rules of an election. Only rarely can foreign governments do the same. Their best role might be to finance and support both local and international NGOs, providing leverage at critical moments. There are times when a particular foreign government can indeed play the role of enforcer, but in the area of extending and preserving democracy, indivi-dual governments should take a back seat to the UN and regional organizations.

Democracy, of course, is more than just elections. To consolidate and deepen democracy, institutions need to be built. NGOs and IGOs should help their local counterparts to develop civil societies and advise them as they establish political parties, legislatures, and judicial systems.

The Collective Defense of Democracy

A distinguished line of scholars and statesmen from Immanuel Kant to Woodrow Wilson has sought to solidify democracy by devising sys-tems of collective defense. Carlos Tobar, an Ecuadoran diplomat, recom-mended that governments deny recognition to a regime that comes to power by violent means until it holds a free and popular election. The Tobar Doctrine was embedded in the Central American Peace Treaties of 1907 but was pretty much ignored.[6]

Fifty years later, Venezuelan president Romulo Betancourt reju-venated and modernized the doctrine. He urged nonrecognition of de facto regimes and their expulsion from the OAS. His proposal failed at the time because most OAS members were dictatorships, but by 1991, almost every country in the Americas had held competitive elections. In Chile in June of 1991, the OAS General Assembly passed the "Santiago Commitment," which deplored unconstitutional changes in government and called for an emergency meeting of OAS foreign ministers to discuss appropriate action if such an event were to occur.

Three months later, the Haitian military overthrew President Jean-Bertrand Aristide, and the Santiago Commitment was put to the test. During the next three years, the OAS and the UN gradually ratcheted up sanctions against the military regime, culminating finally with UN Security Council Resolution 940 in July 1994 authorizing member states to use whatever means necessary to implement UN resolutions calling for Aristide's return.

President Clinton's leadership produced this watershed event, marking the first time that the UN defined the interruption of democracy as a threat to international peace and authorized force to respond to that threat. Armed with this resolution and President Clinton's decision to use force, former president Jimmy Carter, Senator Sam Nunn, and General Colin Powell negotiated an agreement that returned Aristide to power without an actual invasion. I was privileged to advise that mission and asked to remain in Haiti to ensure that the agreement was implemented. It was the most intense negotiation that I ever witnessed. The threat of force preoccupied the minds of the Haitian military, but the only reason why the negotiations succeeded was that Carter, Nunn, and Powell did not brandish that threat: They allowed the Haitian military the space to define their exit.

Haiti was the most forceful example of collective intervention on behalf of democracy, but there were many other important cases where the international community called to account those leaders who appeared to endanger a democratic transition. Shortly after President Alberto Fujimori of Peru closed his country's Congress in early 1992, the OAS General Assembly met. Fearful of being condemned by his colleagues, Fujimori journeyed to the meeting in the Bahamas. This was an unprecedented session, the first time that a sitting president had felt the need to explain and defend his actions before a committee of his neighbors. Fujimori promised the group that he would conduct elections for a constituent assembly soon.

Though Fujimori fulfilled his promise, many member states remained worried about the precedent that had been set. Thus the following year, on 25 May 1993, when Guatemalan president Jorge Serrano illegally closed his country's Congress, the international community was much more forceful and worked closely with an alliance of Guatemalan businessmen and military officers to replace the president with a human rights lawyer, Ramiro de Leon Carpio. In Paraguay in May 1996, army commander General Lino Oviedo rejected an order by the newly elected civilian president. The next day, Oviedo changed his mind, after receiving warnings from Brazilian and Argentine generals acting on the orders of their civilian presidents. Much had changed from the time 15 years earlier when generals in Brazil and Argentina gave orders to civilians and rejected any interference in their countries' internal affairs.

In December 1992 in Managua, the OAS met again and fulfilled Betancourt's request: They passed an amendment to the OAS Charter that would expel any regime installed by an unconstitutional seizure of power. At the same time, new civilian leaders explored innovative ways to strengthen their new democracies. Brazil, Argentina, Uruguay, and Paraguay attached a "democracy clause" to their common-market agreement, Mercosur. The agreement provides for the automatic expulsion of any member country in which the democratic process is interrupted.[7] Since 1991, the European Union, which earlier had used the attractiveness of its market as an incentive for southern European nations to democratize, has insisted on a "democracy clause" in each trade agreement it signs with a Third World government. The Organization on Security and Cooperation in Europe and the Council of Europe also have both played key roles in sustaining democracy in Europe.

In the last five years, Africa has experienced the widest swings between elections and military coups. The presence of international observers, according to Michael Bratton, has been "crucial in helping to extend or withhold political legitimacy to elected governments."[8] Despite the swing back to authoritarian governments in some African countries, there are some encouraging developments on the continent—for example, the Organization of African Unity's strong reaction when Sierra Leone's military overthrew its elected government in June 1997 and the efforts by Nigeria and other West African states to facilitate free elections in Liberia.

A Global Strategy

With the rapid spread of democracy throughout the world, scholars have debated whether to give priority to its consolidation where it has recently emerged or to its extension elsewhere. Samuel Huntington recommends that we concentrate on deepening new democracies in those Western countries (especially in Latin America) that have conducted competitive elections.[9] There is no doubting the fragility of the political institutions in these "electoral" democracies. The army retains considerable power and autonomy. The congress and the judiciary are often suborned by criminal elements or intimidated by the army or the president. If the third wave recedes, many of these democratic castles would turn to sand.

Consolidation is a precious task, but it is not clear why one has to choose between it and the "extension" of democracy, since substantial external resources are not needed to pursue either strategy. Still, if one must choose, I would favor extension over consolidation. In the course of reviewing the critical factors explaining the success of the democratic revolution in Portugal, U.S. Ambassador Frank Carlucci concluded: "It was the election [of 25 April 1975] which turned the situation around."[10] His perception is true not just for Portugal but for many other countries.

The "founding election" is a watershed event. Before crossing that threshold, a government can and usually does ignore its people and the "opinions of mankind." But once elections are accepted as the source of legitimacy and international observers are invited, an electoral logic takes hold. It becomes costly to manipulate the process, and as Panama's General Noriega learned in 1989, the cost of nullifying an election is greater than that of not having an election at all.

A democracy is not made by a single election, but it is not possible without it. As governments join the community of democratic nations, they encounter new constraints, both domestic and international, on undemocratic behavior. These constraints are the product of demands made by civil society, political leaders, and the international environment. The international community should aim to encourage as many countries as possible to step on the election treadmill so that they will begin to experience these constraints. At that point, a strategy to deepen these "electoral democracies" becomes not only possible but essential.

To promote the extension of democracy, democratic governments should forge caucuses in each region to improve collective defenses of democracy and to develop strategies to facilitate transitions and prevent reversals. The OAS, as we have seen, has taken a number of decisions to strengthen the collective message to potential coup-plotters. The record in preventing or overturning coups in the hemisphere in the 1990s has been good. Other regional institutions have also taken useful steps, and some leaders have offered new ideas.

Václav Havel, president of the Czech Republic, has proposed that NATO expand in a way that secures democracies in Central Europe.[11] This is a logical and powerful argument. Security in Europe today relies on democracy; the problem is that, rhetoric notwithstanding, NATO is a conventional military alliance that has given little thought to the problem of securing democracy. NATO did nothing to help Portuguese democracy when it admitted the Salazar dictatorship in 1950. And in June 1997, its position on the creeping military coup in Turkey was, at best, ambiguous. The process of expansion offers NATO leaders an opportunity to set up a working group not of military strategists but of experts on democratization to craft provisions for a new NATO charter that will give the organization the power to preserve democracy among its members.

Leaders might develop guidelines for monitoring threats to democracy and accept procedures to defend against those threats.

While no simple formula can be applied mechanically to all cases, there is a powerful idea that can be extracted from previous experience. Significant differences in religion, race, ethnicity, geography, language, and wealth exist within every state. Authoritarian regimes suppress these differences. Democratic governments, on the other hand, offer the best way to sort out such differences, guarantee the rights of minorities, and reduce the fears of all. The essence of the democratic challenge is to find a way to give all groups a stake in a process of peaceful change.

In the last decade, the international community, including governments, NGOs, and IGOs, has moved gradually but seriously to support national democracy. Yet much of its work has been uncoordinated and ad hoc. On this anniversary of the approval of a document that has inspired all peoples, I propose that the democratic leaders of the world dedicate themselves to a global strategy of democratization. By forging new bonds of solidarity, democratic governments and international institutions can create incentives for authoritarian governments to begin democratic transitions and can embarrass or sanction those that do not. The American comedienne Lilly Tomlin once quipped: "Together, we are in this alone." This statement neatly summarizes the democratic challenge confronting the world's nations. Democracy must be built by the people of a nation, but it can succeed only if the international democratic community is willing to help.

NOTES

1. Cited in Josef Joffe, "America the Inescapable," *New York Times Magazine,* 8 June 1997, 43.

2. Cited in *Recollected Works of Abraham Lincoln,* compiled and edited by Don E. and Virginia Fehrenbacher (Stanford, Calif.: Stanford University Press, 1997).

3. Quoted in Samuel P. Huntington, "The Modest Meaning of Democracy," in Robert A. Pastor, ed., *Democracy in the Americas: Stopping the Pendulum* (New York: Holmes and Meier, 1989), 24.

4. See Robert A. Pastor, *Condemned to Repetition: The United States and Nicaragua* (Princeton, N.J.: Princeton University Press, 1987).

5. See Jennifer McCoy, Larry Garber, and Robert Pastor, "Pollwatching and Peacemaking," *Journal of Democracy* 2 (Fall 1991): 102–14; David Carroll and Robert Pastor, "Moderating Ethnic Tensions by Electoral Mediation: The Case of Guyana," *Security Dialogue* (Oslo), (June 1993): 163–73; and Jennifer McCoy, "Mediating Democracy: A New Role for International Actors," in David Bruce, ed., *Security in A New World Order* (Atlanta: Georgia State University Press, 1992).

6. For an interesting essay on the Tobar Doctrine and why it failed in Central America in the first two decades of the twentieth century, see Charles L. Stansifer, "Application of the Tobar Doctrine to Central America," *The Americas* 23 (January 1967): 251–72.

For other ideas, see Robert Pastor, *Whirlpool*, ch. 10, "Promoting Democracy"; Robert Pastor, ed., *Democracy in the Americas*, ch. 11, "How to Reinforce Democracy in the Americas: Seven Proposals"; Tony Smith, *America's Mission: The United States and the Worldwide Struggle for Democracy* (Princeton, N.J.: Princeton University Press, 1994); and Gregory Fossedal, *The Democratic Imperative: Exporting the American Revolution* (New York: Basic Books, 1989).

7. "Inter-American Affairs: Mercosur to Adopt Democracy Clause," *O Estado de Sao Paulo*, reprinted in *FBIS* 26 (June 1996), 3.

8. Michael Bratton, "Deciphering Africa's Divergent Transitions," *Political Science Quarterly* 112 (Spring 1997): 81.

9. Samuel P. Huntington, "After Twenty Years: The Future of the Third Wave," *Journal of Democracy* 8 (October 1997): 3–12.

10. Kenneth Maxwell, *The Making of Portuguese Democracy* (Cambridge: Cambridge University Press, 1995), 115.

11. Václav Havel, "NATO's Quality of Life," *New York Times Magazine*, 16 May 1997.

IV

Religion, Morality, and Belief

10

PROMOTING DEMOCRACY, PEACE, AND SOLIDARITY

Andrea Riccardi

Andrea Riccardi is president and founder of the Community of Saint Egidio, a lay Catholic nongovernmental organization whose activities he describes in this essay. Saint Egidio received the 1997 World Methodist Peace Award for its successes in brokering the 1992 Mozambique Peace Accord, of which Professor Riccardi was one of four mediators. He has published more than ten books and is the main promoter of the international meetings on Prayers for Peace. He is also professor of history at the University of Rome.

On 4 October 1992, the government of Mozambique signed a peace agreement with leaders of the Mozambican National Resistance (Renamo) insurgency, ending the terrible civil war that had torn the country apart for well over a decade. This agreement was possible in part because of the mediation provided by the Community of Saint Egidio, a Rome-based lay Catholic nongovernmental organization. This happy episode raised the Community's profile and occasioned numerous questions about it. Was it, for instance, an emanation of the Vatican? Was it somehow an agency of the Italian government? How could it be that a Community so committed to the poor and to their needs had played such an active part in a diplomatic process? The answer to each of the first two questions is no. As for the third, I can best suggest its answer by offering my reflections and my witness regarding the 30-year journey of a group of people who have been struggling to make democracy, peace, and solidarity realities in their own lives and in that of the world.

The experience of the Community of Saint Egidio has been centered on this effort. We are not an emanation of anything but a group of men and women, Christians, free lay people, who try to live out the true meaning of democracy, peace, and solidarity in Rome and the larger world. We were born in 1968, a time of crisis in Western democracy, as the young revolted against political, religious, and educational institutions, questioning their profound contradictions and demanding authenticity. As one of the students of '68, the Italian Jewish novelist Miro Silvera, has written in his novel *Il prigioniero di Aleppo* (The prisoner of Aleppo):

> In 1968, everything was up for discussion: bourgeois love, family, work, political commitment. One could have said almost anything about us, but surely not that we were arrivistes. We did not even know where we wanted to arrive; we wanted to change everything, while those who want to arrive do not want to change anything. Our generation was a laboratory generation that tested on its own skin the discomfort and the purity of change, losing every time.[1]

I agree with these words, except perhaps for the last part about "losing every time." It is not our history always to lose. In 1968, one had the feeling that everything could be changed, especially in the world of young people. This feeling expressed itself more in conflict than in construction—conflict in political life, in the Church, in the education system, in Western culture, and so on. This conflict contained a strong demand for authenticity.

In Europe and in the Americas, the well-to-do sons and daughters of the West, university students, felt an urge to be at the center of things. Many undertook a search for authenticity that took very different paths, some of them terrible. As for myself and some of my high-school classmates in Rome, all of us the children of rather affluent families, the thrust of 1968 met with another important force: the discovery of the Gospel of Christ. This "good news" saved us from the most tragic or ideological currents of '68. I remember the first meetings, the first steps, the first experiences; I remember the strong sense of encountering the Gospel as a word of truth, a word that would never mislead. If I had to identify the two major thrusts that moved the Community of Saint Egidio at its inception, I would have to add to the crisis of democracy in 1968 some mention of the Second Vatican Council. The Council, a three-year series of meetings of the world's Catholic bishops convened in 1962 by Pope John XXIII (1958–63), outlined a new path for the Church in the contemporary world. This path is one of faithfulness to the Gospel and, at the same time, of empathy for contemporary men and women.

The Council's premier document, the *Pastoral Constitution on the Church in the Modern World* (known as *Gaudium et spes,* from the first words of its Latin text), begins by speaking of this empathy: "The joys and the hopes, the sadness and the anguish of the people of today, especially of the poor and of all those who suffer, are the joys and the hopes, the sadness and the anguish of the disciples of Christ, and there is nothing genuinely human that cannot find an echo in their hearts." Sometimes, certain words signify well the world into which one is born. The Gospel, we realized, is a word of empathy—unquestionable, inasmuch as it comes from God—offered to contemporary men and women. This word generated an attitude of respect, but at the same time an attitude of closeness in which the hopes and anguish of all were shared.

Dialogue and Solidarity

For our generation, the Second Vatican Council signified a profound detaching of Christian experience from political authoritarianism. This was no secondary matter, for the lack or incompleteness of such detachment had been *the* problem of the Catholic world between the two world wars. The Council ushered in the full acceptance of religious freedom and pluralism. Also vital is the conviction that Christian life matures more profoundly in democracy and freedom. We have distanced ourselves from the negative utopia of the authoritarian state that rules by imposition and that does not favor the appeal to conscience. Sometimes those who are the carriers of values, whether because of an ancient authoritarian tradition, a lack of conviction, or a fear that the required spiritual change will be too great, find it hard to accept the diversity of the other. This is the story of many religious, national, or ideological fundamentalisms, but it is one that I do not have room to explore here.

For our generation, pluralism and democracy are the path for believers, and the presence of Christians along this path has been crucial. Democracy, in fact, stimulates the responsibility for one's own convictions and not a confused conscience. I have always been touched by what Albert Camus, the great secular French writer, said to the Dominican priests and brothers of Latour-Maubourg in 1946, at a time in which it was not easy for Catholics and nonbelievers to talk to each other:

> I shall not try to modify anything of what I think or of what you think to reach a conciliation that would be pleasing for all. On the contrary, what I want to say to you today is that the world needs true dialogue, that the opposite of dialogue is, at the same time, lies and silence, and thus there is no possible dialogue if not between people who remain as they are and who speak sincerely. This brings me to say that the world of today needs Christians who remain Christians.[2]

The season of pluralism and democracy in which we live needs men and women who hold strong convictions, but who at the same time realize the need for dialogue. In the heart of '68 as in the following years, on the streets of Rome, on the roads of the world, and in the poorer areas of cities, the Community of Saint Egidio has lived a commitment to dialogue, believing that this is the true expression of convinced Christians who are rooted in the Gospel. Indeed, a Christian community *is* a dialogue: between men and women, between different generations, between different cultures. Faith itself, as Pope Paul VI said in his encyclical *Ecclesiam Suam,* is "dialogue between God and men." No one can impose a world made in his or her own image.

But I would not like to give the impression that Saint Egidio is an organization of intellectuals. First as young people and now as not-so-young people, we have lived our dialogue in solidarity with the other. During our years of existence, we have lived in close proximity to the poorest, both in Rome and in the slums of many other cities of the world. These are the truly other, so often excluded from solidarity and from dialogue. We students discovered another world, the world of misery, a misery that was close at hand but often ignored.

This is how the 15,000 members of the Community live. We share the joys and hopes, the anguish and sorrows, of all, but especially of the poor. For us, solidarity does not mean trying to substitute for public institutions. We have considered the poor as friends and relatives of ours. This is the spirit that moves our work and the services provided by the members of the Community of Saint Egidio, whether helping immigrants, the elderly, those with mental or physical handicaps, the homeless, or people with AIDS. All this work is done in a completely voluntary way, in addition to each community member's job and ordinary civic commitments. Everyday people with families and jobs, the members of the Community of Saint Egidio listen to the Gospel and live in concrete solidarity with the poor. This is solidarity inside the great urban misery, where the difficulty of living is made heavier by loneliness and isolation.

I could cite many forms of poverty, but here I only want to talk about one, that of the elderly. Contemporary societies have achieved great success in prolonging life, but in a subliminal way they send the message that old people have to be put aside. The continent of the elderly, and indeed it is already a continent, is the land of sunset—a land where economic, religious, and political figures rarely venture. This land is foreign to our dreams, but it is nevertheless the land where all of us will eventually dwell (at least we all hope to live long enough to get there). It is the land of frailty. The Community has always lived in profound solidarity with the world of the elderly. In a book by Paolo Barbaro, *La casa con le luci* (The house with lights), an old lady living in a retire-ment home tells a young girl: "Anything can knock down old people. A little bit of wind is enough. Down they fall. Here the wind is always strong, very strong. They fall down like leaves."[3] There is an old person inside each of us. The effort to run away from aging is the folly of our society.

Solidarity is the recognition that the poor and the nonpoor share a common destiny. It is the affirmation of a kinship that our society wants to deny. The culture of solidarity is, furthermore, a challenge to the view that competition is the only guiding value. It is a reservoir, an oasis of concern for the world of the poor, who are so far from our attention and who count for so little.

Working for Peace in Mozambique

What is Saint Egidio? Carlo Maria Martini, a Jesuit priest and Scripture scholar who worked with the Community in the 1970s and is now the cardinal archbishop of Milan, once said:

> What attracted me to them? They are the Church beginning once again from its origins. With the poverty of these situations and the Christian enthusiasm of the origins, Saint Egidio took its first steps. Their attention to the people who lived in the Roman slums explains their discovery of the themes, images, and sorrow which are proper to that reality: the cold of winter, the loneliness, the disease, the situation of women.[4]

Daily solidarity is the commitment of Saint Egidio, a Community that today is present in many European, African, and Latin American countries. On the day the Mozambican peace agreement was signed, a journalist from the *Washington Post* asked me when we had left our work with the poor in order to take up diplomatic work. I answered that they are the same work. I am still convinced of that. The struggle against poverty leads to struggle against war, the mother of all poverty. This is the story of our work in Mozambique. There we were working in the humanitarian and social field, but we realized that this was useless in a country paralyzed by war. The first problem was peace. We gradually realized that a group such as ours, even if it is not a government agency, may nonetheless bring a certain strength to bear on the side of peace.

The problem of peace has been decisive for Christian conscience in this century; as Christians, we have become aware of the absurdity of war. This awareness, however, penetrates slowly. Not until years after the Second World War, for instance, did we become aware of the full extent of the tragedy of the Holocaust. The long Cold War period was characterized by easy recourse to war, with many local conflicts serving as "proxy wars" between the two large blocs. After the end of the Cold War and its bipolar balance, dreams of peace gave way to other nightmares as the fragmentation of the older geopolitical framework allowed the use of armed conflict to spread even more widely. Since 1989, warmaking has become the province not only of the state but of groups below or outside the state. Political factions, criminal gangs, ethnic militias, and insurgent movements of various kinds have all learned that terrible weapons are widely available for use in winning disputes or forcing political changes.

The growth in recourse to war has been particularly pronounced in Africa, where the state is so often weak. Sometimes war becomes a chronic disease. But our experience has taught us that if war is possible for many, so also is peace. Many can work for peace, and not only states. Working for peace involves more than affirming principles or taking part in public demonstrations. To work for peace, we must move from affirmations of principle to actual encounters with those who make war.

Let us consider Mozambique in this context. The country suffered 16 years of war. A million Mozambicans lost their lives, while close to a million others became refugees, forced to flee to neighboring countries. The strife was said to be a conflict "by proxy" within the larger Cold War framework. In actuality, however, it resulted from a complex process that combined several different factors. Analysts declared at the time that there would be no stopping the war as long as South Africa remained under the apartheid regime. The government of President Samora Machel and his Mozambique Liberation Front (Frelimo) proposed at most to grant amnesty to the Renamo guerrillas, whom it dubbed "armed bandits." In reality, these "bandits" had drawn together most of the discontent that was roiling the country, particularly its northern and central regions, as a result of various changes that the Marxist-Leninist Frelimo government had made. These included efforts to reduce the power of traditional institutions and to suppress organized religion. Renamo achieved a degree of military success, though it remained incompetent in the area of civil politics and had no realistic prospect of coming to rule the country.

We were sure that the war could have dragged on with no clear result. The problem was to overcome the inhibitions that prevented all sides from entertaining the idea that peace was possible. Rejecting the predominant notion that peace would have to be imposed on Mozambique from the outside, we believed that peace could be—had to be—something that developed between the contending parties. But there were huge obstacles even to the basic task of setting up talks. The government feared that such contacts would tend to legitimate the guerrillas, while Renamo's leaders lacked the skills and political culture to conduct negotiations.

We decided that our first order of business was to get to know Renamo. For months, we worked with Archbishop Jaime Gonzálvez of Beira to establish a stable contact with Renamo's leaders. Our aim was to get them to come to Europe, where we hoped to make a convincing case that they should abandon the logic of purely military opposition. The moment at which the resolve to start talks ripened was when both sides realized that no one could win the war. Negotiations began in July 1990. They took place on the neutral ground of Saint Egidio, the old building in the Roman district of Trastevere that gives our Community its name.

The government's strategy was to treat the insurgency as a problem purely internal to Mozambique, while Renamo wanted to "internationalize" the conflict. The government pressed for an immediate cease-fire, while the guerrillas were adamant that they would not give up their weapons until a peace agreement was signed. The first major issue was the "status" of Renamo. It was resolved by a "preamble" to the talks that the parties adopted in the summer of 1991. In this document, the parties pledged to work together for peace. Renamo agreed to recognize the Frelimo regime as the government of Mozambique, while the government agreed to recognize the guerrilla movement as the opposition. This represented a success for Renamo, which now entered directly into the framework of the dialogue as a counterpart to the government, but it was also a success for the negotiations as such, for it entailed the affirmation that Mozambique had a state, with a political and juridical system. This underscored the existence of a common destiny and hence of a common interest in bringing an end to the unwinnable war.

The problem for peace was to pass from an armed struggle to a political one within the common framework of the state. At the beginning, a great number of mutual accusations—not all of them unfounded—seemed to hinder mutual recognition. My response was to acknowledge that there were great problems, both those left behind by the past and those lying ahead for the future. Aware of the potential for any problem to generate misunderstanding, I recalled a favorite expression of Pope John XXIII: "Let us try to find what unites us and put aside what divides us."

Readers should grasp the severity of the conflict that we were addressing. Many atrocities had been committed, as a matter of deliberate strategy, by both parties. Renamo wanted to put the government on trial; the government called Renamo a band of terrorists. There was also a certain "pathology of memory" at work: Each side's memories were important to its conception of its own legitimacy and could not be given up, but the bitter memories harbored by each side widened and deepened the great gap between them. How could we overcome the impasse and avoid the repetition of all those tragedies? The answer was to bring the government and the guerrillas to a recognition of each other as parts of the same country and the same state—parts in conflict, to be sure, but parts of the same entity nonetheless.

In the midst of these excruciatingly difficult negotiations, what instruments could we, the "nonprofessional" mediators, use to bring pressure to bear? We did not want our initiative to be isolated, and so worked to get the governments of various countries involved: Italy entered the mediation process directly, while the United States, Portugal, France, and Great Britain were accredited as observers. Private and public entities were thus united in a common effort. We had no economic leverage, but we did have the strength of representing Mozambican public opinion, which wanted peace. I will never forget how, at a critical juncture in the talks, we laid on the bargaining table a great number of petitions for peace submitted to us by Mozambican Christians. Among the many letters, the leader of the Renamo delegation found one from a parish in Beira that bore the signature of his father, whom he had not seen for years.

The negotiations lasted for two and a half years, including a six-month interruption that began in December 1990. Over time, they fostered evolution in the political culture of the guerrillas. The mentality of a guerrilla fighter feeds on unquestionable certainties and shapes itself in fierce opposition to a demonized enemy. This evolution took time, of course, but only a change of mentality could truly guarantee the passage from armed struggle to a political one. The government, for its part, faced the challenge of abandoning the logic of one-party rule and accepting democratic pluralism.

Also crucial was the climate of trust that we created. Both sides recognized our moral authority and our disinterestedness. The whole process, however, was more than a matter of human relations. On the contrary, it was a considerable achievement in terms of negotiations and documents. One indispensable achievement was the unification, under a June 1992 agreement reached at the Rome talks, of the two contending armed forces. The elections of October 1994 never could have gone forward—much less have enjoyed a chance of success—had the government forces and the insurgents waited for the returns with guns in hand, ready to take the field in the event of adverse result.

Avoidable Clashes

I have said a lot about our work for peace in Mozambique in order to explain something of the Community's methods. Other situations in which we were or are engaged include those in Burundi, Kosovo, Albania, Guatemala, and Algeria. In the last country, we have not had a mediating role, but we have denounced a violent crisis that is devouring an entire society. In the January 1995 Platform of Rome, signed by secular and democratic parties and by the Islamic Salvation Front (FIS), we proposed negotiations as a way of escaping the imprisoning logic of terrorism and state repression. The aim is to reestablish democratic institutions (such as elections) in hopes of linking democracy to a wider area of consensus. If democratic life does not resume, Algerians will remain hostages to the blind violence of terrorists and their opponents in a repressive, authoritarian regime. This is how a society becomes corrupted. The women who have been raped, the journalists who have been murdered, the children whose throats have been slit are representative victims in an Algeria that is the hostage of an insane war. Since January 1995, when we offered the opposition an opportunity to engage in dialogue and to propose a peace platform, twenty thousand more people have died, bringing the death toll to more than sixty thousand since 1992. Our most urgent goal is to avert the "Somaliazation" of Algeria. We are also striving to prevent any more sectors of Islamist opinion from drifting, tragically, toward the terrorism of the Armed Islamic Group. Although the situation does not appear very tractable, we will not resign ourselves to accepting such a devastating conflict.

Our commitment to peace is rooted in the conviction that some clashes are indeed avoidable, whether they be between opposing forces within a given country, or even between civilizations, cultures, or religions. It was in order to prevent such an avoidable clash that in 1993 we became involved in Kosovo, where the ethnic-Albanian majority living under the power of the Serb minority had begun a nonviolent struggle for cultural autonomy and political independence. Even without a profound knowledge of the Serb-Albanian conflict, we realized that the situation of the majority was unbearable. Hence we favored an agreement between Yugoslav president Slobodan Milošević and Ibrahim Rugova (the Albanian president of Kosovo) that would permit the reopening of the schools. We knew that the risk of violent explosions was high if the Albanian-speaking Kosovars were not guaranteed the possibility of living normally, without extra burdens and hardships imposed on them merely because of their ethnic identity. Events in the spring and summer of 1998 have borne us out. Our method in such volatile situations is to seek a negotiated *modus vivendi* regarding crucial aspects of life in the region (education, health care, and the like) while leaving open the larger question of a future settlement of the overall conflict.

Since 1989, we have seen religious identities play a crucial role both in cementing national identities and in hardening national conflicts. Many even speak of the resurgence of religious wars (I do not agree with this characterization, but it does suggest how religion can add fuel to the flames of war). As the case of the former Yugoslavia emphasized, the divide between Western civilization (secular and Christian) and the Muslim world is becoming a frontier of misunderstanding and sometimes of conflict. Fundamentalism is revealing a disturbing face, with its desire for the "totalization" of control over society, ostensibly for the sake of religion.

The Spirit of Assisi

In 1986, Pope John Paul II invited the leaders of Christian churches and of the great world religions to join him in Assisi, the birthplace of Saint Francis. They met to pray, not to debate. Amid Cold War divisions, the pope's intuition was simple and basic: Religions should encounter one another, without syncretism but also without hatred, never again one *against* the other. Despite all difficulties, the Community of Saint Egidio has sought to implement this initial intuition of Assisi. The power for peace that is present in the depths of each religion must emerge. For every religious tradition, peace is a fundamental and sacred value, even if in the historical experience of religions there have been seasons in which this value was either ignored or profaned. It is only by plumbing the depths of one's own religious tradition, stimulated by the problems of the world, that one can retrieve that sacred value. This purges hearts of their anger and educates to peace. The aim of religions—through different paths, to be sure—is to purify and pacify hearts: Holiness and peace, ethics and peace, prayer and peace, they all signify the same thing. Since 1986, the Community has invited leaders of different religious traditions to speak to one another, to pray together. I recall one such meeting on 1 September 1989 in Warsaw, a city that was anxiously thinking back exactly half a century to the beginning of the Second World War but that was also concerned about the contemporary changes that were taking place. I remember the pilgrimage to Auschwitz: Jews, Christians, and Muslims together. Every year this movement of people of faith, assembled to talk and to pray and to put peace at the center of their reflections, has grown.

Today, different religious worlds coexist in nearly every part of the planet. This can lead to growing respect for freedom and the identity of the other, or to tension and conflict. At the end of the twentieth century, a faith that does not develop a "theology of the other" is impoverished indeed. We have worked toward this end, not by convening congresses of intellectuals, but by promoting the encounter of religious leaders who, in some way, represent their people. I think of the first appeal that was signed by religious leaders in Rome at the end of the 1987 meeting: "Religion does not want war. May the word of religion always be peace! May men and women never find in the patrimony of their own religious traditions reasons or incitements to hate one other, to fight, to use war and oppression!"[5]

A path has opened, a path of religious recognition of "the other," of faith-inspired work for peace, of dialogue (undergirded by religious values) that enhances democratic respect for others. The Community of Saint Egidio has animated a pilgrimage shared by people from different religious traditions—Jews, Christians, Muslims, Buddhists, and Hindus. This pilgrimage has been complicated and yet simple. Our aim has not been some impossible unification but rather understanding of and respect for "the other" in all its diversity. Far from being a crusade of religions against secularism or modernity, this pilgrimage has always been intended to celebrate an important aspect of peace, that is, the ability to live both as an actively convinced and self-conscious bearer of one's own tradition and identity, and as a participant in fraternal and open dialogue.

These meetings, which typically gather about three hundred religious leaders from all over the world, have also been attended by important representatives from the secular world. I recall the words of Mário Soares, the former president of Portugal, who attended one of the meetings in Assisi: "[Religions] should not fight among themselves. I would ask religions—especially all the churches that are represented here—to multiply their initiatives for peace. Religions . . . must continue to promote encounter between people, united in the dignity of their own condition and of the immense mystery of living."[6]

A prominent Italian journalist listening to President Soares asked, "What, then, is faith, and what is the difference between a secular and a religious faith?" Such are the questions that arise along this path of dialogue, that of a pluralism which is full of a desire for interaction and full of strong convictions.

I realize that my account of our Community may seem fragmentary, moving through reflections on bringing peace out of war, on the need for dialogue among peoples and traditions, on the importance of a concrete solidarity with the poor, and on democracy. These are the elements of our life, fragmented and yet possessing a coherence of its own. This is our task, that of meeting people in the concrete circumstances of their lives, of going beyond walls, whether of diversity or ideology. The world of today displays a rich and complex diversity, but that does not mean that it is doomed to conflict. In closing, let me recall the words of the Koran (Chapter 5, Verse 48): "For every one of you We appointed a law and a way. And if Allah had pleased, He would have made you a single people, but that He might try you in what he gave you. So vie with one another in virtuous deeds. To Allah you will all return, so He will inform you of that wherein you differed."

NOTES

1. Miro Silvera, *Il prigioniero di Aleppo* (Milan: Frassinelli, 1996).

2. F. Chavanes, *Albert Camus: Un message d'espoir* (Paris: Cerf, 1996), 11–12.

3. Paolo Barbaro, *La casa con le luci* (Turin, Italy: Bollati Boringhieri, 1995).

4. Carlo Maria Martini, address to the Community of Saint Egidio on the occasion of the celebration of its 27th anniversary, 1995.

5. Final appeal of the Second International Meeting "People and Religions," Rome, October 1987.

6. Mário Soares, "Politica e religioni nella prospettiva della pace," in *Costruire la pace* (Cinisello Balsamo, Italy: Sanzanobi, 1996), 95–104.

11

BUDDHISM, ASIAN VALUES, AND DEMOCRACY

His Holiness the Dalai Lama

The Dalai Lama, the spiritual and temporal leader of the Tibetan people, fled Chinese-occupied Tibet into exile in India in 1959 with 80,000 Tibetans. When it became clear that they would not be able to return to their homeland any time soon, he established a government-in-exile with a democratically elected parliament in the hill town of Dharamsala in northern India. One of the world's great exponents of nonviolence, His Holiness was awarded the Nobel Peace Prize in 1989.

While democratic aspirations may be manifested in different ways, some universal principles lie at the heart of any democratic society— representative government (established through free and fair elections), the rule of law and accountability (enforced by an independent judiciary), and freedom of speech (exemplified by an uncensored press). Democracy, however, is about much more than these formal institutions; it is about genuine freedom and the empowerment of the individual. I am neither an expert in political science nor an authority on democracy and the rule of law. Rather, I am a simple Buddhist monk, educated and trained in our ancient, traditional ways. Nonetheless, my life-long study of Buddhism and my involvement in the Tibetan people's nonviolent struggle for freedom have given me some insights that I would like to discuss.

As a Buddhist monk, I do not find alien the concept and practice of democracy. At the heart of Buddhism lies the idea that the potential for awakening and perfection is present in every human being and that realizing this potential is a matter of personal effort. The Buddha proclaimed that each individual is a master of his or her own destiny, highlighting the capacity that each person has to attain enlightenment. In this sense, the Buddhist world view recognizes the fundamental sameness of all human beings. Like Buddhism, modern democracy is based on the principle that all human beings are essentially equal, and that each of us has an equal right to life, liberty, and happiness. Whether we are rich or poor, educated or uneducated, a follower of one religion or another, each of us is a human being. Not only do we desire happiness and seek to avoid suffering, but each of us also has an equal right to pursue these goals. Thus not only are Buddhism and democracy compatible, they are rooted in a common understanding of the equality and potential of every individual.

As for democracy as a procedure of decision making, we find again in the Buddhist tradition a certain recognition of the need for consensus. For example, the Buddhist monastic order has a long history of basing major decisions affecting the lives of individual monks on collective discourse. In fact, strictly speaking, every rite concerning the maintenance of monastic practice must be performed with a congregation of at least four monks. Thus one could say that the Vinaya rules of discipline that govern the behavior and life of the Buddhist monastic community are in keeping with democratic traditions. In theory at least, even the teachings of the Buddha can be altered under certain circumstances by a congregation of a certain number of ordained monks.

As human beings, we all seek to live in a society in which we can express ourselves freely and strive to be the best we can be. At the same time, pursuing one's own fulfillment at the expense of others would lead to chaos and anarchy. What is required, then, is a system whereby the interests of the individual are balanced with the wider well-being of the community at large. For this reason, I feel it is necessary to develop a sense of universal responsibility, a deep concern for all human beings, irrespective of religion, color, gender, or nationality. If we adopt a self-centered approach to life and constantly try to use others to advance our own interests, we may gain temporary benefits, but in the long run happiness will elude us. Instead, we must learn to work not just for our own individual selves, but for the benefit of all mankind.

While it is true that no system of government is perfect, democracy is the closest to our essential human nature and allows us the greatest opportunity to cultivate a sense of universal responsibility. As a Buddhist, I strongly believe in a humane approach to democracy, an approach that recognizes the importance of the individual without sacrificing a sense of responsibility toward all humanity. Buddhists emphasize the potential of the individual, but we also believe that the purpose of a meaningful life is to serve others.

Many nations consider respect for the individual's civil and political rights to be the most important aspect of democracy. Other countries, especially in the developing world, see the rights of the society—particularly the right to economic development—as overriding the rights of the individual. I believe that economic advancement and respect for individual rights are closely linked. A society cannot fully maximize its economic advantage without granting its people individual civil and political rights. At the same time, these freedoms are diminished if the basic necessities of life are not met.

Some Asian leaders say that democracy and the freedoms that come with it are exclusive products of Western civilization. Asian values, they contend, are significantly different from, if not diametrically opposed to, democracy. They argue that Asian cultures emphasize order, duty, and stability, while the emphasis of Western democracies on individual rights and liberties undermines those values. They suggest that Asians have fundamentally different needs in terms of personal and social fulfillment. I do not share this viewpoint.

It is my fundamental belief that all human beings share the same basic aspirations: We all want happiness and we all experience suffering. Like Americans, Europeans, and the rest of the world, Asians wish to live life to its fullest, to better themselves and the lives of their loved ones. India, the birthplace of Mahatma Gandhi and of the concept of *ahimsa,* or nonviolence, is an excellent example of an Asian country devoted to a democratic form of government. India demonstrates that democracy can sink strong roots outside the Western world. Similarly, our brothers and sisters in Burma, Indonesia, and China are courageously raising their voices together in the call for equality, freedom, and democracy.

The fact that democratic reforms are on the rise around the globe, from the Czech Republic to Mongolia, and from South Africa to Taiwan, is testimony to the strength of the ideals that democracy embodies. As more and more people gain awareness of their individual potential, the number of people seeking to express themselves through a democratic system grows. These global trends illustrate the universality of the desire for a form of government that respects human rights and the rule of law.

The Case of Tibet

I am deeply committed to the political modernization and democratization of my native Tibet and have made efforts to develop a democratic system for Tibetans living in exile. In 1963, I promulgated the democratic constitution of Tibet, and our exiled community has, under difficult circumstances, responded well to the challenge of this experiment with democracy. In 1969, I declared that whether the institution of the Dalai Lama should continue to exist depended on the wishes of the Tibetan people. And in 1991, our legislature, the Assembly of Tibetan People's Deputies, adopted the Charter of Tibetans in Exile, which expanded the Assembly's membership and transferred from me to it the power to elect the Cabinet. While this Charter was modeled on constitutions from established democracies, it also reflects the unique nature of the Tibetan culture and system of values: It protects freedom of religion, upholds the principles of nonviolence, and emphasizes the promotion of the moral and material welfare of the Tibetan people.

In 1992, in order to guide our efforts to have an eventual impact on Tibetans living in Tibet, I announced the Guidelines for Future Tibet's Polity. This document is based on my hope that, before too long, we will achieve a negotiated settlement with the Chinese government granting full autonomy to the Tibetan people. I believe that once such an agreement is reached, it is the Tibetans inside Tibet who will bear the major responsibility for determining Tibet's future governance and that the officials presently serving in positions of leadership in Tibet shall bear an even greater responsibility in the future.

> *Respect for basic human rights, freedom of speech, the equality of all human beings, and the rule of law must be seen not merely as aspirations but as necessary conditions of a civilized society.*

Unfortunately, Tibetans living in Tibet have not shared in the democratic freedoms that we have implemented in exile. In fact, over the last several decades, our brothers and sisters in Tibet have suffered immeasurably. Through direct attacks on all things Tibetan, the very culture of Tibet has been threatened. I believe that the Tibetan people have a right to preserve their own unique and distinct cultural heritage. I also believe that they should be able to decide their future, their form of government, and their social system. No Tibetan is interested in restoring outdated political and social institutions, but we are a nation of six million people with the right to live as human beings.

As we Tibetans have begun moving toward democracy, we have learned that to empower our people we must give them a sufficient understanding of their rights and responsibilities as citizens of a democratic society. For this reason, I have focused considerable attention on education. The more the Tibetan people learn about their individual potential and their ability to play a role in their own governance, the stronger our society will become.

In some respects, I have been the unluckiest Dalai Lama, for I have spent more time as a refugee outside my country than I have spent inside Tibet. On the other hand, it has been very rewarding for me to live in a democracy and to learn about the world in a way that we Tibetans had never been able to do before. Had I continued to live in and govern Tibet, I would certainly have made efforts to bring about changes in our political system, but it is quite probable that I would still have been influenced by the conservative political environment that existed in my homeland. Living outside Tibet has given me an invaluable perspective. I know that our previous political system was outdated and ill-equipped to face the challenges of the contemporary world.

Today, the world has become increasingly interdependent. In this age of cross-border cooperation and exchange, it is very important for the United States and other democratic countries to help preserve and promote democratic trends around the world. For example, the dismantling of the Soviet Union was seen as a significant victory for democracy and human rights. In fact, many Western leaders, including those in the United States, took credit for the Soviet Union's demise. Today, however, conditions in Russia are dire, and many of the former Soviet republics face the prospect of political and economic chaos. The failure of Russia's experiment in democracy would have adverse repercussions throughout the world and could give power and strength to democracy's detractors. I therefore believe it is the responsibility of the democratic free world to come to the aid of those countries who took the courageous step toward democracy and now are struggling to make it work.

I also understand that it is the right of all people to be concerned with the security of their nation. But it is surely more important to help create stability in troubled areas like the former Soviet Union, through economic and other means of support, than to invest in increasingly sophisticated weaponry and a soaring national defense budget. Furthermore, despite the fact that each nation has the right to determine its own security needs, I believe that a nonviolent approach is the most constructive path to securing peace in the long term.

In conclusion, I would like to stress once again the need for firm conviction on all our parts in acknowledging the universality of the key ethical and political values that underlie democracy. Recognition of and respect for basic human rights, freedom of speech, the equality of all human beings, and the rule of law must be seen not merely as aspirations but as necessary conditions of a civilized society.

12

DEMOCRATIC REMEDIES FOR DEMOCRATIC DISORDERS

Gertrude Himmelfarb

Gertrude Himmelfarb is professor emeritus of history at the Graduate School of the City University of New York. She has served on the Board of Trustees at the Woodrow Wilson Center, the Council of the National Endowment for the Humanities, and the editorial boards of the American Historical Review, *the* American Scholar, *and other journals. Her many books include* The De-Moralization of Society: From Victorian Virtues to Modern Values *(1995) and* The Idea of Poverty *(1994). This essay was previously published in the Spring 1998 issue of the* Public Interest.

A famous passage in the *Federalist* calls for "a republican remedy for the diseases most incident to republican government." The diseases the American Founding Fathers had in mind were those associated with factions: the pursuit of special interests to the detriment of the general interest. And the main remedy they proposed was federalism: the general interest to be represented in the national legislature, local and particular interests in the state legislatures.

Today, it is America's democratic society, rather than its republican government, that is problematic. And the diseases incident to that society are moral and cultural rather than political: the collapse of ethical principles and habits, the loss of respect for authorities and institutions, the breakdown of the family, the decline of civility, the vulgarization of high culture, and the degradation of popular culture. Three-quarters of the people in a recent poll said that the main cause of America's problems is "moral decay."

In their most virulent form these diseases manifest themselves in illegitimacy, crime, violence, drug addiction, illiteracy, pornography, and welfare dependency. Some of these conditions have improved in recent years, but there is little cause for complacency. If the number of births to teenagers has decreased, the proportion of out-of-wedlock births, to adults as well as teenagers, continues to increase (and this country still has the dubious distinction of having the highest rate of teenage pregnancy in the industrialized world). If divorce is tapering off, it is because cohabitation is becoming so common; people living together without benefit of marriage can separate without benefit of divorce (and do so with greater facility and frequency). If there are fewer abortions, it is in part because illegitimacy has become more respectable. (Indeed, the term "illegitimacy" is taboo; the preferred terms in official circles are "non-marital childbearing" or "alternative mode of parenting.") If one drug falls out of favor, another takes its place; and the decline among adults is more than offset by an increase among young people—and progressively younger people. And in spite of the recent decrease of crime (which, penologists warn us, may be reversed when today's baby boomers become tomorrow's delinquents), teenage boys, regardless of race, are still more likely to die from gunshot wounds than from all natural causes combined, and homicide is the second leading cause of death for all young people and the leading cause for young blacks.

From a longer perspective, even the good news may give us pause. The decline or stabilization of some of the indices of social disarray does not begin to bring us back to the status quo ante—that now-maligned period of the 1950s before the precipitous rise of those indices. With a divorce rate more than twice that of the 1950s, half of the marriages today, and well over half of the remarriages, are expected to end in divorce. Illegitimacy has increased sixfold, and the number of children living with one parent has risen from less than one-tenth to more than one-quarter. Violent crime, although considerably lower than it was only a few years ago, is still almost four times that of the 1950s. And the much-heralded reduction of the percentage of families on welfare has brought us down from five times that of the 1950s to three and one-half times.

If some of the good news is only equivocally good, some of the bad news is unequivocally bad. The escalating violence on TV, the ready accessibility of pornography and sexual perversions on the Internet, the "dumbing down" of education at all levels, and the "defining down" of deviancy of every kind—these too are part of the social pathology of our time. And this pathology, which affects not only the "underclass" but the entire population, shows no signs of abating; on the contrary, these diseases are becoming more acute and more pervasive. Affluence and education, we have discovered, provide no immunity from moral and cultural disorders.

This situation is all the more distressing because it violates two of our most cherished assumptions: that moral progress is a necessary by-product of material progress and that enlightened legislation will solve our social ills. The 1960s witnessed both an expanding economy and a heightened social consciousness. Yet it was precisely then (for reasons abundantly analyzed elsewhere) that the "moral statistics," as the Victorians called them, took a turn for the worse. And not only in this country but in most Western countries, which is why Vietnam is not the crucial factor it has sometimes been made out to be. If single parenthood or welfare dependency do not preoccupy most Europeans (with the notable exception of the English), this is more a reflection of the permissive ethos in those countries than of the objective conditions. And if Americans are more acutely aware of these conditions, if we perceive them as serious social problems, it is because we pride ourselves on being not only the most democratic nation but also the most moral one ("moralistic," our denigrators would say). Thus we are preternaturally alert to the moral diseases incident to democratic society and anxious to find democratic remedies for those diseases.

The Civil-Society Solution

One remedy looks to the most democratic branch of the government, the legislature, to pass laws designed to promote the moral well-being of the country (income-tax measures favoring married couples) or to nullify those laws that have contributed to our ill-being ("no-fault" divorce laws that facilitate and may encourage divorce). Another remedy is the devolution of power from the federal government to state and local governments, on the theory that the latter reflect the moral temper of the people more faithfully than the remote Washington bureaucracy; this is the rationale behind the recent welfare bill making the states responsible for relief. A more radical remedy looks to the Constitution for redress—an amendment, for example, to forbid or limit abortion.

These are all efforts to find political remedies for our social and moral disorders. Recently, a nonpolitical remedy has been proposed, to near-universal acclaim. This is the restoration and revitalization of civil society—families, communities, churches, civic and cultural societies. It is an attractive idea because it calls upon nothing more than such natural, familiar, universal institutions as families and communities. Moreover, it is preeminently a democratic idea. It is democracy on the smallest scale—the "little platoon" that Burke described as "the first principle (the germ as it were) of public affections." It is also an attribute of democracy on the largest scale—Tocqueville's "voluntary associations," which have the crucial task of mediating between the individual and the state. In addition, it serves as a corrective to that other democratic flaw identified by Tocqueville: "the tyranny of the majority," the power of the collective mass of the people that may be inimical to the liberty of individuals and minorities.

Today, civil society is asked to assume yet another task: that of repairing the moral fabric of democratic society. The institutions of civil society, we are told, are the "seedbeds of virtue." It is here, in families and communities, that individual character takes shape, that children become civilized and socialized, that people acquire a sense of social as well as individual responsibility, that self-interest is reconciled with the general interest, and that civility mutes the discord of opposing wills. And all of this is achieved naturally, organically, without the artificial contrivances of government, without the passage of laws or the intrusion of bureaucracies, and without recourse to the coercive, punitive power of the state.

It sounds too good to be true. And it is too good to be true. The intentions of the proponents of civil society are admirable, and today more than ever the idea of a mediating structure between an unrestrained individualism and an overweening state is commendable. The difficulty is that civil society—not as it once was, as Burke or Tocqueville or even our parents (or ourselves, of a certain age) knew it, but as it now is— cannot bear the burden of the charge placed upon it. Civil society has been described as an "immune system against cultural disease." But the fact is that much of civil society has been infected by the same virus that produced that disease—the ethical and cultural relativism that reduces all values, all standards, and all authority to expressions of personal will and inclination. Even the family, the traditional bedrock of civil society, has not been spared. Civil society, then, is a necessary but not a sufficient remedy for the diseases incident to democratic society.

Religion in America

When the Founding Fathers devised a "new science of politics" based upon the principle of divided powers and interests, they understood that that "science" alone was insufficient to sustain a proper republican government, that the best political arrangements were of no avail in the absence of "virtue and wisdom."

> I go on this great republican principle [Madison said], that the people will have virtue and intelligence to select men of virtue and wisdom. . . . To suppose that any form of government will secure liberty or happiness without any virtue in the people, is a chimerical idea.

Tocqueville, visiting America half a century later, found that a democracy, even more than a republic, is threatened by an egalitarianism that undermines liberty and an individualism that saps "the spring of public virtues." America's saving grace was the proliferation of the "voluntary associations" that mitigate the worst effects of democracy and maintain a sense of public virtue. And among the most important of these associations were the churches.

"The religious atmosphere of the country," Tocqueville wrote, "was the first thing that struck me on arrival in the United States." Unlike France, where the Enlightenment had seen to it that religion and freedom were "almost always marching in opposite directions," in America they were "intimately linked together in joint reign over the same land." It was religion in the service of virtue that made freedom possible. And American religion was uniquely able to do this because it was not an established religion. Americans cherished the idea of religious freedom, the separation of church and state, as much as they cherished their particular church or sect. Religion was "the first of their political institutions" precisely because it was not, strictly speaking, a political institution at all.

Again and again Tocqueville reflected upon the relationship of religion to morality and of both to freedom:

> While the law allows the American people to do everything, there are things which religion prevents them from imagining and forbids them to dare.

> Freedom sees religion as the companion of its struggles and triumphs, the cradle of its infancy, and the divine source of its rights. Religion is considered as the guardian of mores, and mores are regarded as the guarantee of the laws and pledge for the maintenance of freedom itself.

> Despotism may be able to do without faith, but freedom cannot. Religion is much more needed in . . . [a] republic . . . than in . . . [a] monarchy . . . and in democratic republics most of all. How could society escape destruction if, when political ties are relaxed, moral ties are not tightened? And what can be done with a people master of itself if it is not subject to God?

Tocqueville anticipated the objection commonly heard today that this view of religion is demeaning, even irreligious, because it is concerned more with the utility of religion than with its spirituality. "I do not know," he admitted, "if all Americans have faith in their religion—for who can read the secrets of the heart?—but I am sure that they think it necessary for the maintenance of republican institutions." Every religion, he noted, has two dimensions: one that elevates the soul above the material and sensory world, and the other that imposes upon each man an obligation to mankind. These are complementary functions, and both are essential for the self-government that is at the heart of democracy.

Like Tocqueville, a visitor to the United States today may well be struck by the "religious atmosphere of the country." He will also be struck (again, like Tocqueville) by the conspicuous contrast between the United States and Europe. In most European countries, there is an inverse relation between religious commitment and education; the least educated tend to be the most religious. In the United States, there is a high level of both education and religion. In the United States, 43 percent attend church at least weekly; in Britain, 14 percent; in France, 12 percent; in Sweden, 4 percent. In the United States, 49 percent say that religion is very important in their lives; in Britain, 17 percent; in France, 10 percent; in Sweden, 8 percent. The French press was startled recently by the million or so young people who flooded Paris to hear the Pope celebrate Mass. But only half of French youth even call themselves Catholic (compared with almost

90 percent who did so three decades ago), and fewer than half of these practice their faith. At a conference in Prague about the same time, the president of the Czech Republic, Václav Havel, defined the central problem of our time as "global atheism" and called for a revival of those values and principles that all religions hold in common.

America is notably exempt from that "global atheism." "The churching of America," as sociologists call it, is reflected in a variety of statistics, some almost incredible. A staggering 96 percent of Americans profess to believe in God or a "universal spirit" and 90 percent in heaven. (In good American fashion, only 65 percent believe in the devil and 73 percent in hell.) Sixty-seven percent identify themselves as members of a church; 60 percent say they attend church at least once a month, and 43 percent that they had attended in the previous week; 90 percent say that they pray at least once a week and 75 percent daily. With only small variations, these statistics hold for the better-educated and the less-educated, for the rich and the poor. Indeed, those earning more than $75,000 a year are more likely to have attended religious services in the previous week than those earning less than $15,000. It may well be that people are reporting what they think they ought to be doing rather than what they actually do. But this too is significant, reflecting values that are believed in even though they may not be observed in practice.

Other statistics demonstrate the social effects of religious affiliation and observance. The practice of religion has a high correlation with family stability, communal activity, and charitable contributions; and a low correlation with suicide, depression, drug addiction, alcoholism, and crime. Black Protestants and white Catholics, with similarly high church attendance, have similarly low divorce rates. Those who seldom or never attend church have seven times the cohabitation rate of those who do. (This spills over into the following generation; children whose mothers frequently attend services are half as likely to cohabit as adults as those whose mothers are not church-goers.) Not "safe sex" but the regular practice of religion is one of the most important factors in preventing out-of-wedlock births. Religion has even been shown to be conducive to physical well-being. Regular church attendance is correlated with lower mortality rates from heart, liver, and lung diseases. Older adults who attend church regularly are twice as likely to have strong immune systems as those who do not.

An Ethics Gap

These comforting statistics about religion would seem to be at odds with the discomforting ones about our social and moral condition. If religion is so important in America, and if it seems to have such positive effects, why is the country in the state of moral decay reported by so many people?

The anomaly may be accounted for, in large part, by the changing character of the mainline churches, so that religious attendance or prayer is no longer a reliable indicator of cultural and moral dispositions. Tocqueville, living in a less secular, less permissive age, could assume that "each sect worships God in its own fashion, but all preach the same morality in the name of God." That is no longer the case. The churches do not preach the same morality; some do not presume to preach any morality. Many ministers happily preside over marriage services where the pledge of "until death do us part" has been replaced by the new dispensation, "for as long as we both shall love."

One pollster speaks of an "ethics gap" between religious faith and religious practices. More to the point is the gap between religious faith and moral practices. Thus Episcopalians tend to be liberal and latitudinarian in their social attitudes as well as in their theology, whereas Evangelicals and Mormons are typically fundamentalist in theology and traditionalist in morality. (The violent crime rate in Utah, which has the largest Mormon population, is less than half that of the United States.)

The ethics gap cuts through religions and denominations. Southern and Northern Baptists differ sharply not only on such subjects as the ordination of women and homosexuals but on cultural and moral values in general. And among Southern Baptists themselves the disagreements are severe enough to have very nearly caused a schism in recent years. Some Reform Jews regard marriage with an Orthodox Jew almost as a species of intermarriage, and would actually prefer their child to marry a non-Jew who shares their values rather than an Orthodox Jew who does not. Traditionalist Catholics are at odds with modernists. Even on the subject of abortion, where one might expect agreement, the rift is significant, with little more than a third of modernist Catholics subscribing to a pro-life position. And Protestants allied with the Christian Coalition have as little in common with those in the National Council of Churches as they do with secularists or atheists; indeed, they may be better disposed to the latter because they do not contaminate the well of religion and morality.

The religious revival we are now experiencing is not only—perhaps not so much—a religious revival as a moral revival. This is not to deny or belittle its religious impulse, only to recognize its ethical as well as spiritual character. (The resemblance to the Wesleyan movement in the eighteenth century, which also had a strong ethical component, is striking; even today's televised gospel meetings recall Wesley's open-air meetings.) It is significant that the revival has not affected the mainline churches. On the contrary, as the evangelicals have doubled in size and the Mormons have quadrupled, the mainline churches have declined by a fourth.

The revival, which has no parallel abroad, may well bewilder a foreign visitor. It is even bewildering to those Americans who have no strong religious convictions and are fearful of the intrusion, as they see it, of religion in the public sphere. It is especially disconcerting to those academics who believe religiosity to be obsolete. Peter Berger and others have long since refuted the idea that modernization necessarily implies secularization. But intellectual habits die hard in the academy, and that theory has persisted, perhaps because it is congenial to the secular disposition of most professors. Even some professors who loudly deplore the decline of civic virtue and call for a restoration of civil society do not look to religion for the recovery of virtue or to the churches for the revitalization of society.

Journalists, who are also disproportionately liberal in politics and secular in belief, are no less dismissive of religion. A few years ago, a front page story in the *Washington Post* described evangelicals as "poor, uneducated, and easy to command." Protests from readers obliged the *Post* to retract that statement. But the media continue to report upon the religious revival *de haut en bas,* as if describing the antics of some barbarian tribe.

Two Nations

This suggests a larger "ethics gap" in our society—a gap serious enough to warrant a revival of the term "two nations." Only a few years after Tocqueville completed his *Democracy in America,* Disraeli, in his novel *Sybil,* described the very different society of England, an England that comprised not one but two nations:

> Two nations; between whom there is no intercourse and no sympathy; who are as ignorant of each other's habits, thoughts, and feelings, as if they were dwellers in different zones, or inhabitants of different planets; who are formed by different breeding, are fed by a different food, are ordered by different manners, and are not governed by the same laws.

Disraeli's two nations were "the rich and the poor." The two nations in America today are distinguished neither by money nor by class. Nor are they the two racially divided nations described by Andrew Hacker in his 1992 book, *Two Nations: Black and White, Separate, Hostile, Unequal.* Nor are they the two nations within the black community, the elites and underclass, identified by Henry Louis Gates, Jr., in his 1995 book, *Two Nations . . . Both Black.*

The distinctive features of our two nations are ethos and culture rather than class, race, or ethnicity. Jean Jaurès, the French socialist and member of the Chamber of Deputies early in this century, is reputed to have said, "There is more in common between two parliamentarians, one of whom is a socialist, than between two socialists, one of whom is a parliamentarian." So, an American might now say, there is more in common between two church-going families, one of which is working-class, than between two working-class families, only one of which is church-going; or between two two-parent families, one of which is black, than between two black families, only one of which has two parents. (The statistics support this: Blacks and whites who grew up with two parents have low crime rates; blacks and whites who grew up in broken homes have high crime rates.)

The two-nations divide runs through race, religion, ethnicity, class, party, and sex. It is because their identity is defined primarily by moral and cultural values that many inner-city black parents send their children to Catholic schools, not because they themselves are Catholic (they often are not), but because they want their children to have a more rigorous education in a more disciplined environment than is available in the public schools. For the same reason, some non-observant Jews send their children to Jewish day schools rather than public or even secular private schools.

The divide makes for strange bedfellows. Some Orthodox Jews are finding, to their surprise, that they have more in common with Protestant fundamentalists and Catholic traditionalists (on such subjects as school vouchers, gay marriage, or sex-education in the schools) than with their brethren in the Reform or even Conservative denominations. And the old animosity between Catholics and Protestants is giving way to a sense of common cause between traditionalists in both religions. It is not unusual to find, at a conference of the Christian Coalition, an Orthodox rabbi, a Catholic priest, and a black Baptist preacher sharing the head table with evangelicals. The Christian Coalition itself has spawned a Catholic Alliance that is committed to the same social and moral values. James Davison Hunter refers to the "pragmatic alliances being formed across faith traditions," with cultural conservatives pitted against progressivists. Others speak of a shift from "ethnocultural" to "ideological" coalitions, leading to "cross-tradition alliances" of liberals against conservatives.

As religious alliances are reconstituting themselves on moral and cultural grounds, racial segregation is also breaking down. In the past, only liberal denominations were integrated. Now conservative ones are as well, with white Southern Baptist churches beginning to open their doors to blacks, and evangelical organizations endorsing the principle of "racial reconciliation." Political affiliations have undergone similar realignments. It was the state of the culture, not "the economy, stupid," that prompted many working-class Democrats to switch their lifelong allegiances and vote for Reagan in 1980. And the voting patterns in 1996 show a division not between Protestants and Catholics but between traditionalists and modernists in both religions.

The two-nations image was surely overdramatized by Disraeli and can easily be exaggerated today. Then, as now, a large part of the population falls somewhere between those two nations. Yet that image did illuminate an essential aspect of early Victorian England. And it does help explain the peculiar, almost schizoid nature of our present condition: the sense of moral disarray on the one hand, and the visible, even dramatic evidence of a moral-cum-religious revival on the other. This disjunction is apparent in small matters and large—in the fact, for example, that gangsta rap and gospel rock are each among today's fastest growing forms of music. Or that, amid all the evidence of family break-down, we also have the Promise Keepers, the half million men who assembled in Washington for a day of prayer and atonement, pledging themselves to Christian observance, marital fidelity, and familial responsibility. (In local meetings of fifty thousand or so, they pay for the privilege of participating in these demonstrations.)

The moral polarization of society is most conspicuous in such hotly disputed issues as school vouchers, prayer in public schools, partial-birth abortions, pornography on the Internet, or homosexuality and adultery in the military. But it has larger ramifications, affecting beliefs, attitudes, and values on a host of subjects ranging from private morality to public policy. It is, in fact, more profoundly divisive than the class polarization that Marxists looked to as the precondition for their revolution.

The Counterculture

Having been spared a class revolution, we have finally succumbed to the cultural revolution. What was, only a few decades ago, a subculture or counterculture in society is now the dominant culture. For some time conservatives resisted acknowledging this, convinced that "the people" were still "sound," still devoted to traditional values, and that only superficially and intermittently were they (or more often their children) seduced by the blandishments of the counterculture. That confidence has eroded, as surely as the values themselves have. By now, it is evident that the counterculture of yesteryear is the dominant culture today. "Alternative lifestyles" that only a few decades ago were frowned upon by polite society are now not only tolerated but given equal status with traditional lifestyles. An "adversary culture" once confined to artists (and *artistes manqués* known as "bohemians") has been democratized and popularized. Family values once taken for granted are now, if not derided as "bourgeois values," then widely ignored and violated with impunity.

Like all cultures, the dominant culture today exhibits a wide spectrum of beliefs and practices. At one end is the "elite culture," as it has been called, represented by the media and academia. Statistics confirm what we all know, that the views of the media and academia are consistently more permissive and "progressive" than those of the public. Thus only a third of the public, but 90 percent in the media, support the right to abortion without qualifications. Or well over half of the public, but only 5 percent of leading filmmakers, say that they attend church at least once a month. Or more than three-quarters of the public, but fewer than half in the media, say that adultery is always wrong. (Both adultery and promiscuity are portrayed frequently and sympathetically in films and television. The favorable portrayals of casual sex on TV outnumber the unfavorable by 20 to one.) The story of the professor who says that he cannot understand how Reagan could have been elected, when he knows no one who voted for him, is not at all apocryphal; I have had that said to me in almost exactly those words on more than one occasion.

But the elites are only a part, if a most visible and influential part, of this culture. The bulk of the people are acquiescent and passive. Even when they express conservative views on some subjects, they do not feel strongly enough to take a vigorous or consistent stand on them. They believe in God, but they believe even more in the autonomy of the individual. They say that one cannot legislate morality, but what they mean is that one should not adjudicate morality. They find it difficult to judge what is moral or immoral even for themselves, still more for others. Thus they take refuge in such circumlocutions as "Who is to say . . . ?" or "Personally, I oppose abortion, but . . . ."

Most people have misgivings about "sexually active" teenagers, and with good reason; according to a recent survey, one-fifth of 15-year-olds and one-half of 17-year-olds have had sex, many on frequent occasions and with multiple partners. But the same people tend to be tolerant of sexually active college students and adults. Only one-quarter think that premarital sex is always wrong, while two-fifths think that it is not wrong at all. Almost half of parents with young children say that their primary goal is to raise a moral child, compared with over a third who give priority to the happiness of the child. But what they mean by morality is not specified in the poll, and probably not clear to themselves. Nearly everyone professes to believe in "family values," but the concept of the family has radically changed. It is not only sociologists who define the "postmodern family" as almost any combination or permutation of members; some dismiss the very idea of "family" (encapsulated in quotation marks) as having no objective meaning at all. More significant is the fact that almost three-quarters of the public reject the traditional (and until recently legal) concept of family as people related by blood, marriage, or adoption, in favor of the expansive notion of "a group of people who love and care for each other."

The Counter-Counterculture

If the dominant nation expresses the values of what was once the counterculture, the "other" nation may be said to represent a counter-

counterculture. Here too, one finds a spectrum of beliefs and behavior, ranging from a rigid adherence to traditional values only occasionally violated in practice, to a somewhat more lenient set of values more often violated. But even the laxer members of this other nation are more assured in their values and less diffident about expressing them than their counterparts in the dominant nation. "Who am I to say . . . ?" and "Personally . . . but" are not in their lexicon.

As the dominant elite becomes more audacious in defying conventional values, it risks provoking a reaction on the part of an otherwise acquiescent public.

At one end of the spectrum of this other nation (paralleling the cultural elite of the dominant nation) is the "religious right." This is the hard core of the other nation—a determined and articulate group of evangelical Protestants. In a recent survey, 18 percent of the public identified themselves under this label. Yet even they are not homogeneous either in theology or politics; they vary in the degree of their fundamentalism and conservatism. Forty-three percent of the public describe themselves as "born-again" Christians, but only one-third of these associate themselves with the religious right. The other nation, then, extends well beyond the religious right. It includes traditionalist Protestants, Catholics, Mormons, some Orthodox Jews (the latter a very small number proportionately), and individuals of no particular religious affiliation but of strong traditional moral convictions.

Although this other nation is an important and often vocal presence in the polity (neither party can ignore it with impunity), it is a minority of the population. A recent survey of the "political culture" (in which moral attitudes and issues loom large) produced a typology of six categories: the two traditional groups ("traditionalists" and "neo-traditionalists") constituting 27 percent of the population, the two liberal ones ("communitarians" and "permissivists") 46 percent, and the two intermediate, moderate ones ("pragmatists" and "conventionalists") 29 percent. The other nation is clearly outweighed numerically. As a result, it labors under the disadvantage of being perennially on the defensive. Its elite—gospel preachers, radio talk-show hosts, a few prominent columnists, and organizational leaders—cannot begin to match that of the dominant nation occupying the commanding heights of the culture: the professors who preside over a multitude of young people who have to attend their lectures, read their books, and pass their examinations; the journalists who determine what information, and what "spins" on that information, come to the public; the television and movie producers who provide the images, models, and values that shape the popular culture; the corporate leaders who willingly produce whatever the public will buy, indeed, are ingenious in creating a market for new and ever more meretricious products. An occasional boycott by the religious right of the Disney enterprises can hardly counteract the cumulative, pervasive effect of the dominant culture.

Backlash

Yet as the dominant elite becomes more audacious in defying conventional values—"pushing the envelope," as is said—it risks provoking a reaction on the part of an otherwise acquiescent public. Even those who have been long inured to such excesses may be repelled by the latest TV serial that is acclaimed as "push[ing] the limits of network television" and "stretching the acceptable"—that is, setting new standards of violence, profanity, and prurience; or by the new game on the Internet by the creators of "Sesame Street," which has the dual distinction of being one of the goriest yet produced and a tremendous commercial success; or by the Pulitzer Prize–winning drama celebrating not so much homosexuality as pornography and obscenity; or by the "Distinguished Professor" who flaunts her sexual relations with her students as a higher form of scholarship and pedagogy.

Some professors are beginning to complain that their students are resisting the prevailing academic fashions and are becoming conservative—career-minded, they contemptuously call it—and even religious. The *Chronicle of Higher Education* reports upon a surge of religious activities on college campuses. And pollsters tell us that half of teenagers attend church, and an increasing number do so of their own accord rather than because of pressure from their parents. Young people are also becoming less enchanted with their sexual liberation. In the past few years, the number of college freshmen who believe abortion should be legal declined from 65 percent to 56 percent, and those who approve of casual sex from 51 percent to 42 percent. This tendency cuts across class lines: 83 percent of inner-city high-school juniors and seniors, asked about the ideal age to have sex, gave an age older than that when they themselves had had sex.

Their elders are also reconsidering the sexual permissiveness of their own youth. More than half of those who now say that premarital sex is always wrong themselves had sex before marriage, and a fourth of those who say that sex for a young teenager is always wrong had sex at that young age. Twenty-five years ago, one-seventh of those in their twenties said that premarital sex was always wrong; today, one-fourth of that generation (now in their forties) believe it is always wrong. At that time, one-third of the twenty-somethings thought divorce should be more difficult to obtain; today, almost half of those in their forties do (and somewhat less than half of those now in their twenties).

The dominant ethos, then, is still dominant, but a reaction against it is growing—among young people who will shape the culture of the future, and among their elders who have personally experienced the effects of a revolution that promised liberation and brought, all too often, grief and disaster.

Alternative Measures

Historians have not been notably successful in predicting the future. They are not even, as some wit has said, very good at predicting the past. Some observers of the religious revival predicted the demise of religion when the Moral Majority disbanded in the late 1980s. They were woefully wrong. More recently, others have predicted a new religious "Awakening" that would transform the ethos and culture of the United States as did the Great Awakenings of the eighteenth and nineteenth centuries. I have more modest expectations. I think the religious-cum-moral revival will continue to invigorate the other nation, without succeeding in converting the dominant nation. It will however, serve the vital function of keeping alive an alternative ethos and culture— an alternative that will not necessarily have a religious character.

Those who urge us to be tolerant of "alternative lifestyles"—and not only to be tolerant of them but to give them full credence and legitimacy—have in mind such lifestyles as single-parent families, gay marriages, or cohabitation and procreation without benefit of marriage. But there are other alternatives, traditional lifestyles, that are reasserting themselves within that other nation and even beginning to be reflected in public policies.

The welfare bill, for example, is not merely an alternative way of administering welfare. It is an attempt to promote an alternative ethos, a new attitude toward dependency and all the ills associated with it. Critics say that the reform has not yet had a measurable effect on out-of-wedlock births. But it does represent a significant change in public opinion, which (if the reform is sustained) will eventually be reflected in the statistics. In the meantime, it has succeeded in reducing the relief rolls and, more important, in inspiring a new appreciation for what was once derided (in some circles, is still derided) as the "bourgeois work ethic." A poll of women on welfare in New Jersey, which has a "family cap" policy denying additional benefits for new births to mothers already on the relief rolls, showed two-thirds of them judging the policy to be fair and more than four-fifths praising it for promoting responsibility; only one-half said that it hurt children, and one-third that it interfered with a woman's right to have a baby.

Other alternatives are the charter schools and voucher system, which enable poor parents to do what the rich have always done—send their children to the school of their choice. Still another is the "covenant marriage" instituted by Louisiana, according to which couples forfeit their right to no-fault divorce and agree to a more binding marriage contract. Implicit in both cases is the recognition that the dominant culture will not soon be changed; the public school system is not likely to be significantly reformed in the near future, and the no-fault divorce law is not about to be repealed. But the alternatives are important not only because they make available other modes of education and marriage but also because these modes have been legitimized and institutionalized by the state.

Some alternatives do not require the intervention of the state. They require only that the state forbear from intervening. Private schools, and especially religious schools, have long been available, but are now far more numerous than they have ever been, in the suburbs as well as inner cities and appealing to all classes and races. (Jewish day schools now cut across denominational lines; the largest number are still Orthodox, but they are being joined by nondenominational ones that include adherents of the Conservative and even Reform movements.)

A more radical alternative is home schooling; it is estimated that a million or more children are now being educated at home. This movement has advanced to the point where a new two-year college is being planned especially for home schoolers. Analogous to home schooling is the "TV-free" home. At a time when television is becoming increasingly intrusive and aggressive, more and more parents are making the deliberate decision not to have television in their homes. Two million households, most of them with children, now practice this kind of "cultural abstinence"— yet another means by which the other nation voluntarily opts out of the dominant culture.

Internal Exiles?

This other nation, then, is not a cure for the diseases incident to a democratic society, but it is a way of containing and mitigating those diseases. Moreover, it does so in an eminently democratic fashion, consistent with the original Federalists who assumed that virtue—and religion of sorts, if only of the deist sort—was a necessary attribute of the citizens of a large republic, although not a direct or primary responsibility of the government. The other nation, reconciled to its minority status in what is now a very large and varied republic indeed, has no ambitions to impose its values upon others; it only seeks to promote and protect those values for itself. It does not want to alter the constitutional arrangements separating church and state, but only resists the efforts of the courts to go beyond that separatism by creating a hostile environment for religion as such. Nor does it desire a more active role for government than that which has been traditional in America until very recently, as exemplified in the principle of community standards applied to pornography. More often than not, restoring traditional practices means favoring a less intrusive government (as in the matter of sex-education).

The other nation is self-selecting and self-sustaining. It is not, however, entirely self-sufficient. Even within this other nation, there is no guarantee of immunity from the diseases afflicting society; the dominant culture is too pervasive and powerful. Nor would it be desirable to immunize this other nation entirely, even if that were possible. The dominant culture has too much of value to warrant the kind of segregation or quarantine that would require. Opting out of the culture is hardly an ideal solution. School vouchers and home schooling are defensive measures, a last resort against a seriously flawed public school system that was once the pride of our democracy. So, too, gated and segregated communities are understandable but unfortunate expediencies in a country that values openness and mobility. The parents of TV-deprived children have good reason to worry about the "forbidden fruit" syndrome. And even covenant marriages have unwitting side effects. The requirement of premarital counseling, like prenuptial contracts, may induce a premature sense of doubt and uncertainty where there should be confidence and security. And any alternative form of marriage makes the conventional one seem even more precarious, an open invitation to divorce.

TV "abstainers" have been called "a band of internal exiles." It would be regrettable if the other nation were reduced to that lowly status. One can only hope that eventually the diseases will run their course, and the nations will, more or less, reunite. This is, after all, what happened in Disraeli's time, when industrialism and education gradually diminished the gap between rich and poor, so that by the end of the nineteenth century they had become mere classes rather than distinctive nations. It is not unreasonable to suppose that our own two nations will evolve in the same fashion. And it is very much the desire of the other nation that this happen. A 1996 survey conducted by the Roper Organization finds that the supporters of the Christian Right are "among the most unwavering in their commitment to the American political system." Forty-eight percent score high in "respect for the political institutions in America," compared with one-third of the general population; 71 percent take pride in living "under our political system," compared with 61 percent of the whole; 68 percent feel strongly that "our system of government is the best possible system," compared with 53 percent of the whole; and 85 percent "support our system of government," compared with 65 percent of the whole. They are disaffected, to be sure, with the present condition of the political culture, but entirely loyal to America as a country, a creed, and a polity—a single nation.

A Moral Majority

The example of Victorian England emboldens me to make another prediction. There too the religious revival, inspired by the Methodists and Evangelicals, had from its inception a strong moral impulse. And there, in the course of the nineteenth century, the moral part of that revival gradually overshadowed the religious part, so that by the end of the century, the moral-reformation movement counted among its followers not only Methodists and Evangelicals but also high-church Anglicans, Catholics, dissenters of every denomination, and, not least, a good body of secularists.

This is already becoming evident in the United States. As religious groups begin to feel more self-confident and less beleaguered, they will shed some of their sectarianism and intransigence. This is already occurring; witness, for example, the shift in tactics from a constitutional amendment reversing *Roe v. Wade* to a policy designed to chip away at abortion incrementally. They will also become more hospitable to those secularists who share their values. Indeed, this was anticipated 20 years ago, when the Christian Right associated itself with the secular New Right. It was then that Jerry Falwell, inaugurating what he optimistically called the Moral Majority, defined it as including "fundamentalists, Protestants, Roman Catholics, Jews, Mormons, and persons of no particular religious convictions at all who believe in the moral principles we espouse."

It is in this latitudinarian sense that the Moral Majority might become just that—a majority of Americans of all religious creeds, and of none, sharing a common ethos. By then, too, the religious element may have become so attenuated that historians will have to remind their contemporaries (as we have been reminded in our own time) that they are living off the religious capital of a previous generation and that that capital is being perilously depleted. Society may then find itself caught up in yet another cycle of de-moralization and re-moralization, including, perhaps, another Great Awakening.

But such prophecies take us far into the future. For the moment, let us be content with the knowledge that the two nations can live together in the present (as they did in early Victorian England) with some degree of tension and dissension but without civil strife or anarchy. And (recalling the example of late Victorian England) we may even look forward to something like a reconciliation of the two nations—at the very least, to an abatement of the diseases incident to democratic society.

13

DEMOCRACY AND UTOPIA

François Furet

François Furet, until his death in July 1997, was director of the Institut Raymond Aron at the Ecole des Hautes Etudes en Sciences Sociales in Paris and also a professor at the Committee on Social Thought at the University of Chicago. In March 1997, he had been elected a member of the Académie Française. An eminent historian who wrote a number of pathbreaking books on the French Revolution, he was also the author of Le passé d'une illusion *(1995), a widely discussed study of the idea of communism in the twentieth century that appeared in English translation in 1999 as* The Passing of an Illusion. *The text that follows, based upon a lecture that he delivered in Lisbon in January 1997, was translated from the French by Philip J. Costopoulos.*

The subject of democracy and utopia may be approached in a philosophical fashion. Since the eighteenth century, democracy has presented itself to the modern individual as a promise of liberty, or more precisely, of *autonomy*. This is in contrast to earlier times when men were viewed as subjects, and consequently were deprived of the right of self-determination, which is the basis of the legitimacy of modern societies. Ever since the democratic idea penetrated the minds and peoples of Europe, it has not ceased to make inroads nearly everywhere through a single question, inherent in its very nature, that crops up continuously and is never truly resolved. That question, which was posed very early on by all the great Western thinkers from Hobbes to Rousseau and from Hegel to Tocqueville, was as follows: "What kind of society should we form if we think of ourselves as autonomous individuals? What type of social bond can be established among free and equal men, since liberty and equality are the conditions of our autonomy? How can we conceive a society in which each member is sovereign over himself and which thus must harmonize the sovereignty of each over himself and of all over all?"

In the course of these probings into the central question of modern democracy, one is necessarily struck by the gap between the expectations that democracy arouses and the solutions that it creates for fulfilling them. In the abstract, there is a point in political space where the most complete liberty and the most complete equality meet, thus bringing together the ideal conditions of autonomy. But our societies never reach this point. Democratic society is never democratic enough, and its supporters are more numerous and more dangerous critics of democracy than its adversaries. Democracy's promises of liberty and equality are, in fact, unlimited. In a society of individuals, it is impossible to make liberty and equality reign together or even to reconcile the two in a lasting way. These promises expose all democratic political regimes not only to demagogic appeals but also to the constant accusation of being unfaithful to their own founding values. In premodern systems, legitimacy, like obedience, found its guarantee in *la durée*. In the democratic world, neither legitimacy nor obedience is ever lastingly secured.

A century and a half ago, one of the best minds of French liberalism, Charles de Rémusat, explained how the congenital instability of liberal democracy is a consequence of the limitless vistas that it makes available to the human imagination:

> The speculations of social philosophy, particularly when everyone gets involved in them, have an inconvenient way of making people disgusted with real things, of blocking all contentment while the dream of the absolute remains unrealized, and of casting discredit upon all the opportunities for improvement and progress that fortune offers to nations. All that is not yet ideal is misery. If the principle of authority is not established without restriction, all is anarchy. If pure democracy is still to come, all is oppression. There is never anything to do in the present except start a new revolution, and it is necessary to agitate incessantly, to roll again and again the dice of politics in an attempt to turn up some abstract number that may not even exist.

Thus the modern world is a place that is particularly sensitive to the claims of utopia. It is necessary, in this context, to give the word "utopia" a slightly different meaning than it had in earlier centuries. Before the modern era, the word referred either to a literary genre or to an eschatology tied to Christianity. In the first case, it attached to that type of work in which the author imagines a perfect social universe, exempt from human vice and wickedness, outside of space and time. In the second, it designated the messianic emotions that animated a number of popular insurrections in Christian Europe, notably at the end of the Middle Ages, through the passion for obtaining eternal salvation by means of action here below. The utopia of democratic times, however, belongs to a third category, one that was unheard of until the French Revolution. While it also can be bookish, as so many political works from the nineteenth and twentieth centuries attest, it is never outside of time and space; on the contrary, it tends to be based upon time—in the guise of "history"—and to incarnate itself within a specific territory. It has severed all ties with religious hopes and seeks only earthly human happiness. It is charged with emotions of a political kind. These emotions are nourished by the frustrations engendered by the promises of democracy and seek to fulfill these promises by making liberty and equality finally *real*. The commitment is merely terrestrial, but it is so total that the legitimacy of the social contract depends upon the fulfillment of these promises.

We might thus undertake a philosophical analysis of the psychological inevitability of utopianism in modern politics by listing the traits that characterize it during the contemporary age in contrast to the past. But I prefer to follow a mode of exposition that is more historical than philosophical. Let us trace the course of democratic utopias from their first appearance during the French Revolution up to our own day, the end of the twentieth century, in the hope that in studying their history, we might clarify their nature and profundity.

The French Revolution and the American Revolution

Let us begin, then, with the French Revolution, that laboratory of modern democracy. And let us consider its first objective: to make a *tabula rasa* of the past. This was a goal that was shared by the American Revolution, but which in France carried a particular utopian charge.

In both cases, the notion of erasing the past bespeaks modern artificialism, the obsession with *constructing* society rather than considering it as given by the natural or divine order of things, with founding it upon nothing but the free consent of its members. Thus the original founding is clothed in a particular reverence and solemnity. "Original" does not necessarily mean "definitive," since, as Jefferson once said, society must be refounded every 20 years so that each generation may have the opportunity to correct or remake the constitution according to its own will. Yet this attempt to institutionalize revolution at periodic intervals merely emphasizes the extraordinary character of a society whose members must never be bound by a contract that they would not have freely subscribed to themselves.

United by this common ambition to invent a society that would be the product of free wills, the American Revolution and the French Revolution nonetheless display a capital difference in this regard. The former did not need to overturn an aristocratic social order to institute a society of free and equal individuals. The American colonists had left the aristocratic social order behind them when they left England or Europe to live in freedom and equality in a new land: It was the trans-Atlantic voyage that effected a revolutionary rupture, which emancipation from the British Crown would later merely reinforce. The difference from the French case is so great that Tocqueville, drawing a contrast with what happened in France in 1789, saw in the American case an example of the *nonrevolutionary* establishment of democracy. "The Americans' great advantage," he wrote, "is to have arrived at democracy without having suffered democratic revolutions, and to have been born equal instead of becoming equal." For Americans, the conventional founding of society by the will of its members accords with the reality of their history.

Lacking the option of moving to a new territory, the French at the end of the eighteenth century had to deny their nation's feudal and aristocratic past in order to invent themselves as a new, or to use the vocabulary of the time, *regenerated,* people. It was on this condition only that they could act out the grand drama of the *social contract,* which so many philosophers of the age had identified as the basis of legitimacy. That is no doubt why they tended to go too far in the vein of democratic philosophy and the universality of natural rights. The Americans had no need to make a great effort of abstraction in order to proclaim themselves free and equal, since their social condition was not too far from these ideals.

The French, by contrast, had to insist all the harder on the normative character of their "Declaration of the Rights of Man and Citizen," for which their history offered neither precedent nor support. On the contrary, it was precisely under the *ancien régime* that these rights were trampled underfoot. In its French setting, then, the idea of "revolution" was inseparable from the condemnation of the past, which sharpened the will to exclude or eliminate those corrupt beneficiaries of the old order, the aristocrats. The American revolutionaries, it is true, also had to fight a certain number of their compatriots who rallied to the English cause. But the American republic, once it became independent, possessed only a single history, which served as a source of pride and unity. The French, on the other hand, quickly became—and long remained—that strange people incapable of loving their whole national history, for loving the Revolution meant detesting the *ancien régime,* and loving the *ancien régime* meant detesting the Revolution.

This tendency penetrated more and more deeply into the national consciousness, extending the revolutionary *tabula rasa* into the future and renewing the emotion surrounding it for the generations of the nineteenth and twentieth centuries. Yet this tendency also perpetuated a fiction by hiding the Revolution's relationship to the past from which it sprang—namely, absolutism. While the Anglo-Americans formed a new people by means of their exodus from the Old World, the French of the late eighteenth century became obsessed with a passionate desire to cut themselves off from their past, and thus were condemned to overlook that this passion for separation was itself a legacy of this past: The ancient constitution of the kingdom already had been destroyed by a series of absolute monarchs before the men of 1789 made their solemn proclamation of a new starting point and principle of regeneration. Revolutions, wrote Guizot, "are far less the symptom of something beginning than the declaration of something that has already occurred." Viewed from this angle, the two revolutions of the late eighteenth century, the American and the French, are the offspring of two preceding revolutions. The American reinforced what had begun when people left England in the name of individual liberty. The French was heir to the subversion of the traditional order by the administrative monarchy. This was a subversion that the Revolution appropriated and completed through the proclamation of the *tabula rasa,* before weighing its consequences for the reconstitution of a body politic. Yet the failures that the Revolution met in this very enterprise would constantly give new life to the idea of an absolutely fresh start: If this enterprise failed in 1789 or 1791, it had only to be resumed in 1792 or 1793. In France, revolutionary consciousness combined the view of the times as a curse with the view of the times as a new dawn.

This consciousness was thus free of any reference to a restoration, to say nothing of a return to a golden age. Like its opposite, the idea of the *ancien régime,* this consciousness constituted itself very quickly, taking the form of a universal promise opening out onto an unlimited future. In this sense, as Michelet wrote when trying to characterize the spirit of 1789, "time no longer existed; time had perished." Yet this fictitious exorcism of an accursed past did not exempt the French Revolution from also being, in its turn, a history, constantly judged against its promise and therefore constantly obliged to begin anew its efforts to fulfill it. The American idea of revolution found its fulfillment in the founding of an independent republic through the federal Constitution of 1787 and the constitutions of the several states. The French idea of revolution passed from one phase to the next of revolutionary history, searching for a fulfillment that it could never attain.

Restarting the Revolution

The French Revolution was utopian in the sense that it had nothing but abstract objectives, and thus no foreseeable end. It left in its wake an initial, failed Revolution (that of 1789) in order to begin its course anew, this time solemnly decked out with a new calendar dating time from the beginning of the Republic on 21 September 1792. Its goal was no longer to embody itself in constitutional law but rather to ensure that liberty and equality would triumph over their enemies—an indispensable first step in the making of a new man, delivered from his age-old subordination to his fellows. This is why the Revolution stressed its character as an annunciation, which gave a unique value to its course. It was the extraordinary contrasted with the ordinary, the exceptional contrasted with the quotidian, to the point where the adjective that appeared to define it could only be tautological: The Revolution was "revolutionary," just as the circumstances were "revolutionary" and the government was "revolutionary." It was no longer solely a question of the health of the fatherland, as in the great perils of the monarchy, or of a Roman-style temporary dictatorship, as described in Rousseau's *Social Contract*. It was a regime new to history, as Robespierre underlined in his famous speech of 5 Nivôse, Year II (25 December 1793), where he drew the contrast between "revolutionary" and "constitutional" government. His goal was not to preserve the Republic but to *found* it, getting rid of its enemies by means of the Terror.

Hence his superiority to the law and consequent independence from it: What authorizes the provisional suspension of law thus goes beyond the public safety; it is the higher imperative to found society upon the virtue of its citizens. The Revolution inherited corrupt and denatured human beings from the *ancien régime;* before the Revolution could be ruled by means of the law, it would have to regenerate each actor in the new social contract. What for Rousseau constitutes the difficult, even almost impossible passage from man to citizen became for Robespierre the meaning of the Revolution, to be realized through the radical actions of the revolutionary government.

Thus the Revolution of 1789 found itself pregnant with a second Revolution, that of 1792. The latter aimed at being both a correction and an expansion of the former: more radical, more universal, more faithful to its emancipatory goal than its predecessor had been. By means of this intensification, it unfolded in a movement of negation and self-transcending that had no limit. Its horizon—the regeneration of humanity—was so abstract that it fostered political passions that tended toward the quasi-religious, although invested in the world of here and now. It is this which imparts to revolutionary politics its character of ideological intolerance and, at the same time, leaves it open to a constant upping of the ante. Yet this is also what protects the revolutionary idea against its own eventual failure: Those who take it up again find its seductive power intact, for the revolutionary idea contains all that modern politics can offer in the way of messianic charm. It is thus that the French Revolution overflows its chronological definition and escapes being trapped amid the prosaic shoals of Thermidoreanism. To those who came after, the Revolution bequeathed the memory of its ambition, which the nineteenth century would not cease to refashion.

The political impasse had been grasped at the end of the Terror by the actors in or witnesses of the Revolution themselves. To understand this, one need only think back to the period that followed Robespierre's fall, after the month of Thermidor, Year II (July 1794). Circumstances demanded the rehabilitation of the "legal" at the expense of the "revolutionary" by writing the Revolution into the law—hence the Constitution of the Year III. Those who had toppled Robespierre found themselves caught between two contradictory imperatives. They neither wished nor were able to renounce the Revolution, since it alone had made them what they were. Yet they could not totally endorse it, since the Terror had been part of it. It was the young Benjamin Constant, a newcomer to Paris in 1795, who furnished the solution to this dilemma by distinguishing two types of revolutions. The first results from a gap between the institutions and the ideas of a people and consists in the violent adjustment of the former to the latter; it is the manifestation of a historical necessity. The second, on the contrary, comes about when the revolution, lost within utopia, has passed beyond the progress of the human spirit. The revolution loses itself in the unreal, the impossible, and the arbitrary, eventually provoking the threat of an about-face. Yet this young Swiss thinker's historicist philosophy was too biased to avoid appearing as a rationalization of power or to erase the messianic dimension of revolutionary hope.

Moreover, at the very moment when Benjamin Constant was seeking to "fix" the Revolution within the movement of history, Gracchus Babeuf was working to start the Revolution up again, since it had produced merely the bourgeois world, such a far cry from its revolutionary promises. Constant invoked the laws of history; Babeuf, the Jacobin cult of will. For the former, the Revolution was the achievement of a necessity; for the latter, it was the invention of a future. The European left would thenceforth ceaselessly explore these two alternatives, contradictory yet born of the same event. Marx would spend his intellectual life trying to reconcile them, but he would remain too deterministic for his voluntarist side, and too voluntaristic for his determinist side. The principal charm that Bolshevism held for some imaginations, 120 years after the French Jacobins, was that it reprised the revolutionary enterprise within this combination of necessity and will.

The Role of Religion

Yet before we turn to that, we must highlight a final aspect of the revolutionary idea, one that has furnished a foundation for democracy in Europe—namely, the notion that the promise of a good society is no longer inscribed in sacred texts (as in the English case), or in political and religious harmony (as in the American example), but must be fulfilled solely by the unfolding of history. This story is too long and too complex to go into here, but we may at least attempt to sketch its consequences by continuing my comparison, following many historians of the last century. The English Revolution of the seventeenth century offers an example of the mutation of a religious revolution into a political revolution, with the former laying down the spiritual and moral basis of the latter. The American republic, founded at the end of the following century, was born out of an insurrectionist movement that was never cut off from its Christian roots. In France, on the contrary, the men of 1789 were forced to break with the Catholic Church, one of the pillars of the hated *ancien régime,* without ever succeeding in substituting another Christian or post-Christian cult in its place. At that time, Protestantism's hour had passed, and deist rationalism, whatever form it took, left people indifferent. The upshot was that the spirit of the Revolution revealed merely politics pure and simple, even though by virtue of the universal character of its promise, this politics shared something with the message of the gospels. The paradox of modern French history lies in recovering the spirit of Christianity only through revolutionary democracy. Or to put it another way: The French Revolution renewed universalism without ceasing to limit itself to the level of the political. The French divinized modern liberty and equality without giving the new principles any support other than the historic adventure of a people still otherwise faithful to the Catholic tradition. For a republican historian like Edgar Quinet, this contradiction spelled out the inherent failure of the French Revolution. It is also by means of this contradiction that we can best come to understand the utopian dimension of the Revolution and of the tradition that it inaugurated.

The problem, moreover, is older than the Revolution. It was already present within the philosophy of the Enlightenment, which in its French version was not more antireligious but surely more anticlerical than any other in Europe. The Catholic Church and its priests in France were the quintessential targets (think of Voltaire) of that great movement toward the reappropriation of man by man that formed the basic tendency of the age. But eighteenth-century philosophy, unlike that of the sixteenth, showed itself powerless to fashion any religious renewal or even any new spiritual principle from the critique of tradition. Voltairean deism, parliamentary Jansenism, the doctrine of Rousseau's Savoyard vicar, the natural religion of the physiocrats, and Masonic esotericism were all alike in this regard: They served more to embellish political expectations than to shape collective beliefs. The France of the Enlightenment lived under the empire of the political even before it became the France of the Revolution. And those elements of religion it retained, as Tocqueville perceived, were reinscribed within the core of the political: the universalism of "civilization," faith in progress, and the emancipation of the human race. Marx also keenly sensed this; he defined the French Revolution, at the time when he was seeking to decode its mystery, as "the illusion of the political."

The boundless investment in historical action, a flame that burned brightest during the years of the Jacobin dictatorship, led the French revolutionaries toward such utopian objectives as the regeneration of humanity. Condemned to waste away under the weight of actual history, as can be seen after Thermidor and under Napoleon, this messianic hope nonetheless survived the event that formed it, as a universal promise of

earthly salvation, oriented simply toward the future. There may be found
its link with Bolshevism, to which I now turn.

The October Revolution

If you will allow me, I would like to take a giant step across the
nineteenth century to examine our own, which is richer still in the utopian
idea. Indeed, if we take the nineteenth and twentieth centuries together,
we can consider them as belonging to the same category, for between
them they constitute the European experience of democracy. Yet they
may be viewed as two separate *epochs,* each of which possesses (both
by itself and in relation to the other) enough distinctive traits to have its
own *esprit du temps.* Nineteenth-century Europe, which followed upon
the French Revolution, mastered the storm that preceded it. Despite the
revolutionary upsurge of 1848, the nineteenth century offers the spectacle
of a relatively stable ensemble of nations and regimes sharing a single
vision of moral and political civilization. (It is true that it combined
many aristocratic elements with what it had already acquired in the way
of democracy.) The twentieth century, however—if we accept the idea
that it began with the First World War in 1914—has known two world
wars and several radically contradictory types of social and political
organization. If it is finally ending up before our eyes in a sort of
universalization of humanity thanks to the dual impact of the market
and the democratic idea, this is only after having passed through tragedies
without precedent. From the utopian standpoint, it should also be readily
apparent that our own century is the one in which the idea of a collective
salvation by history has exerted its full fascination over the masses—a
thought sometimes expressed by saying that it has been, in the words of
Raymond Aron, the age of "secular religions." Ours has been the first
fully democratic century in human history (given that the nineteenth
remained partially aristocratic), and it is not by chance that it has also
been the one in which the utopian vision of politics has played an
essential role.

Hence I come to the question that I sought to understand in my most
recent book, *Le passé d'une illusion.* This question was not the history
of communism. It was rather the very different one of the sway that the
communist idea held over so many minds during the twentieth century:
a sway so deep and so vast that it gave rise to a universal belief whose
geographic reach exceeded that of Christianity. Born in Europe during
the nineteenth century, the idea of communism spread throughout the
whole world during the twentieth. I mean by this not that it dominated
everyone's imagination but simply that it was endowed with an exceptional ubiquity; not that it failed to arouse adversaries but simply that it
was more universal than any known religion. Whether in its soft or hard
versions, whether reassuring or demanding of sacrifices, it spanned

nations and civilizations as a prospect inseparable from the political order of every society in the modern epoch.

Yet this prospect presented the paradoxical character of being linked to a historical event and a historical reality: the October Revolution of 1917 and the regime to which it gave birth. Without the October Revolution, without the USSR, the communist idea would have remained what it had been in the nineteenth century: a vague promise, a far horizon, a post–bourgeois-alienation world that each could imagine according to his own inclination. It was October 1917 and the USSR that gave this vision its unity, its substance, and its force. Its voyage through the century would never stop depending on discussion of the regime that was supposed to illustrate it. The communist idea was no longer free, as it had been in the preceding century, but subordinated to the constraint of a constant affirmation of the veracity of its Soviet incarnation. This was its strength—that the idea had taken root in history—but also its weakness, for the idea was dependent upon its manifestation in reality. The interesting thing is that its strength triumphed over its weakness. Until its end, the Soviet Union managed to embody for millions of people the promise of a new society. The mere fact of its existence and its expansion justified its claims. No amount of massive, organized violence committed by its government and no failure in the economic realm could ever snuff out the dogma of its superiority to capitalism. The mystery of the communist idea in this century is thus that of a hope grafted onto a tragedy.

Another way to make the same observation is to consider the recent end of the USSR. This end came about in a nonrevolutionary fashion, through the self-dissolution of the metropolitan regime—which had itself set the stage for the fall of the satellite regimes—without a purge of old personnel from the new system. Yet what was a gentle transition for the system's personnel (so different in this respect from the liquidation of fascism in 1945) stood in stark contrast to the radical abandonment of communist ideas: The ex-communist countries all tried to base their rebirth on the very "bourgeois" principles that they once had claimed to have abolished and surpassed. As a result, the presence or return to power of former members of communist parties did nothing to change the fact that communism had come to an end along with the regime that had taken it as its banner; communism died with the Soviet Union. The proof is that the European of the present *fin de siècle* finds himself bereft of a vision of the future. If bourgeois democracy is no longer what comes before socialism but rather what comes after it, then those living in bourgeois democracy can no longer imagine anything beyond the horizon within which they now dwell.

Thus nothing less than the disappearance of the USSR was required to break the spell that had linked the regime born in October 1917 to the idea of a better society. The hour of general disillusionment came not from the spectacle of Soviet history but only from its end. This permits us to attach precise dates to the lifespan of the illusion, from Lenin to Gorbachev, and also to gauge the extent to which, powerful though it was, it possessed a very ephemeral character: The illusion did not survive beyond its object, that is, it was to last less than three-quarters of a century. Hence the word *illusion,* in the title of my book, does not designate the same type of belief that Freud had in view in his *The Future of an Illusion.* He was writing about religion, whereas I attempted to analyze the brief trajectory of a political idea tied to the history of a government and a regime. If I have used this same term, illusion, it has been to indicate that while the object may be earthly rather than divine, a comparable psychological investment is at stake. Moreover, the idea of the universality of men forms a minimal common ground between Christianity and communism. Finally, this particular illusion, unlike religious belief, has the advantage (for the observer, at least) of no longer having anything but a past. Today, the history of communism is closed and thus can be documented. This is not to say that modern democracies shall henceforth live without political utopia; I believe the contrary. But in the form through which it exerted such power over men's minds during our century, the communist idea has died before our eyes and will not be reborn. The mystery of its strength and its short lifespan forms the subject of my book.

The Political Imagination of Twentieth-Century Man

I had no intention particularly to focus on the case of intellectuals. If I accorded them a large role, it is because they write things down and thus leave testimony behind—and God knows that, in our time, they have written a great deal on politics! But what is interesting about them is less their case in itself than what it reveals about opinion in general. Contrary to what is usually written, the communist illusion was not peculiar to those who write and think for a living. It was far more widespread, and the intellectuals drew it from the atmosphere of their times, where they found it in all its forms, from a militant faith to a vague notion about the meaning of history. But in every case it endows the political universe with much vaster stakes. It superbly illustrates the character of an epoch when politics was the great dividing line between good and evil. In the illusion of communism, in the imaginary and fraught journey of the communist idea, I have tried to recover one of the starting points, perhaps the principal one, from which twentieth-century man has imagined his situation in the world. My book is a contribution to the history of the political imagination of twentieth-century man.

At the heart of this political imagination stands the figure of revolution, established since the end of the eighteenth century in the minds of Europeans—even those who hate it—as the quintessential means of historical change. The revolution took place in order to inaugurate the reign of the bourgeoisie over the feudal world. It must recommence in order to inaugurate the reign of the proletariat—precursor to the emancipation of humanity—over the bourgeois world.

The idea is first of all nourished by hatred of that which it seeks to destroy. Its mainspring is the rejection and even the hatred of the bourgeois, the central personage of modern society and the scapegoat for all the troubles that this society is constantly fostering. The bourgeois is the symbol of man's division within himself, first diagnosed by Rousseau, and this existential difficulty has weighed ceaselessly upon his destiny. All his inventions turn against him. He rises by means of money, which has allowed him to dissolve aristocratic gradations of "rank" from within, but this instrument of equality transforms him into an aristocrat of a new type, even more the prisoner of his wealth than the noble was the prisoner of his birth. He inaugurated the Rights of Man but in fact prefers the right of property. Liberty frightens him, and equality scares him even more. He was the father of democracy, in which every man is the equal of every other, associated with all in the construction of the social order, and in which each one, by obeying the law, obeys only himself. Yet democracy has exposed the fragility of bourgeois governments along with the threat posed by the masses, that is to say, by the poor. Thus the bourgeois is more reticent than ever about the principles of 1789, even though they facilitated his spectacular entrance into history.

If the bourgeois is the man of denial, it is because he is the man of falsehood. Far from incarnating the universal, he has but one obsession, his interests, and one passion, money. It is money that arouses the worst hatred against him, that unites in opposition to him the prejudices of the aristocrats, the jealousy of the poor, and the contempt of the intellectuals, past and present, who expel him from the future. The source of his power over society also accounts for his weak hold over the imagination. A king is infinitely more vast than his person, an aristocrat derives his prestige from a past far older than he is, a socialist preaches struggle to bring forth a better world where he will no longer exist. But the rich man is only what he is: rich, that is all. Money is not a sign of his virtue, or even of his labor, as in the Puritan understanding; instead, it is a sign of his luck or his greed. Money, moreover, divides the bourgeois from his fellows without bringing him the respect that allows the aristocrat to govern his inferiors; it reduces the bourgeois to a private condition by closing him up within the economic realm. The bourgeois has no appeal against this political deficiency, since it arises from a handicap of birth. It is at the very moment when the consent of the governed becomes explicitly necessary for the government of men that it is the most difficult to unite them.

The revolution represents the inversion of the bourgeois world as well as the principal sign of its having been transcended. As its inversion, the revolution is the revenge of the public on the private, the triumph of politics over economics, the victory of will over the everyday order of things. As the transcending of the bourgeois world, the revolution tears society away from its past and its traditions in order to undertake anew the construction of a social world. The revolution carries modern artificialism to its absolute form by rejecting all traditions. If bourgeois interests foiled the French Revolution's drive to wipe the slate clean, the only thing to do is to direct the struggle against them.

Necessity, Will, and the Revolutionary Idea

I am well aware that there is another version of the revolutionary idea, one that does not attribute such a Promethean role to the human will. Far from it, since this version consists not in making but in waiting for the revolution, as one waits for fruit to ripen, from the maturation of mentalities and things. The analogy with a natural cycle indicates that a more or less deterministic vision of the evolution of societies has taken the place of the creative virtues of human initiative. In both versions, the revolution constitutes the privileged mode of history's unfolding; but the second leaves nothing or almost nothing to the poetry of action, while the first exalts political invention without stripping from it the dignity of a necessary accomplishment. Marx never ceased oscillating between the two conceptions, and his heirs have done so still more. One of the Bolsheviks' great charms, perhaps their main one, was their extreme voluntarism, drawn from the example set by the Jacobins: What could be more extraordinary than to make a proletarian revolution in the land of czars and *muzhiks?* Yet Lenin managed to drape even this extraordinary event in the authority of science: The revolutionary party had grasped the laws of history. He thus recovered the necessity of the revolution yet did so by putting it at the service of political decision. It matters little that the two ideas are contradictory. Their peculiar marriage beguiles the imagination as the union of liberty and science. There, modern subjectivity finds both its plenitude and its guarantee.

As a rupture in the temporal order, although it fulfills history's promises, the revolution is invested with almost infinite social expectations. It must free the world from the bourgeois curse: from the reign of money, from the alienation brought by the market, from the division of classes, and even from the division within man himself. For it emancipates not only the proletarian, or the poor, but also the bourgeois, or his son. It makes everything depend upon history, which henceforth becomes the arena of human salvation, and upon politics, through which people choose their destiny: Everything can be achieved by a good society, if one can be established. Modern society disrupts the social bond by imprisoning individuals within the obsessive urge for money. Burdened from the start with a political deficit, it ignores the idea of the common good, since all those who compose it, plunged in relativism, have their own good. Such a society is incapable of forming a community of members freely associated around a collective project. The revolutionary idea is the exorcism of this unhappiness. It divinizes the political so as to avoid having to be contemptuous of it. In these traits we can recognize the hopes invested in the foundation of socialism by the revolution of October 1917.

Now one of the features—and one of the novelties—of the twentieth century is fascism's appropriation, to the profit of the right, of the revolutionary idea. One can easily understand this by looking back through the thought of the nineteenth century. During that epoch, revolution formed part of a conception of history that was monopolized by the left. It was a conception so powerful that even the right depended on it to a large degree, under the inverted form of its negation: The right was counterrevolutionary. But the idea of counterrevolution was compromised by this very dependence, for it evokes a return to a bygone past, out of which was born the revolution that the counterrevolutionary idea wanted to erase. This return, moreover, could only be achieved by means of revolutionary violence, which the counterrevolutionary idea claimed to detest. Whether seen as an end or a means, the counterrevolution was caught in a contradiction. It offered neither a policy nor a strategy. It was from this impasse that fascism delivered the European right that opposed the principles of 1789. Fascism gave the right a future.

Fascism fought the modern individualism and bourgeois egotism for which the French Revolution had paved the way, but it did not do so in the name of a return to aristocratic society. Fascism had no more esteem for the old aristocracy than it did for the new bourgeoisie. It aimed to destroy both in the name of the people, assembled without distinction of rank or class under the authority of a leader who incarnated that people. To serve this end it stopped at nothing, no matter how violent or illegal it might be, for the national or racial community of tomorrow could be brought into being only at the price of overthrowing the classes in power.

To fascism, then, were annexed all the seductions of the revolutionary idea, so essential to the modern absolutization of history. Fascism presented itself as an uprooting of the past, a violent and radical triumph over the corruption of the world of yesterday, an instance of political will revenging itself upon the alienating forces of the economy. It also fulfilled the conditions for a refoundation of the social, but in the name of the nation. One cannot recover a sense of the popularity that fascism enjoyed during the period between the two world wars unless one considers the promises of which it claimed to be the bearer. One can grasp nothing of our century's tragedies, moreover, unless one sees that the revolutionary idea took not one but two paths into people's minds.

The End of Utopia?

I shall not recount these tragedies here, contenting myself with having underlined what they owed, from the outset, to the divinization of political action that is one of the characteristics of the utopian thought of the democratic age. I would instead like to offer some observations on our situation today, when this type of thought has been discredited by history. Communism never conceived of any tribunal other than history's, and it has now been condemned by history to disappear, lock, stock, and barrel. Its defeat, therefore, is beyond appeal.

But must we conclude from this that it is necessary categorically to banish utopia from the public life of our societies? That might perhaps be going too far, because it would also mean destroying one of the great props of civic activity. For if the social order cannot be other than what it is, why should we trouble ourselves about it? The end of the communist idea has closed before our eyes the greatest path offered to the imagination of modern man in the matter of collective happiness. But it has by the same token deepened the political deficit that has always characterized modern liberalism.

In reality, this collapse affects not just communists, nor even just the left. It forces us to rethink convictions that are as old as democracy, especially that famous notion of a clear direction of history that was supposed to have anchored democracy in time. If capitalism has become the future of socialism, and the bourgeois world has succeeded that of the "proletarian revolution," what becomes of this conviction about time? The inversion of the canonical ordering obscures the articulation of epochs along the road of progress. History again becomes a tunnel where man enters as in the darkness, without knowing where his actions will lead, uncertain of his destination, dispossessed of the illusory sense of security about what he is doing. Most often bereft of belief in God, the democratic individual of our *fin de siècle* sees that the divinity called history is trembling on its foundations. From this comes an anguish that must be dispelled.

The democratic individual finds himself poised before a closed future, incapable of defining even vaguely the horizon of a *different society* from the one in which we live, since this horizon has become almost impossible to conceive. We need only to look at the crisis into which political language has been plunged in today's democracies in order to understand this. The right and the left still remain, but they are stripped of their reference points and almost of their substance: The left no longer knows what socialism is; the right, deprived of its best argument (namely, anticommunism), is also searching for something which can distinguish it. The political scene both in France and in Italy offers good examples of this situation.

Can such a situation last? Will the end of communism deprive democratic politics of a revolutionary horizon for long? With this question, I take my leave.

INDEX